PUNISHMENT IN DISGUISE
PENAL GOVERNANCE AND FEDERAL IMPRISONMENT OF WOMEN IN CANADA

In *Punishment in Disguise*, Kelly Hannah-Moffat presents a look at some current forms of penal governance in Canadian federal women's prisons. Hannah-Moffat uses women's imprisonment to theorize the complexity of penal power and to show how the meaning and content of women's penal governance changes over time, how penal reform strategies intersect and evolve into complex patterns of governing, how governing is always gendered and racialized, and how expert, non-expert, and hybrid forms of power and knowledge inform penal strategies.

The author posits that although there has been a series of distinct phases in the imprisonment of women, the prison system itself, given its primary functions of custody and punishment, is consistent in thwarting attempts at progressive reform. While each distinct phase has its own corresponding ideology and discourse, the individual discourses have internal complexities and contradictions that have not been adequately recognized in the general literature on penology.

Avoiding universal and reductionist claims about women's oppression, Hannah-Moffat argues that relations of power are complex and fractured and that there is a need to explore the specific elements of institutional power relations. Backed by solid research, *Punishment in Disguise* makes a strong contribution to criminology and feminist theory by providing an alternative approach to analysing the governance of women by other women and by the state.

KELLY HANNAH-MOFFAT is an assistant professor in the Department of Sociology at the University of Toronto.

Punishment in Disguise:

Penal Governance and Federal Imprisonment of Women in Canada

KELLY HANNAH-MOFFAT

UNIVERSITY OF TORONTO PRESS
Toronto Buffalo London

© University of Toronto Press Incorporated 2001
Toronto Buffalo London
Printed in Canada

ISBN 0-8020-4690-8 (cloth)
ISBN 0-8020-8274-2 (paper)

Printed on acid-free paper

Canadian Cataloguing in Publication Data

Hannah-Moffat, Kelly, 1967–
   Punishment in disguise : penal governance and federal imprisonment
   of women in Canada

   Includes bibliographical references and index.
   ISBN 0-8020-4690-8 (bound)   ISBN 0-8020-8274-2 (pbk.)

   1. Reformatories for women – Canada – History.   2. Women prisoners –
   Canada – History.   3. Female offenders – Rehabilitation – Canada –
   History.   I. Title.

   HV9507.H36 2001   365'.43'0971   C00-931944-1

This book has been published with the help of a grant from the Humanities
and Social Sciences Federation of Canada, using funds provided by the
Social Sciences and Humanities Research Council of Canada.

University of Toronto Press acknowledges the financial assistance to its
publishing program of the Canada Council for the Arts and the Ontario
Arts Council.

University of Toronto Press acknowledges the financial support for its
publishing activities of the Government of Canada through the Book
Publishing Industry Development Program (BPIDP).

1 × 2

To Paul, Alexandra, and our families

Contents

Illustrations follow p. 124

Acknowledgments

As we wander along the numerous paths of life, we are inspired by various individuals, a number of whom do not know how much they have contributed to our growth. While I cannot begin to acknowledge all the individuals who have influenced my work and supported this project, I want to express my appreciation to some who contributed directly and indirectly to this project. I had the good fortune to benefit from the kindness and support of many individuals.

I am grateful for the generous support of the faculty and students at the Centre of Criminology, University of Toronto. I would like to thank Rita Donelan, Gloria Cernivivo, Beatrice Caulfield, Lisa Steigmann-Gall, and Fiorella Arcara for their administrative support. I extend a special thank you to Monica Bristol, who always had words of encouragement and the time to listen. I am grateful to the past and present staff of the Criminology Library – Catherine Matthews, Tom Finlay, Renana Almagor, and Jane Gladstone – and to various students and faculty members who were always willing to talk about undeveloped ideas. Each of the following individuals contributed to my knowledge and success: William Bateman, John Beattie, Tony Doob, Richard Ericson, Don Evans, Carolyn Strange, William Watson, Lorna Wier, Clifford Shearing, and Philip Stenning. Some of my fondest memories are of intellectual and recreational experiences shared with friends like Marc and Heather Copolino, Willem Delint, Simon Devereaux, Kevin and Deirdre Freiheit, Kevin Haggerty, Amanel Iyogun, Kirsten Johnson, Tammy Landau, Maeve McMahon, Voula Marinos, Allyson May, Anna Pratt, Brian and Beatrice Schoenhofer, Greg Smith, Kim Varma, Mary Lynn Young, and many others. I also appreciate the support of my colleagues at Brock University and the University of Toronto.

A special note of appreciation to Anne-Marie Singh, one of my most supportive friends and colleagues, whose late-night e-mails and phone calls from England helped me complete this project. I am also indebted to the Friday reading group – Annette Bickford, Janice Hill, Lucy Luccisano, Paula Maurutto, Carol Anne O'Brien, and Jacinth Samuels – and to the 'Toronto History of the Present' group. I would also like to remember the friendship of Kevin Carrière, a dear friend, who died while this work was in progress. Kevin taught me to appreciate and value my friends and work, and to always maintain a balance between the two. His love of art and life will not be forgotten.

I have Dan Coughlan to thank for cultivating my enthusiasm for criminology and for sharing stories about his experiences working in Ontario Corrections. My fond memories of St Patrick's days and engaging afternoon discussions inspired me to pursue a graduate career in criminology.

This work would not have been possible without the support of the staff of several organizations, including the Canadian Association of Elizabeth Fry Societies, Correctional Investigator, Correctional Service of Canada, the Elizabeth Fry Society of Toronto, the Federally Sentenced Women's Program, the George Railton Salvation Army Archives, the Ontario Council of Elizabeth Fry Societies, the Kingston Penitentiary Museum Archives, the National Archives of Canada, and the Toronto University Women's Club Archives. I extend special thanks to Nancy Webb, Leslie Kelman, Claire Price, Kim Pate, Patricia Monture, Elizabeth White, Vera Cherry, Joan Peeling, and Dave St Onge for their support of this project. I also owe thanks to all of the women at the Prison for Women, and others who directly and indirectly contributed to this project through formal and informal interviews. Many women have lost their lives to imprisonment, both literally and figuratively. Their suffering must not be forgotten or minimized.

While attending to this project, I spent a great deal of time working for the Commission of Inquiry into Certain Events at the Prison for Women. During this time I had the opportunity to work with a number of inspiring and dedicated individuals who, on a daily basis, work towards ideals of justice: Justice Louise Arbour, Patricia Jackson, Guy Cournoyer, Tammy Landau, Sheila-Marie Cook, Julie Cyr, Karen McFarlane, and many others.

I am grateful for the expertise and support of Virgil Duff and Barbara Porter and the staff at the University of Toronto Press. I thank them, and the anonymous reviewers of this manuscript, for their insights and direction, and Matthew Kudelka for his detailed copy-editing.

I am especially grateful to Marnie Crouch, Kellie Leclerc, and Dawn Moore for their support, comments, and exceptional editing skills. I owe special thanks to Madeleine Weiler for her multiple administrative talents and encouragement during the final stages of this manuscript. I also appreciate the time and energy of Rosemary Gartner, Pat O'Malley, Jim Phillips, Margaret Shaw, and Jonathan Simon, who offered valuable comments on early drafts of these chapters. Over the past few years I have learned a tremendous amount about the skills required to become an excellent scholar. Much of this learning came from working with Mariana Valverde. I thank Mariana for educating and inspiring me on many levels.

There are few who truly understand how much commitment and energy have gone into this book. I would like to acknowledge the unconditional support and tolerance of my family and Sean, Susie, Kayla, Shane, and Katie Hannah; Marcia and Stephanie Smith; Lisa, Brad, Jordan, and Jacob Tamscu; Marie and Grandma Hawkins; John and Eleanor Moffat; and Steve and Helen Macdonald and their girls. Their patience and encouragement over the past several years were greatly appreciated. Special thanks go to my mom and dad, Joan and Al Macdonald, who have always encouraged and believed in me, and to my brother, Sean, whom I admire and find to be a great inspiration. My parents, in-laws, and brother were never more than a phone call away, and no matter what, they have always found a way to make me laugh and persevere. They make visits home a wonderful retreat from work. Their unwavering faith in my abilities contributed greatly to the completion of this project. From them, I have learned that with hard work and determination any goal can be accomplished.

Last but not at all least, thanks Paul for your understanding, acceptance, faith, inspiration, and love. Your logic, humour, and acceptance of my need for 'absolute' silence and personal space is greatly appreciated. We have a special friendship and love that defies description – it is to you, our beautiful daughter, Alexandra, and our families that I dedicate this work.

PUNISHMENT IN DISGUISE

Introduction

It is necessary to move beyond these narrowly conceived conceptualizations and to reconceptualize penal reform as a complex and whole system of action capable of producing different processes and outcomes, which are themselves shaped by wider influences.   (Blomberg 1995: 59)

In the spring of 1995, Canadians were shocked by images of women prisoners being forcefully strip-searched by members of a male emergency response team clothed in black riot gear. These stark images were first aired by the television program *the fifth estate* and later reproduced in nearly every major Canadian newspaper and magazine. In the wake of this videotaped evidence, the Canadian government was widely accused of inhumane and unconstitutional treatment of women prisoners. Advocates and prisoners recounted horrifying stories of prolonged segregation (with women being denied access to their lawyers, clothing, showers, sanitary products, and so on), cross-gender strip searches, and involuntary transfers of some women prisoners to a segregated unit in a notorious men's maximum security penitentiary, and challenged these administrative practices; meanwhile, Corrections Canada either denied that such events occurred or argued that their actions were a legal, reasonable, and justifiable response to prisoners who 'posed a threat to the good order of the institution.' Even though the actions of corrections officials contravened the accepted United Nations standards for the treatment of prisoners, the Canadian Charter of Rights and Freedoms, and various other policies and pieces of legislation, few individuals in Corrections Canada acknowledged that the treatment of these women was morally and legally inappropriate.

These events, which are astonishing enough on their own, occurred in a wider international context of women's correctional reform. These reforms, modelled on *Creating Choices*, the 1990 report of the Task Force on Federally Sentenced Women, involved the design of a new, 'supportive,' women-centred model of punishment that would 'empower women,' create 'meaningful choices,' reinforce notions of 'respect and dignity,' and respond to the unique experiences and context of women prisoners in Canada. That these two contradictory developments shared the same time frame has astounded and perplexed many observers. Over ten years have passed since the project began, during which the government has committed itself politically and financially to a new vision, and during which five architecturally beautiful regional facilities (prisons)[1] have been built with the goal of replacing the antiquated Prison for Women. The language describing women's imprisonment now speaks of empowerment, choice, and healing; yet many argue that little about the regime has changed and that few past lessons have been learned (Frigon 1997, 1999; Hayman 2000; Horii 2000; Martel 2000; Monture-Angus 2000; Morin 1999; Pate 1999). In May 2000, the last prisoner at P4W was transferred, and in July the solicitor general, Lawrence MacAulay, decommissioned the sixty-six-year-old prison in an elaborate ceremony.

The recent 'reforms' are yet another flawed attempt to reconceptualize the meaning and experience of punishment to make it more 'appropriate' and suitable for women. The operational problems experienced by often well-meaning correctional staff and the pressing concerns of critics like the Canadian Association of Elizabeth Fry Societies are not new; in fact, they are inevitable. Many Canadian and international observers believe that the ideas included in *Creating Choices* offer an innovative solution to the specific managerial and political problems posed by the comparatively small female prison population. In 1990, many feminists and reformers within government endorsed this report and its recommendations in the optimistic belief that the five new prisons could operate on principles such as empowerment, meaningful choices, shared responsibility, and respect and dignity, and that by providing a supportive environment they could break the cycle of abuse, neglect and discrimination experienced by imprisoned women. This book situates the repressive and progressive qualities of punishment evidenced by the most recent attempts at reform, in a broader social, political and historical analysis of Canadian women's penality.

This book is titled *Punishment in Disguise* to encourage readers to think about the complex and contradictory elements of punishment and its reform in modern society. While many authors have shown how the best intentions of reformers become 'bastardised versions of reality' (Rothman 1980; also see Brown, Kramer, and Quinn 1988), few have examined the logic and strategies of governing that perpetuate long-established patterns. In this book, I argue that well-intentioned benevolent efforts to improve the conditions for women prisoners and to create a penal regime that addresses historically specific understandings of women's needs reproduces and obscures complex and ambiguous relations of power, and further, that prisons are remarkably flexible institutions that absorb, adapt, and accommodate a variety of competing and sometimes contradictory rationalities. There is a complicated relationship between ideals and penal policies.

This discussion of women's penal reform builds on a Foucauldian analysis of power/knowledge and on the recent contributions of governmentality scholars, who offer certain theoretical tools that are valuable for analyzing governing across social sites. Notwithstanding the many feminist critiques of Foucault's scholarship, many feminist theorists believe that Foucault's concepts can be used to expand our understanding of how women are governed in multiple social sites (Weedon 1987; Smart 1990; Lacombe 1991; Sawicki 1991; Bell 1993). Foucauldian work is useful in feminist scholarship because it allows for a more complex and detailed understanding of the gendered nature of knowledge and of the disciplining of female bodies (Finateri 1999). His theory of power is especially useful for advancing our understanding of penality; the term 'penality' is used intentionally to draw attention to the historical, social, and political aspects of a complex range of institutions and practices that shape modern forms of punishment.

Analyses of power as *productive* rather than *repressive* are either absent from or marginal to feminist reviews of women's penal reform (Freedman 1981; Adelberg and Currie 1987, 1993; Carlen 1990, 1994; Zedner 1991b; Rafter 1992; Shaw 1992a, 1993; Faith 1993). Recent feminist researchers, including Estelle Freedman (1981), Lucia Zedner (1991b), and Nicole Hahn Rafter (1992), have set out to re-evaluate the history of imprisonment to include the experiences of women. Freedman examines the development and feminization of women's prisons and the 'benevolent' role played by American women reformers in caring for their 'fallen sisters.' Rafter offers a more critical analysis of the intersections between gender, race, and class in the development of women's prisons in the United States. She questions Freedman's emphasis on 'sisterliness' and shows how relations between reformers and prisoners are shaped by wider social processes, and how social controls are exercised on women as women. She also shows how men and men's prisons are accepted as 'norms,' from which women and women's prisons are viewed as deviating. She also makes an important contribution to feminist criminology by analysing the relations of power that exist between women of different classes and races: in Rafter's view, the American women's reformatory movement also represents a struggle between 'chaste' white middle-class reformers and women prisoners from less powerful groups. Rafter is concerned mainly with the social control function of the prison and with how reformers use repressive disciplinary techniques to regulate a particular class of women. In a similar fashion, Zedner has examined how notions of appropriate male and female roles figure in the development of penal theory and how gender distinctions affected the entire British penal system.

The few historical Canadian analyses of women's imprisonment (Biron 1992; Adelberg and Currie 1987, 1993; Cooper 1993; Sangster 1999) have focused on the struggle to reform the infamous Prison for Women. With the exception of Strange (1983, 1985) and Oliver (1994, 1998), who examined the regime at the Andrew Mercer Reformatory at the turn of the century, and Hamelin (1989), who studied Soeurs du Bon Pasteur in Montreal in 1876, there have been few detailed efforts to document patterns of governing Canadian women prisoners. These historical studies of women's prisons often undertake somewhat narrow institutional histories, without systematically analysing the disciplinary and other relations that shape the broader field of penality. Recent Canadian scholarship on women's imprisonment and women's criminality consists of either overviews of a wide range of issues (Shaw 1991a; Faith 1993; Bertrand 1998; Hannah-Moffat and Shaw 2000a), or detailed analyses of the gender-specific experiences and characteristics of women's offending (Kendall 1993a, 1993b; Shaw 1994, 1996a; Shaw and Dubois 1995; Comack 1996; Pollack 1999, 2000), or comparative studies (Bertrand et al. 1998). Other work assesses the conditions, needs, and experiences of imprisonment (Berzins and Collette-Carrière 1979; Watson 1980; Adelberg and Currie 1987, 1993a; Walford 1987; Hamelin 1989; Sugar and Fox 1989; Jaccoud 1992; Kendall 1993a; Lemonde 1995; Sommers 1995; Comack 1996; Bertrand 1998; Woodrow 1998; Frigon 1999; Martel 2000). Some scholars, such as Margaret Shaw (1992a, 1993, 1996a, 2000) and Kathy Kendall (1994), have started to explore the implications of promoting a feminist analysis of women's crime and feminist techniques of rehabilitation within existing prison structures.

Most studies of women's imprisonment either avoid theoretical analyses of power/knowledge relations, or they rely on what Foucault calls a 'juridico-discursive' model of power or governing. This model of power involves three basic assumptions: *first*, power is possessed exclusively by certain groups or institutions; *second*, power flows from a centralized source down to the bottom (usually the state); and *third*, power is primarily repressive, involving prohibitions and sanctions (Sawicki 1991: 20). In order to develop analyses that decentre the state as an instrument of power, Foucault conceptualized power as a relation and not a possession of certain individuals or groups. Thus, his analyses of power are not about who possesses or should possess power but rather about how relations of power give rise to and emerge from particular strategies of governing. Further, he argues that power is productive, not simply repressive. Therefore, an examination of the institutional and cultural practices involved in the production of citizens is crucial. While penal governance can be seen as a representation of juridical power and repressive forms of disciplinary power, it can also be analysed as a form of productive power that has the intention of producing individuals who meet certain normative expectations. This view of power underpins Foucauldian attempts to understand penal discipline. Foucault suggests that power is a ubiquitous and heterogenous concept that is at some times concentrated and hierarchically organized, and at other times socially dispersed (Hindus 1996).

The insights of Foucault (1977, 1980, 1990) are useful, because he focuses on the relations of power and technologies of power, which are dispersed through society rather than being located specifically in the state. Foucault (1980) warns that 'we should not assume that the sovereignty of the state, the form of law or the overall unity of domination are given at the outset; rather, these are only terminal forms power takes' (Watson and Pringle 1992: 233). He also notes that 'the idea that the state must, as a source or point of confluence of power, be invoked to account for all the apparatuses in which power is organized, does not seem to me very fruitful for history or one might say that its fruitfulness has been exhausted' (1980: 188).

Foucault is useful to feminist analyses of reform, in that he accords the state no unity, individuality, or rigorous functionality (Smart 1990) but nevertheless provides an important focus on power. Power is exercised in a multifarious network of relations that permeate all aspects of life; it is not a possession of individuals or groups. The state should be seen as an overall *effect* of these relations and cannot be assumed to act coherently as the agent of particular groups (Watson 1990; Pringle and

Watson 1992). Foucauldian analyses of power represent a substantial challenge to those feminist and nonfeminist paradigms that simply ascribe power to men, or to a state operating in a functional or instrumental way to maintain women's subordination (or other objectives of social control).

'Patriarchy' is not a useful analytical term, because it tends to focus our analyses of power on men's oppression of women. It limits our ability to understand the complexity of power relations at a given social site, and to examine power relations among women. Foucault's understanding of power is that it is not simply disciplinary or repressive.

For instance, he uses the concept of *pastoralism* to analyse more benevolent, tutelary forms of power, and to address broader questions of care and welfare. He claims that pastoralism is 'an old power technique which originated in Christian institutions' (1983: 213). The Christian principle of pastoralism, which assumes 'that certain individuals can, by their religious quality, serve others not as princes, magistrates, prophets, fortune-tellers, benefactors, educationalists, and so on, but as pastors,' is central to his definition of pastoral power (1983: 214). He argues that 'this form of power is salvation orientated ... it is individualizing (as opposed to legal power); it is coextensive and continuous with life; it is linked with a production of truth – the truth of the individual himself' (1983: 214).

In short, Foucault claims that this form of pastoral power stresses the Christian aim of salvation and corresponding obligations of individual sacrifice and concern for the salvation of others. While Foucault's idea of pastoral power draws on Christian metaphors and themes, it can be used to understand secular as well as nonsecular practices of care. It is a form of power that focuses on a personalized, prescientific knowledge of an individual's mind and soul. Accordingly, Foucault argued that pastoral power 'implies a knowledge of conscience and ability to direct it' (1983: 214). More recently, Ransom has argued: 'In its secular variant, where leading the flock to safety is no longer at issue, pastoral power continues to concern itself with the health and psychic states of the individual in this world. Thus, psychologists and psychiatrists, as well as others with a less professional façade, diagnose and attempt to address the miseries of modern life' (1997: 64).

Furthermore, Dean (1999: 75) argues that Foucault's concept of pastoralism facilitates a more general understanding of the origins of modern notions of care, and of the expectation that the 'state' should care for the welfare of its citizens. And it also helps us understand a central paradox of contemporary liberal welfare states: that charity, philanthropy, and voluntary activity can be used to both buttress and undermine the ideal of the welfare state.

An analysis of the relationship between pastoral power and disciplinary power can help us understand the complex strategies employed by social workers, community agencies, reformers, and the state to shape programs in ways that promote the 'best interests' of women prisoners. The concept of pastoral power, when combined with Foucault's understandings of other forms of power, such as disciplinary power, juridical power, and governmentality, provides an interesting framework for studying women's imprisonment and the role of evangelical, maternal, and feminist reformers in women's penal reform.

Feminist analyses of women's penality, as well as nonfeminist analyses that rely on Foucauldian concepts, tend to reduce diverse features of penal governance to repressive relations of discipline. For example, Dobash, Dobash, and Gutteridge (1986), in their important history of women's imprisonment, combine feminist criticism with Foucauldian characterizations of disciplinary power to further our theoretical understanding of the governance of women in prison. They show how penal and therapeutic techniques of governing women prisoners are a gender-specific form of disciplinary regulation that are often overlooked by nonfeminist revisionists. Their work offers a valuable critique of revisionist analyses of men's penality (Ignatieff 1978; Rothman 1980, 1990; Foucault 1977) by pointing out how these fail to consider the role of patriarchal and gender-based assumptions in the development of modern prisons (1986: 9). They trace the development of punishment and prison regimes, and discuss the role of criminological/expert knowledges in the formation of those regimes, and show how criminological knowledge reflects and incorporates wider, gender-based assumptions about 'women's nature': 'Over time, the woman prisoner has been transformed from evil to mad and responded to accordingly, with closer and closer forms of control and confinement reaching beyond her body and into her mind and emotions' (1986: 14). Besides providing a rich source of empirical data, Dobash, Dobash and Gutteridge make an important contribution to theory by showing how medical professionals and some reformers play a disciplinary role in the normalization of women prisoners.

Adrian Howe (1994) argues that the contribution of Dobash, Dobash, and Gutteridge is commendable but limited, because 'it does not extend beyond a recognition of the especially demanding nature of disciplinary regimes within the women's prison' (149). Howe also notes that the overwhelming impression left by the Dobash, Dobash, and Gutteridge study is that of 'an oppressive surveillance which renders resistance impossible within the women's prison system in the United Kingdom.' She adds that the introduction of gender into the study of women's imprisonment has not advanced feminist penal theory, and that 'gender-sensitive penal analysts have not realized that gender cannot be reduced to a study of women' (158). She argues that feminist analyses of penality must also consider the role of masculinity in the development of men's prisons, and that feminist analyses must incorporate the insights of other critical analyses of penality (159). While Howe makes a valid point about the atheoretical nature of many feminist histories of punishment, she clearly misses the importance of feminist contributions that document (and in some cases theorize) the experiences of women prisoners and reformers. Howe's comments on the importance of analysing masculinity as it relates to penality, and to crime more generally, are important (see Newburn and Stanko 1994). Here, however, the focus is on developing a more complex analysis of how various constructions of femininity are evoked to define and legitimate different reformers and reform initiatives, with the goal of showing how penal power is gendered, and of analysing the gendered relations of power that exist between women in different social positions. Howe advocates a postmodern Foucauldian approach to the study of women's 'penality' that does not focus explicitly on the prison, but rather on wider strategies of regulating women. She states that 'feminist studies of the disciplined female body have as yet untapped potential to transform our understanding of punishment in the Western world' (206). This is what Dobash, Dobash, and Gutteridge do in their study, but they do not make a direct connection to the postmodern feminist analyses of women's bodies as the site of disciplinary power. In a similar vein, I argue that the historically and culturally specific techniques and rationalities evoked to discipline women's minds and bodies are also used to create knowledge about the female prisoner and to legitimate and support the exercise of disciplinary power in women's prisons.

Howe (1994) equates penality with discipline by examining how women's bodies are policed in accordance with certain normative standards of femininity and sexuality. In her review of postmodern feminist analyses of women she includes a discussion of her own work on the relationship between women's penality and social injury. The term 'social injury' is used in the context of the claims of women prisoners and young women at risk of state intervention (171). She argues that women prisoners are in a position where they are at risk of state harm, and that therefore they need to be empowered. Like several other studies on women prisoners, Howe's work tends to portray women in prison as victims with little or no agency. More importantly, she does not examine the complexity of risk-based governance, or how women in prison are not simply 'at risk' of harm but also perceived by the state and others to be 'a risk' to public safety (Hannah-Moffat 1999). Furthermore, her claims about empowerment are not examined. A feminist political strategy like empowerment is not easily used within the context of penal reform (Hannah-Moffat 1995, 2000). My analysis of the governance of women in prison shows how recent terms such as 'risk' and 'empowerment' can be used to responsibilize and regulate women (see chapter 6). A concept such as 'penal harm' can be useful in politicizing some abuses of prisoners' rights, but it does not further our understanding of penal governance. In short, Howe's 1994 book is an instructive review of some literature; however, she fails to see how power/knowledge/body relations transcend gender, and how studies of imprisonment are linked to wider processes of governing, which are not necessarily disciplinary. The reduction of penality to a functionalist (social control or repressive disciplinary) concept reveals little about the reform process, and it assumes a coherence in operations of power that has not been shown to exist. Instead, I am interested in the relationship between various forms of power – pastoral power, sovereignty, discipline, government – and various forms of knowledge. I argue that penal governance relies on *multiple* expressions and forms of power, and that these forms of power are both productive and repressive, and involve different types of agency (compliant and resistant) and knowledge.

The recent literature on governmentality allows for a more complex analysis of the relations between state power and other modalities of governance, and how power is exercised over individuals (Hudson 1998: 585). It gives those interested in the sociology of punishment an opportunity to re-examine the dynamics of penality.

According to Foucault (1991: 102–4) governmentality marks the emergence of a new way of thinking about and exercising power on societies. Studies of governance that rely on Foucault's notion of government draw our attention to the variety of ways of reflecting and acting that aim to shape, guide, manage, and regulate the conduct of persons – not only other persons but also oneself – in light of certain principles or goals (Rose 1993: 287).

Governance is not a monopoly of the state. As Dean argues, government 'is any more or less calculated rational activity, undertaken by a multiplicity of authorities and agencies employing a variety of techniques and forms of knowledge, that seeks to shape conduct by working through our desires, aspirations, interests and beliefs for definite but shifting ends and with a diverse set of relatively unpredictable consequences, effects and outcomes' (1991: 11). Thus, analyses of government evaluate the governing authority or agency, the forms of knowledge, techniques, and other means employed, the entity governed and how it is conceived, and the ends sought, as well as the outcomes and consequences (11).

Intimately linked to the notion of government as the 'conduct of conduct' is the concept of self-government. Self-government refers to situations where the governor and the governed are two aspects of one actor. As noted by Dean, 'the notion of government extends to cover the way in which an individual questions his/her own conduct (or problematizes it) so that he/she may be better able to govern it. In other words government encompasses not only how we exercise authority over others, or how we govern abstract entities like states and populations, but how we govern ourselves' (12). This characterization of governance allows for a broad-based study of punishment that captures the interdependent and complex roles of state and nonstate reformers in the regulation of women in prison.

Nikolas Rose and Peter Miller (1992: 175–6) argue that political rationalities and governmental technologies are conceptual tools that can facilitate an understanding of the problematic of government. *Political rationalities* are described as 'the changing discursive fields within which the exercise of power is conceptualized, the moral justifications for particular ways of exercising power by diverse authorities, notions of the appropriate forms, object, and limits of politics, and conceptions of the proper distribution of such tasks among secular, spiritual, military, and familial sector,' and *governmental technologies* as 'the complex mundane programs, calculations, techniques, apparatuses, documents and procedures through which authorities seek to embody and give effect to governmental ambitions.'

Rose and Miller (1992: 176) further indicate that in the advanced liberal democracies of the present, an analysis of the intricate interdependencies between political rationalities and governmental technologies can facilitate an understanding of the multiple and delicate networks that connect the lives of individuals, groups, and organizations to the aspirations of authorities. Here, my concern is with the multiple and delicate networks of reform that organize and shape the politics of women's imprisonment. These conceptual tools help us understand how women prisoners are governed through rationalities and technologies of reform and of punishment.

Studies that analyse the problem of government give priority to the question of 'how' we govern and are governed – in the context of this book, 'how' the female prisoner is governed, and how different penal/social domains are constituted as authoritative, and how various knowledges shape or give authority to various techniques and practices that emerge as women's prisons evolve. In this book I examine how women prisoners are governed by reformers and by the state; I do so by analyzing the *political rationalities* and *governmental technologies* that culminate in particular penal reform strategies such as a maternal strategy, a welfare-based therapeutic strategy, a self-governing strategy, and a pastoral strategy.

As noted, this book is based on a view of power as decentralized and heterogeneous. It highlights four strategies of reform and punishment: pastoral, maternal, disciplinary, and empowering/responsibilizing. *Strategies* are conceived of as particular amalgamations of political rationalities and governmental technologies. Strategies of reform are flexible and enabling diagrams of action. At any given historical moment, multiple rationalities and technologies are available to reformers and state agents. In this sense, a *strategy* is a particular process of governance that incorporates a variety of possibly contradictory rationalities and mobilizes several different techniques for the purpose of governing a known object in a particular way.

The strategies discussed (e.g., maternalism, empowerment) are not necessarily unique to the specific reform initiatives in which they are promoted. For example, a logic of maternalism was pervasive in social governance throughout the nineteenth and early twentieth centuries. The metaphor of motherhood was used in conjunction with diverse rationalities (religious, scientific, penal) to justify and legitimate multiple reform projects. Maternal strategies were used by a variety of reformers to morally reform the poor, prostitutes, and alcoholics; to develop home economics courses; and to promote antiwar initiatives, suffrage, and the integration of women in the workforce.

Foucault and others have maintained that power/knowledge relations are linked primarily to expert-based knowledge systems. Foucault (1977) claims that deviance is controlled through strategies that emerge out of processes of identifying the deviant as such and then classifying, monitoring, and treating that individual. These activities are typically associated with experts. A secondary objective of this book is to show how modern penal strategies do not rely solely on expert knowledges as they are typically conceptualized: women reformers, most of whom were not 'experts,' have played a central role in penal governing.[2] This analysis of women's penal strategies shows how everyday systems of governance and nonexpert women's knowledges have been used to reform and regulate prisoners. Nonexpert matrons and women reformers used their everyday knowledge of activities such as mothering to devise specific technologies of reform. Expert-based penal techniques are of course important, but they coexist with and sometimes appropriate everyday techniques of governing. The near absence of experts, whether medical or psychiatric, in the reform of federally sentenced women during the heyday of therapy in prisons (the 1950s and 1960s) is particularly significant. Furthermore, ideas, rationalities, and maternal programs of reform used in prisons by reformers (such as Elizabeth Fry) predate the rise of 'scientific' knowledges and techniques of penal governing. Strategies promoted by 'nonexpert' women were not wholly derived from or rationalized with scientific explanations of women's crime and deviance.

In many ways, it was women reformers' knowledge claims regarding women prisoners that precipitated the development of contemporary women-centred regimes. However, women reformers were in some instances trained in lower-status, feminized professions such as domestic science and social work. They often represented a hybrid of expert and everyday commonsense knowledges about women prisoners. Women like Phyllis Haslam of the Toronto Elizabeth Fry Society and Mrs Hof, a domestic science instructor at P4W in Kingston, are good examples of this hybrid knowledge. These women were professionally trained in the female-dominated professions of social work and domestic science, respectively. They and other women used their professional knowledges and status in combination with everyday commonsense knowledges of maternalism to govern women in prison. Furthermore, the category of 'reformer' changes over time. In the postwar period, women working in Canadian women's prison reform were both professional and nonprofessional women working outside the state and within state institutions.

This book offers a genealogy of some current forms of penal governance. It traces the emergence of Canada's current federal regime of women's imprisonment. It shows how penal regimes rely on various forms of power/knowledge relations, and how they become the target of various programs of reform, and the impact of some of these changes. More generally, this book is about women's engagement with penal reform. It outlines the co-operation, fragmentation, and compromises that resulted from reformers' varied attempts to alter the conditions and terms of women's confinement. The history of women's imprisonment is used to understand the complexity of penal power/knowledge relations and to show how the meaning and content of women's penal governance changes over time. It is not my intention to provide a detailed historical account of Canadian women's imprisonment. Instead, I use specific historical periods to demonstrate the dynamics of a gendered form of penal governance. By no means are the forms of governing discussed exclusive or restricted to a given historical moment.

The book roughly follows the chronology of Canadian women's imprisonment. The decision to emphasize particular times and places is partly intentional and partly a result of the inaccessibility of certain historical data. There are few primary documents that describe the management and operations of federal women's prisons, and there has been very little secondary research that analyses these processes. For primary research, I relied on archival material in the National Archives of Canada, the Correctional Service of Canada Museum, the University Women's Club of Toronto, the Canadian Association of Elizabeth Fry Societies, and local archives of Elizabeth Fry Societies. Where possible, I also obtained official records and reports of commissions and investigations pertaining to federally sentenced women. Also where possible, I supplemented these materials with interviews with reformers, prisoners, government officials, and retired employees of P4W and the Female Unit at Kingston Penitentiary. Notwithstanding this primary research, the data presented here offer only a partial history of P4W and of the newer regional prisons. Many of the records documenting how these facilities were managed are either missing or inaccessible. The present regime at the new regional prisons is difficult to capture because it is experiencing constant changes.

This book was originally motivated by a concern for women in prison, but the final product is not about 'the experiences of women prisoners' – it is about prison policies and programs, with a special focus on the role of nonstate women reformers. The book places the evolution of federal women's imprisonment in a broader international and historical context. It does not analyse the development of provincial and territorial prison regimes for women. A genealogy of provincial women's imprisonment in British Columbia, Quebec, Newfoundland, and other provinces and territories may reveal different patterns of penal governance (see for example, Marie-de-Saint-Benoît 1953; Hernandez 1970; Thompson 1972; Tietolman 1972; Proudfoot 1978; Berzins and Collette-Carrière 1979; Watson 1980; Female Offender Study Committee 1985[3]; Cousineau, Laberge, and Théorêt 1986; Bertrand 1998; Hamelin 1985, 1987, 1989; Biron 1992; Stewart 1993; Woodrow 1998; Frigon 1999; Sangster 1999). For example, the current direction of the Ontario government's reform of provincial women's prisons is quite different. Ontario is closing its only women-only facility – Vanier Centre in Brampton, Ontario – with the goal of co-locating women in a separate unit in a male prison – Maplehurst, in Milton, Ontario (Haq 1999). Clearly, Ontario and the federal government appear to be moving in opposite directions.

Chapter 1 focuses on early maternal and pastoral forms of power, and how these 'kinder,' 'gentler' forms of governing were used by nineteenth-century reformers to soften the pain of imprisonment and to normalize women prisoners. I do not present maternalism simply as an ideology, as others have done; instead, I interpret maternal strategies as a synthesis of various political rationalities and governmental technologies. A maternal logic plays a pivotal role in governance by shaping, guiding, managing, and regulating the conduct of women prisoners, reformers, and state officials. Maternal power is a *strategy* of governance, to the extent that it seeks to render itself technical (Rose 1993) and to incorporate itself into the penal sphere. The strategies and vision of Elizabeth Fry show how maternal, pastoral, and disciplinary forms of power operate to govern other women. Elizabeth Fry, a nineteenth-century British reformer, is an internationally acclaimed pioneer in women's prison reform. Her strategies formed the basis of the American women's prison reform movement. In Canada her legacy inspired the creation of national, regional, and several local Elizabeth Fry Societies – organizations that now play a critical role in Canadian penal politics.

Chapter 2 discusses the interdependence and coexistence of maternal, pastoral, and disciplinary techniques at Canada's first separate prison for women, the Andrew Mercer Reformatory. I argue that Canadian penal politics were influenced by developments in American women's prison reform. Reformers' white middle-class ideal vision of separate spheres led to the construction of separate institutions for women. By virtue of their sex, women reformers were in many respects regarded as 'authorized knowers' with respect to the ills of society, and in particular, deviant women.

Chapter 3 shows how maternal and other more repressive disciplinary logics – not to mention old-fashioned sovereignty – shaped how women were governed at the Female Unit of Kingston Penitentiary, and later at the infamous Prison for Women (opened in 1934). I present a partial picture of the circumstances surrounding the imprisonment of women at Kingston Penitentiary in nineteenth- and early twentieth-century Canada. Here, I focus on the early conditions of penal discipline, the perceived importance of female matrons, the struggle to build a separate custodial prison for women, and the multiple logics informing federal women's imprisonment at the newly constructed P4W.

Chapter 4 examines the role of well-intentioned women reformers in the post–Second World War period, and stresses four interrelated themes: the intersection of various logics and technologies of reform (social work and maternal); the governing of women prisoners by private agents; the interdependence of state and private reformers; and the politicization of the experiences and needs of women prisoners. I show how traditional maternal technologies of discipline were professionalized and integrated into the regime at P4W, and that penal power is not always entirely or even primarily linked to 'expert' systems of knowledge. Even though science and professionalization challenged the authority and legitimacy of women reformers, nonexpert knowledges and techniques of governing played an equally critical role in penality.

Chapter 5 focuses on the importance of 'difference,' and the importance of feminist 'difference politics' in the governing of women's prisons. I discuss at length the feminist/Aboriginal struggle to develop a women-centred prison model that would take into account the differences between male and female prisoners. The feminist criticism of and disappointment with liberal equality strategies contributed to the resurgence of difference strategies that emphasized women's common status as women. I analyse the recommendations of the pivotal 1990 Report of the Task Force on Federally Sentenced Women, and how those recommendations were acted on. The definition and redefinition of a culturally sensitive, women-centred prison is used to rethink feminist engagements with the state, and their role in reshaping women's penality.

In chapter 6, *Creating Choices* – a discussion of the Report of the 1990

Task Force on Federally Sentenced Women – is used to show how feminist reformers came to support neoliberal techniques of penal discipline, which stress 'responsibilization' and the production of self-governing prisoners. Techniques such as 'risk,' 'empowerment,' and 'choice' are very flexible: they are being used by a new generation of reformers to advocate an alternative feminist vision of penality, and by the state to modernize existing disciplinary techniques. These new penal strategies take for granted liberal ideals of autonomy, protection, equality, and choice. The recent report of the Arbour Commission about the gross violations of human rights at P4W reminds us that 'empowerment' can hardly be implemented in a population that never enjoyed the most basic liberal legal rights. The 'woman-centred prison' is a manifestation of this paradox. The woman-centred model acknowledges that women suffer injustices because of their sex, but it fails to acknowledge that a feminist vision of justice can unwittingly reproduce different kinds of injustices by denying the specific experience of incarceration and by viewing women as a homogeneous group. This creates a climate of reform that fails to recognize relations of power among women in different social sites. The governance of women by women can be as problematic as the governance of women by men, especially when the relations among the 'keepers' and the 'kept' are shaped by the institutional dynamics of imprisonment.

Chapter One

Mothering the Flock: Maternal Discipline and Pastoral Power

Ever since the nineteenth century, reformers, administrators, and politicians have attempted to reform women prisoners by establishing women-centred regimes, using softer and gentler technologies of reform. Current and past attempts to create a new regime for women have often been in stark contrast to the quasi-military, anonymous, and strictly uniform regimes imposed on men. Implicit in women-centred models is the idea that the negative attributes of penal discipline are tempered by the influence of women. There have been few critical accounts of the relations that emerge when women govern other women: the power relations among women are either overlooked, or they are naturalized (as in the relationship between a mother and daughter, or between an older and a younger sister). All but a few accounts of women's governance of prisoners overlook the imbalance of power inherent in the relationship between prisoners and guards, or keepers and the kept. The failure to acknowledge these power relations leads to a false impression of women-centred penal regimes. I argue that although women guards, administrators, and reformers have made significant contributions to women's penality and have done much to improve some conditions, their involvement in this realm has led to the production of new relations of power/knowledge.

If we are to understand the successes and failures of present correctional initiatives, it is critical that we understand the dynamics of past reform initiatives and institutional change. The primary objective of this chapter is to show how disciplinary power is both repressive and productive and how it operates in conjunction with other techniques of power – in this case pastoral power, which is more centrally concerned with the care and welfare of individuals in a way that is not 'normalized' in relation to scientific knowledges (Dean 1999: 76).

Studies of imprisonment generally outline the social control functions of the prison and show how related penal technologies operate to repress individuals through coercive and disciplinary therapeutic regimes (Foucault 1977; Ignatieff 1978; Rothman 1980, 1990; Cohen 1985; Garland 1985, 1990; Dobash, Dobash, and Gutteridge 1986; McCormick and Visano 1992; Duff and Garland 1994; Blomberg and Cohen 1995; and Simmons, Cohen, Cohen, and Beitz 1995). Drawing on Michel Foucault's influential text *Discipline and Punish*, many authors have argued that improved penal technologies have increased surveillance capabilities and widened and strengthened the carceral net. These studies have made a valuable contribution to our understanding of penal governance and how it relates to similar patterns of disciplinary regulation in alternate sites.

Studies on the imprisonment of women have outlined the patriarchal oppression of women offenders at the hands of their male keepers throughout the eighteenth, nineteenth, and twentieth centuries (Smart 1979; Moulds 1980; Heidensohn 1981, 1985; Freedman 1981; Carlen 1983; Rafter 1982, 1983, 1992; Dobash, Dobash, and Gutteridge 1986; Morris 1987; Zedner 1991b). Concerns about male power – especially patriarchal relations – dominate many of these studies. While some recent studies have analysed the links between gender, class, and racial oppression in the history of women's imprisonment (Sugar and Fox 1989; Rafter 1992; Adelberg and the Native Women's Association of Canada 1993; Richie 1996; Monture-Angus 2000), penal power has been narrowly conceptualized in terms of repression and social control. For the most part, these studies have emphasized the repressive patriarchal aspects of penal regulation without adequately addressing the complexity of relations involved in the normative production of 'a reformed woman.' The few Canadian analyses of this subject follow a similar pattern (Berzins and Cooper 1982; Cooper 1987; 1993; Axon 1989; Shaw 1992a, 1992b, 1993; Adelberg and Currie 1993; Faith 1993; Comack 1996). Over the past few years, Canadian researchers, such as Hattem (1986, 1991), Adelberg and Currie (1987), Vallières and Simon (1988), Frigon (1997, 1999), Shaw (1991a, 1991b, 1991c, 1992b, 1994), Biron (1992), Kendall (1993a, 1993b, 1994), Shaw and Dubois (1995), Comack (1996), Bertrand (1998, 1999), Woodrow (1998), and Martel (2000), have made significant contributions to knowledge regarding the needs and experiences of incarcerated women. In this, the contributions of feminist researchers have been invaluable. They have provided much-needed descriptive accounts of the conditions of women's confinement and/or narratives of state reform initiatives. They have shown how women prisoners have been neglected by the state and how male models of correctional reform have adversely affected the female offender. From these studies, it can be concluded that the Canadian state has put considerably less effort and fewer resources into researching the needs of incarcerated women than it has into the needs of incarcerated men.

Most authors suggest that conditions for women prisoners improved after women reformers and matrons entered the penal realm. They also note that the women who worked in these facilities received very little administrative support and that their working conditions were appalling. Most authors acknowledge that the problems associated with the incarceration of women were not resolved after women were hired and after separate women's facilities were constructed, but they do suggest that the governance of women by other women was a positive development in the history of women's incarceration. While the degree of improvement varied by institution, it is largely indisputable that as a result of reformers' efforts, there was an improvement in the material conditions of incarceration in many women's prisons across the United Kingdom and North America. Although conditions for women improved, idealized notions of benevolent maternal reform were not easily integrated into the punitive prison culture.

What British and North American studies of women's imprisonment do not show is how women reformers and administrators came to play a central role in the accumulation of knowledge that influenced the regulation of women. The existing analyses do not adequately address the relations of power that emerge when women govern other women. In feminist research on women's corrections there is also a tendency to apply narrow definitions of penal power and to understate the complexity of the role played by women reformers in program development. Canadian feminist literatures on the history of women's penality do not explore the diverse relations of power evident in women's penal reform, or the role of women in penal reform, or the importance of past attempts to create a women-centred penal reform strategy.[1] Rather than reproducing the feminist and Foucauldian claims that the knowledge used to regulate women was based on 'expert' scientific or professional systems of knowledge production and dissemination, I argue that lay women and amateur reformers played a key role in the production of knowledge about women in their care. This point is explained more fully in chapter 4.

Foucault's *Discipline and Punish* (1977) is about the relationship between power and knowledge. More specifically, it is about

> conceptualizing punishment as 'a complex social function,' involving not only 'repressive effects' or 'punishment aspects' of punitive mechanisms, but also a range of 'possible positive effects'; analysing punitive methods 'as techniques possessing their own specificity in a more general field of other ways of exercising power'; understanding the interconnection between punishment regimes and the 'human sciences'; and, finally, determining whether the 'entry of the soul on to the scene of penal justice, and with it the assertion in legal practice of a whole corpus of "scientific" knowledge,' reflects changes in the way the body itself is invested in power relations. (Howe 1994: 89)

Foucault (1977) observes that there is an 'interconnection between punishment regimes and expert human sciences.' This is an important observation; however, it overlooks the links between nonscientific, amateur, or lay knowledges, such as maternalism and evangelicalism, and penal regimes. British scholars such as Garland (1985), Dobash, Dobash, and Gutteridge (1986), Sim (1990), Rock (1996), and Kendall (2000) have shown how scientific knowledge provided by psychiatry and criminology are used to create 'a whole set of assessing diagnostic, prognostic, normative judgements concerning the criminal' (Foucault 1977: 18). These theorists and many others illustrate clearly how scientific techniques and rationalities become entangled with the power to punish. Analyses such as those of Dobash, Dobash, and Gutteridge (1986), Allen (1987a, 1987b), Chunn and Menzies (1990), Sim (1990), and Zedner (1991b) all stress the disciplinary aspects of penal and therapeutic governance of women. However, they fail to show how these disciplinary regimes coexist, intersect and sometimes rely on nondisciplinary expressions of power, such as pastoralism, self-governance, and actuarialism (Hannah-Moffat 1999, 2000). Alternatively, I argue that several forms of power/knowledge operate simultaneously.

Spiritual and maternal rationalities play a critical role in shaping the governance of women prisoners. Maternal metaphors, coexisting with the disciplinary logic of punishment, allow for the development of a form of penal discipline that naturalizes the exercise of power. Maternal power is based on an ethic of care that relies on a mother's duty and obligation to do whatever she can within her power to protect her child and ensure the production of a healthy and obedient citizen. There are few limits on the extent of this power. Mothers are as justified in punishing their children for inappropriate behaviour as they are in rewarding them for compliance, as long as neither occurs in excess. The disciplinary actions of a mother are generally understood as being in the best interests of her child. In the context of women's prisons, the disciplinary aspects of maternal strategies are concealed. Maternal strategies in some cases seem less invasive and regulatory than other forms of penal power; nevertheless, they *are* an exercise of power. Positive maternal techniques such as 'teaching child-rearing or home-making skills,' 'keeping in touch,' 'helping with discharge plans,' and 'acting in a woman's best interest' are used to normalize deviants and reinforce desirable behaviours without overt displays of force. Each of these strategies encourages women to take part in events designed to ensure that they conform to certain normative standards of behaviour.

In the nineteenth and twentieth centuries, maternal reformers and the ideal of motherhood played a key role in the governance of women prisoners and in the reform of women's prisons. I argue that the malleable character of maternal power has created diverse and at times contradictory situations. This chapter shows how women prisoners are governed through maternal reform strategies, in combination with pastoral and disciplinary modes of governing. Elizabeth Fry, a nineteenth-century British reformer, is discussed because she was an internationally acclaimed pioneer in women's prison reform and because her strategies formed the basis of the American women's prison reform movement. In Canada, her legacy inspired the creation of national, regional, and several local Elizabeth Fry Societies – organizations that now play a critical role in Canadian penal politics (see chapter 4).

Rethinking Maternalism: Maternal Rationalities and Strategies

The invocation of maternalism by so many different social actors compels us to re-evaluate its ambiguous meanings and uses.   (Koven and Michel 1993: 4)

Maternalism has typically been characterized as an ideology that emphasizes the tasks and qualities of motherhood; it is often associated with a woman's duty and responsibility to mother. Maternalism implies that women have natural abilities and capacities that are specific to their biological sex. Some of these qualities include nurturing, caring, selflessness, restraint, and household management. However, beyond claiming to promote the role of mothering and the 'qualities of a mother,' maternalism appears to have little specific content. Rather than discussing 'maternalism' in general, it is more instructive to discuss the specific dynamics of maternal ideologies and logics and strategies. Maternalism operates 'in relation to other discourses about citizenship, class relations, gender difference, and national identity, to name a few – and in reaction to a wide variety of concrete social and political practices' (Koven 1993: 125). Maternal images and narratives are compelling and flexible rationalities that can be easily linked to several technologies or techniques of governing.

Maternalism does not refer to a specific movement, but rather to the mobilization of a particular image of motherhood in combination with other rationalities. In a discussion of women's voluntary action on child welfare in nineteenth-century Britain, Seth Koven notes that women reformers often chose 'to invoke maternalism in making specific claims about why they as individuals, and women as a sex were specifically qualified to shape welfare policy and provide care for working class children' (1993: 125). While reform strategies that invoke maternalism are similar in content and approach, they are constituted in historically and culturally specific ways to accommodate a variety of agendas (cf. Koven and Michel 1993). Various maternal strategies draw on several political rationalities to define and legitimate reform initiatives and institutional technologies. These rationalities include the cult of true womanhood; Victorian morality; domesticity; separate spheres; religious ideals; and feminism. For example, the suffrage movement[2] used maternal as well as feminist rights-based arguments to help it secure the vote for women; the Women's Christian Temperance Movement used maternal, moral, and evangelical strategies to promote prohibition; educational reformers used maternal ideals, domesticity, and separate spheres ideology to promote domestic science training; and prison reformers have used all of these images at one time or another to rationalize the treatment of women prisoners.

Motherhood is a volatile political image that is 'capable of stirring women to support repressive campaigns under some circumstances as well as progressive causes under others' (Strange 1990: 222–3). My conceptualizations of 'maternal logics' and 'maternalism' differ from previous uses of these terms. The phrases 'maternal feminism' and 'social feminism' appear in a variety of historical discussions about the women's movement and, more generally, the history of women's activities. Maternal feminism and social feminism are terms often used to describe the activities of women prison reformers at the turn of the century (Freedman 1981; Rafter 1992; Oliver, 1994). The use of these terms specifically in penological literature is problematic. By collapsing 'maternalism' and 'feminism' into one descriptive phrase we lose sight of the differences and conflicts between the feminist and maternal ideologies and strategies that have shaped women's reform initiatives.[3] The power, flexibility, and contradictory aspects of these distinct rationalities are obscured. The incompatibilities between these rationalities, and the sites of resistance that emerge through their interaction, need to be recognized. Separating the term 'maternal feminism' into two distinct terms, 'maternalism' and 'feminism,' allows us to identify the distinctness of each reform strategy. It also allows for multiple interpretations of maternalism. It is widely recognized that there is more than one type of feminism; however, the multiple meanings of maternal logics and maternal politics are not so widely understood.

Maternal reform strategies were often inconsistent with feminist objectives. Many maternal reformers and their organizations, such as the Salvation Army and the Elizabeth Fry Society, would not have identified themselves *as* feminist, or *with* feminists. With respect to prison reform, at different historical junctures, maternalists united with feminists to advocate and lobby for the recruitment and employment of female matrons, police officers, parole officers, and social workers for women-only institutions. Similarly, the professionalization of women's voluntarism in areas such as social work can be linked to both feminist and maternal initiatives. However, the agendas of these reformers were not always compatible. While prison reformers often had important feminist insights with respect to the experiences of women and sexual inequalities, early reformers rarely became women's rights activists. Early American and Canadian prison reformers accepted traditional institutions of crime control: 'They wanted to improve the penal treatment of women, and to do so they eventually became keepers in their own prisons' (Freedman 1981: 2). However, reformers with a feminist rationality were more likely to challenge and question the authority of criminal justice institutions.

Christian Mothering as a Social Reform Technique

The mobilization of a maternal image or narrative varies according to local politics and objectives. In spite of the popularity of the ideal of motherhood in nineteenth- and twentieth-century reform, this status of womanhood was not always quite as celebrated.[4] Eighteenth-century paradigms of womanhood stressed the relationships between women and God, and Christian women and men as a wife and social companion (Bloch 1993). Between 1785 and 1815, authors and ministers began to place more emphasis on the moral and spiritual power of mothers. During this time of change, 'women eventually came to be seen as society's primary child rearers and motherhood often came to be viewed as a powerful vehicle used by women to wield broad social influence' (115). This valorization of motherhood elevated the public and political status of women in the United Kingdom, and later in North America.

Maternal imagery captured the variety of 'ideologies and discourses that exalted women's capacity to mother and applied to society as a whole the values they attached to that role: care, nurturing, and morality' (Koven and Michel 1993: 4). Women were increasingly portrayed as more virtuous than men and, in turn, more suited to the task of conserving society's morals. In keeping with these perceptions, women in many Western societies organized themselves in the name of social purity and moral reform, and mobilized available technologies and images to promote their mission. Maternal strategies stressed the ideal of the virtuous, pious, and understanding 'moral woman,' as well as the importance of reaffirming family values in the domestic sphere. Throughout the nineteenth century, the image of motherhood and the activity of public mothering gained prominence. Women were expected to be housekeepers of the state – that is, to restore and preserve the moral values of society, which were perceived as being threatened by the ills of industrialization and social change.

By the late 1830s the notion of an 'ideal' or 'true' woman was closely linked to her maternal and domestic capacities within the family and in the home. Family stability was perceived as central to middle-class morality; in the same vein, the family was a sanctuary for traditional moral and religious values (Zedner 1991b: 12). The ethic of motherhood was used to symbolize women's charity, nurturing, and moral vision. Maternal virtues operated on two levels in social reform: they promoted the ideal of domesticity; at the same time they legitimated women's public relationship to politics and the state, to the community, to the workplace, and to the marketplace (cf. Koven and Michel 1993: 6; Koven 1993: 98). Throughout the nineteenth and early twentieth centuries, maternal reformers in Britain and the United States used the image of the mother and an ideology of separate spheres to gain entry into certain institutions and to legitimate their presence in these predominately male bureaucracies.[5]

However, reformers' interpretations of the qualities and responsibilities of a 'public' mother were neither uniform nor homogenous. At different historical junctures and under certain circumstances, understandings and definitions of motherhood varied considerably. Social reformers' strategies relied on multiple, selective interpretations of motherhood for particular purposes. Many reformers combined images of motherhood with wider religious motifs (or symbols). For example, evangelical perspectives of motherhood in the mid-nineteenth century stressed the religiosity and moral superiority of women. Evangelical images of motherhood epitomized Christian virtues, feminine graces, purity, and domestic skills (Bloch 1993: 119). The symbol of Mary was prominent in Victorian constructions of a virtuous and moral maternal ideal. Religious images of women and motherhood reinforced the ideology of sexual purity and the notion of separate spheres. The evangelical ideal of motherhood 'broke with tradition by attributing to women a strong moral authority and granting them an important field of expertise' (120). This image was especially relevant to evangelical-based charity, philanthropy, and reform campaigns because it entitled women to a considerable amount of autonomy in the public sphere. Maternal and religious metaphors were flexible enough that reformers were able to construct dual images of ideal women. In some instances, religious images of women directly contradicted and undermined the maternal ideal. For example, nuns (one typical portrayal of the ideal Christian woman) challenged the conventional domestic and familial image of woman embraced by maternal reform narratives. The purity and chastity of nuns were given elevated status; even though they did not exemplify motherhood, nuns were able to use the maternal image to their advantage. Religious orders of women were able to mobilize a maternal imagery to legitimate their own programs for fallen women and delinquent girls.[6] Later sections of this chapter show how this imagery and salvationist narratives were also used by Elizabeth Fry to support her own evangelical maternal reform initiatives.

Reformers' responses to female crime were deeply embedded in a complex value system, 'at the heart of which was the highly artificial construct of ideal womanhood' (Zedner 1991a: 320). In Victorian constructions of femininity, paradoxical images of women were highlighted. Thus, women reformers were portrayed as 'virginal,' honest, and sober, and as uplifting moral influences; while criminal or fallen women were constructed as threatening, deceptive, avaricious, and dangerously susceptible to corruption.

Clear distinctions were drawn between different classes of women:

on the one hand, there was the depraved, dirty, misguided, and neglectful criminal mother; on the other, there was the refined, moral, spiritual, caring lady. Social standing played a significant role in the social construction of a 'lady.' The book *Reformatory Prison Discipline* by Mary Carpenter (1872), a mid-nineteenth-century British reformer, clearly articulates this dichotomy. In her descriptions of female convicts she noted that criminal women and women 'belonging to the higher sphere' differ in many respects. Criminal women she described as irrational, less intelligent, and unable to control their passions, and thus prone to 'extreme excitability, violent and even frantic outbursts of passion, a duplicity and disregard of the truth hardly conceivable in better classes of society' (Carpenter 1872 [1967]: 68). Female offenders were often judged against nineteenth-century middle-class standards of morality as encapsulated in the cult of true womanhood, the hallmarks of which were piety, purity, domesticity, and submissiveness (Smith 1990: 69–70). Having failed in all four categories, the female offender was seen as particularly loathsome and dangerous. Having fallen from greater heights by virtue of being born a woman, the female criminal sank to greater depths and was perceived as deserving greater punishment (70). Carpenter suggested that 'the very susceptibility and tenderness of woman's nature render her more completely diseased in her whole nature when this is perverted by evil; and when a woman has thrown aside the virtuous restraints of society and is enlisted on to the side of evil, she is far more dangerous to society than the other sex' (1864b, 1: 31–2; cited in Zedner 1991a: 321). Also:

> The expense which a bad woman is to the public, who come forth from a lengthened confinement in a Government gaol unreformed, is far greater than any possible cost which might have been incurred reforming her; the evil she has done within the prison to those around her is very great, and extends the poisonous influence to a widely extending circle, when the women she has corrupted go out into the world; on her own discharge she emerges from her seclusion only to plunge into greater excesses than before, and to perpetuate and intensify the pollution of the moral atmosphere from which she had been temporarily withdrawn. (1872 [1967]: 70–1)

The female criminal was, for many, a 'moral menace.' The only way to reform her was to bridge the gap between the feminine ideal and female immorality through an elaborate code of prescribed female behaviour. Reformers such as Carpenter and Elizabeth Fry came to believe that every effort, regardless of the expense, should be undertaken to redeem the female convict. For if she was not reformed (according to the moral criteria of reformers), she would be an ever-present moral risk and continue to corrupt innocence.

The fear and disgust expressed toward the fallen woman can also be linked to the dominant Victorian sexual ideology of separate spheres, wherein white middle-class men and women inhabited sexually different social spaces with distinct values and manners. Eventually, reformers used the ideology of sexual purity to legitimate the moral governance of women. This logic functioned to preserve distinctions between women and men and among women. The stigma of the tainted woman was used to control and regulate the sexuality and morality of women and men. Uncontrolled sexuality was often equated with chaos and social and moral contamination. The religiously inspired portrait of the fallen woman and the accompanying social stigma were powerful regulatory devices for all women. As Freedman (1981: 20) notes, 'the line that separated the pure woman from the fallen woman demarcated privilege on one side and degradation on the other.' By not crossing that line, pure women could retain their virtue and privileges, often at the expense of their alienated and fallen counterparts. Women were expected to be pure in order to enforce male continence and to uphold and protect the morality of society. The ideal of a virtuous, unblemished woman, when combined with images of motherhood and domesticity, gave women reformers immense social and political power.

Middle-class reformers benefited from the dichotomous constructions of women, who were portrayed either as 'risky' moral menaces or as maternal saviours. Unlike the criminal woman or the bad mother, early women reformers were given an exalted status. The image of the reformer paralleled the virginal religious icon, Mother Mary, who was portrayed as the 'divine, guide, purifier, inspirer of man' (Basch 1974: 6; cited in Zedner 1991b: 11). These reformers maintained that if given a chance to bring their feminine influence to bear, they could redeem the fallen woman and make her into a 'true woman' (Freedman 1981). Religious upper-middle-class ladies' domestic and moral prowess made them appropriate and likely candidates for social reform work. Many reformers were spinsters, widows, or unmarried women; even so, their reputable, untarnished character and status gave them legitimacy. Even if middle-class ideals of femininity were internalized by reformed women prisoners, the designation of 'a lady' might never be applicable, given these women's unscrupulous pasts.

Evangelical Maternalism and Women's Penality

When I discuss Elizabeth Fry, it is not to suggest that her logic of governing was operational in early Canadian penitentiaries; rather, it is to situate Canadian developments in a wider social, political, and historical context. Those who have examined the efforts of Fry have tended to stress the benevolent and progressive nature of her work (Lewis 1909; Barne 1962; Kent 1962; Pitman 1969; Smillie 1980; Dobash, Dobash, and Gutteridge 1986; Zedner 1991b; Stewart 1993). While these studies have revealed in detail the unquestionable contribution Fry made to penal reform, they have not critically assessed the wider theoretical and material implications of her work. Rather than offering a revisionist history of Fry, I will use this analysis of her work to show how multiple forms of power coexist in the carceral realm, and how our understanding of power/knowledge relations can be extended to include amateur reformers.

Elizabeth Fry

When Elizabeth Fry, in 1815, rapped at the prison doors in England, she not only summoned the turnkey, but sounded a call to all women in other lands to enter upon a most Christ-like mission.   Susan Barney 1891: 359; cited in Freedman 1981: 22

The 'Christ-like mission' of Elizabeth Fry shows how an amateur reformer used maternalism, Enlightenment principles, and her Quaker (evangelical) beliefs to gain access to prisons and to promote the employment and voluntary reform efforts of other women.[7] The pioneering activities and ideas of Elizabeth Fry (née Gurney)[8] are important because they point to a number of significant changes in the governance of women prisoners that emerged with the rise of maternal penal logic. Some of these changes are evident in American regimes, when the American Women's Reformatory Movement emerges in the mid-nineteenth century. Changes in Canadian regimes are not evident until the late nineteenth century, when the Andrew Mercer Reformatory is opened.

Fry was the first advocate of prison reform to recognize and argue that the needs of women prisoners were different from those of men prisoners. In many ways, Fry exemplified the evangelical mother, in that she devoted her life to the moral reform of fallen and depraved women. She also demonstrated the interconnectedness of disciplinary and pastoral techniques of governing. Maternal images (domesticity, motherhood, parental discipline, caring and nurturing) and pastoral strategies of spiritual redemption and guidance were essential to the attempts by Fry and her Ladies' Committee to domesticate female convicts and, more generally, the prison.

The Quakers were the main proponents of moral and spiritual reform for prisoners. Quaker colleagues like Joseph Fry, Samuel Gurney, Thomas Hancock, and Samuel Hoare joined together to form the Society for the Improvement of Prison Discipline to promote their ideal prison regime: solitude, prayer, and reflection under the spiritual guidance of a chaplain (Forsythe 1987; cited in Zedner 1991b: 103). Fry was a Quaker who, acting on her beliefs, sought to provide spiritual and moral guidance to women prisoners and to 'humanize' female prisons. The Quaker faith included a deep sense of social responsibility (Young and Ashton 1956: 36). Their approach to social reform and social work was premised on the firm belief that all men are equal in the eyes of God. They adhered to a strong individualism which advocated that 'everyone should prove his equality with others by hard work, thrift, upright living and honesty' (38). Even if individuals were living in poverty, they were expected to do everything in their power to become self-sufficient and support their dependants before appealing to others for charity. They maintained that the indigent should not be given charity until self-help had failed. However, unlike some of the other philanthropic organizations, the Quakers recognized that people's misfortunes and mistakes were often determined by a bad environment and not simply wilful sinfulness (41). The Quaker reformers believed that social problems were the result of a bad social environment. Consequently, they devoted much of their energy and charity to the prevention of poverty, crime, and social failure. Prison reform was a small part of their pioneering social work and reform initiatives.

Religious ideas and agendas were central, not peripheral, to the context and content of debates about punishment that preceded the large-scale use of incarceration as a reformative sanction (McGowen 1986, 1987, 1988; Spierenberg 1984). The church was widely recognized as the guardian of moral order and stability of the society; the corollary of this view was that the church had an important role to play in the treatment of those who threatened to upset this moral order and stability (Kerr 1979; cited in James 1990: 40). Many early forms of punishment had a sacred quality. Notions of mercy, pardoning, and sympathy, and the ritual of confession that occurred before corporal punishments were administered, are some examples of this role (Strange 1996). During execution processions, convicted offenders were often expected to seek penitence or divine mercy from clergy at the door of the church. The notion of penitence was also essential to early penal regimes, given that the penitentiary was expected to reach the soul of the criminal and not simply to punish the body of the offender. The concept that the prison should be a place of segregation, isolation, discipline, and systematic punishment alleviated by precise 'injections of hope' by a chaplain emerged with the founding of the modern prison, inspired by individuals such as Jeremy Bentham, John Howard, and Elizabeth Fry (James 1990: 4; also see Ignatieff 1978). In keeping with this tradition, early prison administrators emphasized the merits of moral and religious instruction and education. Once built, prisons, penitentiaries, and reformatories alike relied heavily on religious technologies of reform. Wardens ensured moral and religious reformation through techniques such as reading prayers and Bible chapters and teaching illiterate prisoners to read or spell with scriptures and religious readings (Baehre 1977: 198). Most prisons employed a chaplain to govern religious training. Early chaplains believed that penitentiaries had a much 'nobler aim' and 'higher destiny' than simply punishing the offender; they had an obligation and duty to 'save' the convict (James 1990: 29). Most secular prison authorities accepted and actively supported this approach. Quite predictably, the convergence of religious and secular goals enabled the increased involvement of nonstate agents in the project of 'saving' convicts. Religiously based organizations such as the YMCA, the Sisters of the Good Shepherd, the Quakers, and the Salvation Army played an integral role in the development and execution of a reformative and restorative penality.

Fry was an active member of the Society of Friends, and she was officially accepted as a full minister in 1811. At the time, Quakerism was the only religion that accepted the leadership of women in ministerial capacities. From that time onward, she devoted herself to social reform – or *concerns* as they were called for Quaker women (Kent 1962: 32). Initially, Fry addressed her concerns from the safe confines of her home and within the small circles of the Society of Friends. However, in 1812 Fry decided to make 'a sacrifice of natural feeling, to leave the comforts of [her] own home, and [her] beloved husband and children' (Kent 1962: 32) to take a religious tour of Quaker meetings.

Fry's commitment to penal reform was religiously inspired and motivated. First and foremost, by the example of her own conduct she endeavoured to establish a Christian presence in prisons. The fostering of a Christian ethic in prisons was contingent on the development of a moral and religious reform program designed by and administered by Christian women like herself. Her spirituality complemented her maternal image. This combination gave her credibility in the community and with male bureaucrats, but it also 'created a curiously unstable matrix of mutually reinforcing yet contradictory values' (Koven and Michel 1993: 10). Women were expected to cultivate their womanhood and to provide moral guidance in the home, as well as promote Christian values in their communities through charity and voluntarism. Fry's charitable work conflicted with her domestic duties on a number of occasions. Interestingly, her devotion to penal reform and her absence from her home and family brought her condemnation for being a neglectful mother (Fry and Cresswell 1848; Dobash, Dobash, and Gutteridge 1986). Freedman (1981: 2), reflecting on the similar experiences of early American women prison reformers, notes that mid-nineteenth-century American 'reformers clung to a definition of woman's separate nature that limited their own power and often stifled the inmates they sought to aid.' Elizabeth Fry was no exception.

Pastoral Techniques of Governing

Fry's concern for the general welfare of prisoners and her attention to their special needs is important because it shows how multiple expressions of power coexist in penal settings. Fry's activities in the prison system illustrate what Foucault (1981) called pastoral power, which is often but not exclusively linked to Christianity. Foucault argues that pastoralism is a technique 'orientated towards individuals and intended to rule them in a continuous and permanent way' (227). Unlike centralized forms of state or political power, pastoralism is an individualized power. Foucault (235) indicates that pastoral power concerns the lives of individuals and that the metaphorical role of the 'shepherd' is to 'ensure, sustain, and improve the lives of each and everyone.' He claims that the metaphorical 'shepherd' has an obligation or responsibility to his flock. He is responsible for the salvation of the flock, and this salvation occurs through the expression of 'kindly and individualized' forms of power. The actions of the shepherd are generally geared to the best interests of the flock – he feeds them, watches over them when they sleep, and ensures their safety. He is expected to have an intimate understanding of the needs of each member of the flock, and to tend to those needs. The shepherding relationship implies a significant level of knowledge, and hence power, over the lives of individuals. Foucault argues that the 'shepherd-God-like relation' with the flock allows for the gathering, guiding, and leadership of dispersed individuals. Foucault uses the metaphor of the 'shepherd-flock game' to imply that 'the aim of government is to promote the well-being of its subjects by means of detailed and comprehensive regulation of their behaviour' (Hindus 1996: 118).

The techniques of Christian pastorship (examination, confession, guidance, and obedience) used by the shepherd in the execution of his duties have a wider purpose – that of self-examination (Foucault 1981: 239). As Hindus (1996: 121) notes, 'Christian ideas of sin, attainment and salvation, for example, add to the moral complexity of the shepherd and each member of the flock.' Pastoralism requires a high level of devotion from the shepherd, who sacrifices his own needs for the flock. While the shepherd is not legally compelled to guide the flock, he regards his voluntary work as a virtue and as leading to his own salvation. By tending to the physical and spiritual needs and desires of women prisoners, Fry was able to govern women through clearly benevolent, but still invasive, forms of power. Fry's kindness (providing clothing, bedding, and food, and later tending to spiritual, maternal, and vocational needs) allowed her to gain an intimate knowledge of her flock. She made a number of personal sacrifices to ensure the salvation of criminal women by training them to exercise self-government, and thereby furthered her own salvation. Her power arose from her own benevolence; it was not coercion. Her concern for the 'welfare' of women prisoners predates the formulation of the punishment-welfare nexus, which depends on a more scientific knowledge of crime and penality (see Garland 1985).

Consistent with Foucauldian interpretations of pastoral power, Fry fulfilled a shepherding role for a lost and neglected 'herd' of women. Historical images and narratives that attempt to capture the magnitude of Fry's contribution to women's penality often construct her as a saviour. Angelic portraits of Fry are quite common, as are portraits of her leading women in prayer, or teaching them specific skills such as mothering or quilting. The form of pastoral exhibited by Fry implies a relationship between the ruler and ruled (prisoner) that is more intimate and continuous than most standard 'models of government by consent' would permit (cf Hindus 1996). As noted by Hindus (1996: 118), 'pastoral power as Foucault presents it is concerned more with the welfare of subjects than with their liberty.' It is partly for this reason that regimes of pastoral power of this nature, at this time align with broader penal objectives of reform.

Maternal Discipline: Making Moral Mothers and Industrious Citizens

The main components of Fry's reform program were these: the moral and religious instruction of women prisoners; the governing of women by women; the employment of women prisoners; and the classification of prisoners. Throughout her career, Fry, a mother of nine, relied on the ideologies of motherhood and the innate responsibilities and character-istics of women to legitimate her reform activities and to solicit finan-cial and volunteer support. Initially, Fry's reform efforts were directed towards prisoners' children.[9] She used her involvement with these children to justify her presence in the institution and to gain credibility among the mothers and the authorities. Maternal images also legiti-mated the participation of the 'ladies' in 'cleaning up' the prison re-gime. The more general concept of maternal penal governance marked an important shift in relations of power/knowledge in women's pris-ons. This section examines some of the dynamics of the emergent 'benevolent' regime of evangelical maternal discipline. Fry dealt with her anxieties about the women in Newgate Prison by focusing on their children[10] and on their obligations and responsibilities as mothers. One of her first gestures inside the women's prison was to pick up one of the prisoner's children and begin asking the mother about the child. She stated, 'Friends, many of you are mothers. I too am a mother. I am distressed for your children. Is there not some thing we can do for these innocent ones? Do you want them to grow up to be real prisoners themselves? Are they to learn to be thieves and worse?' (Whitney 1937: 152; cited in Young and Ashton 1956: 155).

One portrait graphically depicts Fry's 'motherly love' and her ges-tures toward the prisoners' children. The prisoners and their children portrayed in this drawing are dirty, impoverished, callous, and suspi-cious of Fry; yet they are also surprised and somewhat humbled by Fry's gestures toward the children. Fry communicated to the mothers their responsibilities for keeping the children clean and disciplined. She preached to them about the risks presented to impressionable children by the depravity of the prison environment. She encouraged the women to organize a school and some productive activities for their children. In her initial contact with the women, Fry introduced the Quaker principle of 'self-help.' At the end of her visit, she left the prisoners with the task of creating a school and choosing a governess for it. That night, when she left the gaol, the officials remarked on the calm and quiet in the woman's unit, the 'cuffing' and disciplining of children, and the increased demands for soap. The women used the soap and whatever water they could find to clean their children and make them more presentable for Fry's next visit. Fry's emphasis on the children's discipline also served as a means for disciplining their mothers and the prisoners more generally. A separate school for women prisoners was developed shortly after the children's school. The prisoners supported the school partly because they wanted to improve themselves through education, but also to break the tedium and monotony of the prison routine. However, Young and Ashton (1956: 156) indicate that the school for women was more difficult to establish than the children's school. The authorities were not interested in supporting the education of women prisoners. To execute her plans for the women's school, Fry called into being the 'Ladies' Association for the Improvement of the Female Prisoners at Newgate.' This committee was composed of ten women, 'who pledged themselves to go daily to Newgate, and to provide materials for reading, writing and handiwork' (Young and Ashton 1956: 156). Eventually, a paid matron was appointed by the Ladies' Committee to supervise the prisoners' work and education.

The prisoners were disciplined through the training they received and the expectation that they would become 'good mothers.' Through their involvement with the school, women were taught to read scriptures and were trained in domestic duties. Implicit in the idea of motherhood, and maternalism more generally, was the notion of discipline: a good mother was expected to control and discipline her children and exercise self-discipline. The prison school became a disciplinary and regulatory tool through which spiritual, maternal, and feminine ideals were promoted. Maternal ideals of discipline were promoted on two levels. First, women prisoners were expected to adhere to certain normative ideals of motherhood to properly train and discipline their own children. By teaching women how to govern their children, Fry, the matrons, and the Ladies' Committee were governing the women themselves. The second level of maternal discipline focused on the relations between the prisoners and their female keepers. Women working in the prison used their maternal status to influence the behaviour of prisoners, who were often infantilized and deemed in need of maternal guidance. Clearly, a naturalized relation of power between mothers and children was being used in conjunction with traditional penal techniques to govern prisoners and staff. Fry, like those who followed her tradition, was deeply concerned about the criminal mother. In many ways, women offenders were double-deviants in that they violated the criminal law and also deviated from the standard norms of motherhood. A drawing from a biography on the life of Elizabeth Fry illustrates this image of a bad mother. In the drawing, the mother is shown holding a naked, open-mouthed baby and drinking from its bottle, apparently placing her own needs before those of her child. Criminal women repudiated the revered qualities of femininity, and 'in doing so they offended not only against the law, but against their ascribed social and moral roles' (Zedner 1991a: 320). Reformers often appealed to the maternal instincts of the prisoners, in the hope that they would improve their own situations for the sake of their children. Women's responsibilities as mothers were a key element in reformers' attempts to have the women govern themselves in an appropriate manner. In keeping with the image of the criminal mother presented in Fry's accounts, Carpenter (1872 [1967]), several years later, recounted similar concerns and attempts to appeal to the maternal nature of prisoners. She noted: 'We had been taken to a large room appropriated to nursing mothers with their infants! The room was full, and the spectacle awful! The faces of those mothers can never be forgotten, for they exhibited every species of hideous vice and degradation. And these were to give the first impressions to the young immortal beings who were unhappily their children, and who were imbibing from them the tainted streams of life' (Carpenter 1872 [1967]: 82).

The reformers of this time were deeply concerned about the effect the criminal mother would have on her child; they were also concerned about the influence of the 'other wicked mothers,' whose 'looks and voices were bad and fiendlike.' In their role as mothers, women criminals were 'identified as a biological source of crime and degeneration' (Zedner 1991a: 308). Corruption in mothers was commonly believed to be a major source of juvenile delinquency (Carpenter 1858, 1864; cited in Zedner 1991a: 327). Increasingly, mothers and especially working mothers were being held accountable for miscreant children.

Later on in England, separate quarters were established for convicts' children. The children were governed by 'respectable women' who cared for them on a daily basis on the institutions' premises. Mothers who exhibited good behaviour during the week were permitted to visit their children. The intention of this practice is obvious. Mary Carpenter[11] (1872 [1967]: 83) noted that this privilege 'produced an excellent effect on the mothers' and encouraged these women, perhaps for the first time, 'to think of their solemn responsibilities as mothers.' The notion of rescuing or reclaiming these women was initially perceived as next to impossible, and at first, few 'respectable' women were willing to involve themselves with women they believed to be beyond reform.

Maternal Power/Knowledge – the Governing of 'Women' by 'Women'

The state often encouraged benevolent activists to establish voluntary networks at the local level to develop and execute programs on behalf of women and children, because such programs often reduced public expenditures while securing or reproducing the dominant social order (Koven 1993: 89–98). Women were often welcomed in reform movements for their 'womanly qualities of nurturing, selflessness, and skill in household management' (Kealey 1979: 6). Consistent with this philosophy and the politicization of women, a number of new professions emerged in the late nineteenth and early twentieth centuries that utilized women's 'special skills.'

One strategy women used to gain credibility for their reform efforts was to construct themselves as experts on particular issues. The strategies of maternal reformers clearly linked the place of women in the home to their work in the wider 'public sphere.' Reformers argued that women were imbued with 'special abilities and capacities' that enabled them to accomplish social and individual reform. Maternal activists also insisted that they were responsible for establishing order and well-being for the country as a whole, not just for their families (Prentice et al. 1988: 169). Ironically, most maternal reformers promoted the belief that a woman's first priority must be her family and that women's involvement in reform should revolve around family-oriented issues. The expertise of these women, many of whom were evangelical reformers, was not challenged until the rise of scientific knowledges and professional social work eventually displaced nonscientific, lay knowledges and feminine virtue.

In the nineteenth century, maternal rationalities figured prominently in the public discourse on women's expertise. Women used several rationalities and strategies to legitimate their reform strategies and, more generally, their involvement in the public sphere. Benevolent philanthropy quickly became an accepted role for a 'disparate group of middle-class women who had created a mission for themselves, which relied on their unique capabilities as women and especially as mothers' (Kealey 1979: 2). As the nineteenth century progressed, women's interests grew beyond the domestic sphere to embrace social, economic, and political activities that had previously been reserved for men. The upper-middle-class voluntary associations that emerged during the nineteenth century in England, the United States, and Canada played an important role in linking the private female world of household and family to the public, male-dominated world of politics (cf. Koven 1993: 94). Women reformers envisioned the development of state policies and institutions predicated on the qualities of motherhood and in which women would play an active role as volunteers, electors, policymakers, bureaucrats, and workers within and outside the home (Koven and Michel 1993: 3). Philanthropy and women's volunteer labour figured prominently in the development of the welfare state.

Maternal reformers like Fry believed that evangelical maternal guidance was an appropriate and necessary technique of women's penal reform. For Fry, the success of an evangelical/maternal disciplinary strategy was contingent on the employment and involvement of proper female role models. The tutelary power of matrons, reformers, and ladies' committees would prove to be a key element in later international developments in women's penality. It was increasingly accepted that imprisoned women had to be treated differently from men. For Fry, Newgate 'offered an extreme example of how badly the dominant masculine upper class could design and administer a prison' (Kent 1962: 33). She argued that the supervision of women convicts by men was fraught with the potential for corruption, neglect, and physical and sexual abuse. However, her reasons for promoting separation extended beyond her fear of sexual relations among the male guards and women prisoners. She recognized that women had different reasons for committing crime, and unique responsibilities such as child rearing. She understood that the needs of women and their offspring were clearly different from those of male convicts and that they could be best interpreted by other women – by female staff and ladies' committees (Stewart 1993: 60). Furthermore, Fry argued that the constructive rehabilitation of women relied on the presence of other women, who would perform the tasks of mother, friend, spiritual guide, and role model. One of Fry's most contentious proposals was that entirely separate prisons for women be constructed, which would include 'no men at all except a chaplain and a medical attendant' (Barne 1962: 141). She further argued that male turnkeys should never be permitted to enter the women's unit:

'When a prison is properly managed it is unnecessary, because, by firm and gentle management, the most refractory can be managed by their own sex' (Pitman 1969: 164). Fry was not able to secure funding and approval for the construction of separate prisons for women, but she did succeed in funding the employment of women matrons.

Fry believed firmly that morally upstanding and conscientious women like herself could improve the living conditions in women's prisons and instil good habits of order, discipline, and thrift in prisoners. She also believed that in order to reform the prison, the bodily well-being of prisoners – 'plenty of ventilation, plenty of sunshine, scrupulous cleanliness, association, as far as possible, with those of sound mind and high principle' – must be carefully attended to (Lewis 1909: 166). Determined to improve the conditions at Newgate, Fry sought the permission of penal officials to design an alternative approach to managing and reforming women prisoners. The cornerstone of her alternative vision was the Ladies' Committee and the eventual employment of matrons. Virtuous ladies and matrons (governed by the ladies) were expected to be role models for the prisoners, and for women more generally. Fry believed that the appointment of the proper women as matrons was critical to ensuring the proper administration of the prison. The matron was expected to live in the institution and to abide by a strict code of ethical and moral conduct. The practice of having women matrons live on the prison grounds was incorporated into some early American and Canadian penal regimes, and in some cases it continued until the mid-twentieth century.

Fry claimed that women had a particular responsibility and duty that required them to do this type of benevolent work. In *Observations*, her book on the subject, she wrote that 'no person will deny the importance attached to the character of and conduct of women with their domestic and social relations ... but it is a dangerous error to suppose that the duties of a female end there' (Barne 1962: 135). She also noted: 'May the attention of *women* be more and more directed to these labours of love; and may the time quickly arrive, when there shall not exist, in this realm, a single public institution [where women] ... shall not enjoy the *efficacious superintendence* of the pious and benevolent of their own sex' (Fry 1827: 8; cited in Freedman 1981: 23). According to Fry, women had an innate capacity for nurturing and disciplining that could and should be applied in penal institutions. This depiction of maternal power/ knowledge shows how pastoral and productive disciplinary techniques combined in the logics informing the governance of women prisoners, and how pastoral and maternal techniques were combined to create a new vision of penal discipline.

In 1817, Fry was able to assemble a group of volunteers to aid her in her efforts at the prison. They called themselves the Ladies' Association for the Improvement of Female Prisoners in Newgate (later shortened to Ladies' Committee Newgate).[12] The objective of this association was to 'provide for the clothing, the instruction, and the employment of women; to introduce them to knowledge of the Holy Scriptures, and to form in them, as much as possible, those habits of order, sobriety, and industry, which may render them docile and peaceable whilst in prison, and respectable when they leave it' (Fry and Cresswell 1848: 262). Cooperation between the Ladies' Committee and the prison authorities was central to Fry's philosophy. Fry believed that such a committee could effectively and efficiently administer and perform practical social work and penal reform (Stewart 1993: 5). In keeping with this objective, she organized weekly visits to Newgate Prison for the Ladies' Committee, and urged women to organize their efforts rather than act on an individual basis.

The value of having women of significant social standing on the Ladies' Committee was not underestimated. Fry believed that 'women of status had the time to devote to charity work, the means to financially support the endeavour of their committees, and the influence to command respect from parliamentarians, prison officers, and prisoners alike' (Kent 1962: 74). These characteristics were important because at first, most reforms, such as the hiring of a matron to supervise the women, were initiated and financed by Fry and her committee (Smillie 1980: 24; cited in Stewart 1993: 5). Reform efforts that were not funded by the Ladies' Committee were often supported through the sale and distribution of books and pamphlets written by philanthropic ladies. After some struggles, the 'ladies' were elevated to positions of authority in the prison, and they rose to the challenge of reforming and instilling good habits of order, cleanliness, and godliness in the prisoners. The women on the Ladies' Committee, and later the matrons, were expected to be virtuous and moral; Fry also demanded that these women have strong religious convictions and commitments. Most of the women who worked in the prison and volunteered their time had a strong Christian background. The emphasis on spirituality can be linked to Fry's emphasis on redemption of the prisoners, who were often conceptualized as sinners.

The hiring and selection of matrons was an important duty (according to Fry and her Ladies' Committee), but there was little agreement about who should be responsible for hiring and supervising of the matron. Initially, Fry and the Ladies' Committee argued that *they* should hire and supervise the matrons. Many penal administrators and prison wardens, who were male, disagreed, arguing that they were capable of supervising the matron and her employees. In many instances the matrons were the wives of wardens in charge of the large male facilities where the women prisoners were detained. This disagreement over supervision of prisoners and matrons was one of the earliest challenges to the authority of the ladies in the penal realm. In response, Fry argued that it was important for female officers to be supervised, where possible, by ladies of 'principle and respectability.' She believed that this type of monitoring was crucial to the maintenance of an orderly institution and proper morals and habits (Pitman 1969: 165). Fry's lobby for an all-female staff was partially supported by penal officials and policymakers. The Newgate governor eventually agreed to pay half the matron's salary. And further, the 1823 Penal Act endorsed the principle that where possible, women should be governed by women (Smith 1962: 106). Throughout the nineteenth century, Fry's ideal notion of women governing women was endorsed by the government and implemented in most large prisons. Nonetheless, these matrons were routinely managed by male penal administrators, not by ladies' committees as suggested by Fry.

The learned 'nonexpert' skills and ideas of women like Fry and her followers made a significant contribution to the development and administration of women's and children's institutions. Even so, these women were eventually disempowered and alienated from their own creations by state bureaucracies. Research by Koven (1993: 100) indicates that in the later half of the nineteenth century, British women reformers were being alienated from policymaking. In exchange for state support and funding, they were expected to relinquish their authority over their own organizational and institutional initiatives.

The Legacy of Elizabeth Fry's Ideas

Fry's original strategy of reform was based on role modelling, motherly love, and spiritual and moral guidance. Two tangible results of Fry's activism were the development of separate institutions for women and the hiring of women matrons.[13] Since Fry's evangelical and maternal logic was in conflict with that of the secular reformers, it is difficult to determine the extent to which her ideas of maternal discipline were incorporated into custodial regimes. Fry was one of the first advocates of after-care services for women. She made several visits to other countries to share information and experiences about the prisons and prisoners she had encountered. As prison reform increased in importance in many countries, the notion of a Ladies' Committee attracted much attention from all types of women, and Fry began to receive letters asking for advice and opinions from all over the world (Barne 1962: 171). The moral organization of women prisoners as attempted by Fry inspired a philanthropic movement that spread throughout the world. The rationalities and technologies employed by Fry would be reproduced by a new generation of women reformers.

Conclusions

The positive images of maternal love and pastoral guidance and the authoritative images of mothers as disciplinarians are ambiguously linked to women's penality. Benevolent lessons in motherhood and pastoral strategies of governing played a critical role in the moral regulation of women and in solidifying a role for women in penal governance. The maternal governing of women by women does not equalize relations of power in penal settings; instead, it *naturalizes* them. Maternal reform strategies are part of a much larger and more complex web of rationalities and technologies governing the punishment of offenders. Besides being influenced by Victorian morality, religiosity, and feminine ideals, maternal penal strategies were also informed by conventional penal ideologies. When maternal strategies are combined with penal techniques, such as imprisonment, a unique form of maternal discipline emerges. The pioneering efforts of Elizabeth Fry in the late eighteenth and early nineteenth centuries provide a good example of how evangelical maternalism is integrated with penal discipline, and how various forms of power coexist.

This chapter highlighted the flexibility and diversity of power/knowledge relations in penality, and the presence of these relations in circumstances where women are governing other women through a well-intentioned and benevolent regime of maternal and/or spiritual governance. When women reformers, volunteers, or matrons govern women prisoners, certain structural relations of power are encountered that are not mitigated by gender sameness. Although women reformers, volunteers, matrons, and prisoners are of the same sex, relations of

power continue to exist between these socio-economically and culturally heterogeneous categories of women. The next chapter analyses a
maternally based, 'women-centred' strategy to show that the governance of women by women fails to rectify some of the problems in penal
governance typically associated with the regulation of women by men.

Chapter Two

Mother Knows Best: The Development of Separate Institutions for Women

The sentimental cult of domestic virtues is the cheapest method at society's disposal of keeping women quiet without seriously considering their grievances or improving their position.
Myrda and Klien 1993

Feminist theorists are sensitive to the ways in which social controls are exercised on women *as women* to encourage conformity to prescribed gender roles. The literature on how women are regulated through paternal logics is fairly well established. What is less developed are analyses of how maternal logics are used by *women* to regulate women and shape institutional agendas. This chapter analyses how maternal discipline is applied in women's penal reform projects. It shows how the metaphor of motherhood and, in particular, the image of mothers' responsibility for correcting their errant daughters was adopted by state and nonstate maternal reformers in the late nineteenth and early twentieth centuries. I analyse certain trends in institutional and prison reform in Canadian and American women's imprisonment as well as the development of maternal reform strategies aimed at reforming rather than punishing the offender.

A pervasive faith in the ability of punishment to change the offender and restore social order has persisted since the Enlightenment. Criminologists and sociologists who study the dynamics of penality and social change have reviewed in detail the successes and failures of past initiatives. Most have concluded that while penal reformers and administrators claim to have benevolent and humanitarian intentions, punishment has been a manifestation of disciplinary power that ultimately serves to regulate individuals through various technologies of social control (Ignatieff 1978; Rothman 1980, 1990). By and large, these studies tend to disregard developments in women's corrections.

Most revisionist studies of the functional and instrumental aspects of penality, although instructive, offer little insight into how penal logics operate and how they affect and are affected by wider logics of reform. David Garland's analysis (1990) of modern punishment offers an alternative approach to understanding some recent changes in penality and can aid in the analysis of women's imprisonment. Garland's project – to understand theoretical developments in the sociology of punishment – makes a significant contribution to this field of inquiry. He notes that penal policy is 'a rich and flexible tradition which has always contained within itself a number of competing themes and elements, principles and counter-principles ... its key terms have been developing a fluid rather than fixed, producing a series of descriptions – *moral reform, training, treatment, correction, rehabilitation, deterrence, incapacitation* – for what it is penal sanctions do' (7; emphasis added). He asserts that these 'competing and flexible themes' have played a critical role in establishing and legitimating technical apparatuses designed to punish and control deviants while simultaneously furthering the social engineering of a 'good' society. For example, Garland (6) suggests:

> In normal circumstances the administrators and employees of a penal system understand and justify their own actions within the established ideological framework – a working ideology. This official ideology is a set of categories, signs, and symbols through which punishment represents itself to itself and others. Usually this ideology provides a highly developed rhetorical resource which can be used to give names, justifications, and a measure of coherence to a vast jumble of things that are done in the name of penal policy. Not the least of its uses is to supply the means to explain (or explain away) failures and to indicate the strategies which will, it is hoped, prevent their reoccurrence.

Garland's argument can be expanded to help us understand and theorize developments in women's penality. For example, maternalism – one prominent working ideology of modern punishment – was employed by both reformers and administrators to challenge the failures of the penitentiary (custodial) model and to justify the creation of separate institutions for women prisoners. The operation of these institutions relied on a maternal logic that was combined with other ideologies informing penal administrations, such as labour, religious, moral, and domestic training. A maternal logic, as an example of Garland's working ideology, provides a 'coherence to a vast jumble of things' that are done to and for women prisoners by well-intentioned reformers and administrators. Besides legitimating the things done to improve conditions in women's prisons, maternal logic can be used to understand some of the failures to change certain repressive elements of custodial regimes, and some of the overtly punitive technologies that were used when women failed to conform to maternal notions of reformability. Maternalism is a versatile concept, one easily linked to a wide variety of disciplinary practices.

The image of motherhood that underpins maternal logic is difficult to contest. Maternal ideals are flexible enough to be combined with a wide variety of penal techniques that also rely on a versatile range of ideologies. Implicit in the concept of motherhood is an almost universally accepted productive or positive discipline, as described in chapter 1. To varying degrees, certain forms of maternalism have been accepted or rejected by institutions at different historical moments. The first section of this chapter places historical developments in Canadian women's imprisonment in a wider correctional context. It examines the impact on Canada of the maternally based American women's prison reform movement, which sought better care for female convicts in custodial institutions. The reformers' maternal critique of custodial institutions, their redefinition of the 'female criminal,' and their promotion of separate prisons, show integration of rather than antagonism between nineteenth-century maternal reformism and penal discipline. In the second section I discuss the flexible and eclectic nature of maternal justice through an analysis of the early history of the Andrew Mercer Reformatory, English Canada's first separate prison for women.

The Creation of Separate Institutions for Women Prisoners

Impact of the American Women's Prison Reform Movement in Canada

Penal theorists and reformers had a profound influence on nineteenth-century penal policy. However, as Zedner notes (1991b: 130), 'the most coherent sources of penal policy for women lay mainly outside government policy making circles and arose from publicized but largely voluntary efforts.' Secular and evangelical penal philosophies were combined with maternal logics to devise a separate strategy of maternal reform for women prisoners. Penal reformers and administrators used maternal logics to forge improbable coalitions that led to women governing female prisoners under the authority of maternal benevolence (cf. Koven and Michel 1993).

By the late 1840s, female prisoners were usually supervised by women officials in makeshift women's wings of mixed prisons. The conditions in these units prompted changes that fundamentally altered the face of women's penality. Throughout the nineteenth and early twentieth centuries, American maternalists, inspired by the work of Elizabeth Fry, spearheaded a reform movement that ultimately affected Canada, Britain, and the United States. The construction of separate prisons for women, based on the principle of maternal guidance, was a result of this wave of reform. The movement affected more than simply women's prisons; it fundamentally changed the governance of women more generally. In the sphere of penality, it led to the hiring of many women matrons – an accomplishment that had several unanticipated consequences. Underpinning these strategies was a reformative maternal logic that incorporated some elements of evangelical maternalism but was largely reliant on moral definitions of criminality and on secular interpretations of women's natural expertise as mothers. In this, it differed from the evangelical maternalism advocated by Elizabeth Fry and her Ladies' Committee.

In order to institute a women-centred program of governance, maternal reformers had to do three things: reconstruct the tarnished image of women convicts; 'sell' the importance of proper maternal guidance; and convince the authorities to build separate prisons for women. These objectives were partially based on a critique of failed custodial models. The establishment of Ontario's Andrew Mercer Reformatory for Women in 1874 was an example of the mobilization of a maternal logic. Once it was built, a women-centred form of governing, envisioned and administered by women, was able to emerge.

Custodial Catastrophes and Maternal Interventions

The American women's reform movement began in 1840, when several individuals and small groups of women, concentrated in New York, Massachusetts, and Indiana, took up the cause of women prisoners as their special mission (Freedman 1981: 22). This movement peaked between 1870 and 1920 with the building of several reformatories for women (Rafter 1992; Freedman 1981, 1996). As Freedman (1981) notes, this movement evolved from a critique of state responses to women's deviance and from the perceived inability of the state to sufficiently care for 'fallen sisters.' While insisting that the state had a moral obligation and duty to appropriately care for and reform female convicts, women reformers attempted to accomplish this task themselves through their own good will and charity. Women reformers' calls for state accountability with respect to the care of female convicts and for an endorsement of their own strategies significantly altered women's penality. The strong involvement of American women in this reform movement occurred only after certain state bureaucrats appealed to the evangelical maternal duty of women to come to the aid of their estranged kin. For example, Freedman (1981) reports that in 1819 the male managers of the New York Society for the Prevention of Pauperism were appalled at the condition of the women's quarters at Bellevue Penitentiary and disturbed by women's lack of interest in helping their less fortunate sisters. The managers declared, 'Why this melancholy spectacle of female wretchedness has claimed no more attention, and excited no more sympathy, in a city like ours, where scenes of exalted benevolence and acts of religious devotion are continually displayed, we cannot say' (in Freedman 1981: 7). The belief that women 'messengers' had a role to play in cleaning up this atrocious mess prompted a small but significant reform initiative.

The early activities of these women were similar to those of Elizabeth Fry: reformers visited the women in custody, advocated improved conditions, and eventually developed associations to help women prisoners reintegrate into their communities. In an effort to improve conditions in American women's prisons, women reformers donated their time and money (used to hire matrons and acquire basic amenities, such as soap and food). The advocacy and persistence of these women led to the hiring of a few matrons and female staff (when deemed necessary by administrators), the development of women's prison associations, and eventually, the construction of separate institutions. The first separate custodial institution for women was Mount Pleasant Female Prison at Ossining, New York, which opened in 1835. According to Rafter (1992: 16), the founding of this institution was a milestone in women's corrections because it was the first women's prison in the United States that was deliberately established; before then, women's units had been haphazardly developed as appendages to men's prisons. Mount Pleasant Prison was governed by two innovative women, Eliza Farnham and Georgiana Bruce, who experimented with reformational techniques. These foreshadowed the 'great reformatory movement' just ahead (Rafter 1992: 16–17).

Prior to the development of a semi-organized reform movement, a few dedicated American reformers worked, often in isolation, within the system and with administrators to improve the conditions of women prisoners, most of whom were held in men's prisons. It was the interest of charitable women such as Dorthea Dix, Abigail Hopper Gibbons, Mary Wister, and Sarah Doremus that inspired changes in penal practice and policy and encouraged a new generation of reformers, who eventually succeeded in designing specific programs for normalizing women prisoners. When early American reformers encountered resistance to their ideas about specialized institutions for female criminals, they established private institutions (Pollock-Byrne 1990: 42). Before the emergence of separate prison facilities and institutional programs for women, these reformers opened homes and designed private reformative programs for prostitutes, pregnant women, wayward girls, and orphans.[1] These early manifestations of maternal concern helped generate a strong current of reform that eventually swept most women out of men's prisons and into institutions run entirely for and by women (Rafter 1992: 16; Freedman 1981).

The maternal reform agenda was facilitated by growing international scepticism about the ability of existing penal regimes to effect meaningful change in criminals (Beattie 1977; Rothman 1980, 1990). Reform efforts were stimulated by the appalling conditions of women's incarceration and by concerns about the state's irresponsible and negligent management of women under its care. However, the benevolent efforts of maternal reformers in custodial facilities did not lead to significant changes in a harsh penal system that was inconsistent with wider maternal ambitions (Rafter 1992). Maternalists firmly maintained that the custodial model of punishment exhibited by the penitentiary was a masculine model: 'derived from men's prisons, it adopted their characteristics – retributive purpose, high security architecture, a male dominated authority structure, programs that stressed earnings, and harsh discipline' (Rafter 1992: 21). Given the reformers' and matrons' inability to reform women prisoners under custodial regimes, the emphasis of the reform movement eventually shifted to stress the inadequacy and masculine characteristics of these regimes. This new approach led to the construction of an alternative, women-centred reformatory.

The Importance of Maternal Guidance

Profound changes in the administration of women's penal regimes occurred after reformers identified the source of the problem: women were being held in institutions designed for men and administered by men (Rafter 1992: 16). Once the locus of the problem was identified, the obvious solution was to develop an institutional framework that specialized in the unique needs and experiences of women in conflict with the law, and, more generally, women who breached the boundaries of social norms. In an effort to feminize justice for women, maternal reformers embarked on a campaign of institution building that emphasized the attributes of a loving, moral mother. The architectural ideal for the reformatory differed from that for the penitentiary. Reformatories for women were to be based on a cottage plan rather than a congregate model. This artificial 'home' was to be an embodiment of domestic and maternal ideals. This female ethos created a distinct disciplinary rationality that promoted the matriarchal role of a mother (or older sister) in a traditional, white, middle-class familial setting.

In the late nineteenth century, many penal administrators and male bureaucrats began to embrace, with women reformers, the notion of separate and specialized institutions for the correction and normalization of criminal women. By the late 1800s, several states (as well as certain parts of Britain and Canada) were beginning to construct reformatories for the rehabilitation of female convicts.[2] This emphasis on the separation of female convicts was consistent with the emerging philosophies of new penologists, who underscored the importance of classifying inmates by age, sex, and offence history. These projects were part of a much broader shift in social expectations vis-à-vis the role of punishment and the obligation of the state – a shift characterized as 'welfare penality' (Garland 1985) or 'socialized justice' (Chunn 1992). While these institutions continued to segregate and incapacitate, punishment under the reformatory model had a new purpose: to rehabilitate the inmate. For women, 'rehabilitation' had specific meanings. Rafter (1992: 159) argues that the reformatory regime served two important reformative purposes: to train women to accept a standard of propriety that dictated chastity before marriage and fidelity afterwards; and to instruct women in homemaking, a competency they would use upon release as either a dutiful wife and mother or as a domestic servant in someone else's home. The main objective of women's reformatories was to address the needs of the female convict and regulate her through feminized techniques of benevolent social control. These techniques included familial discipline, the sympathy of other women, maternal and spiritual guidance, and domestic training.

This regime was based on faith in women's innate capacities to reform. The expectation was that a mother's love and power could become a model for regulating, correcting, and normalizing deviant women. This women-centred strategy of governance advocated by state and nonstate reformers relied heavily on normative and corrective technologies that are analogous to those forms of maternal discipline most often associated with middle-class nuclear families. These techniques embody normative assumptions about gender, class, race, and sexuality. The reformatory model exemplified several of the themes expressed decades earlier by Elizabeth Fry: religious and moral regulation of women; the employment of an all-female staff; vocational training (particularly in domestic services); and the classification and separation of different types of offenders. While the concept of offender reform was not new to the reformatory, the notion of an institutionalized maternal logic was a unique innovation.

The hiring of virtuous female role models was deemed essential to the effective operation of a women-centred maternal strategy. The employment of women was predicated on the belief that the female prisoner by nature required special treatment that could only be provided by other women. Reformers argued that women's natural capacities and moral force qualified them for employment in women's prisons. Many well-intentioned reformers moved beyond philanthropic advocacy to secure employment and status in the new reformatories. Female administrators, influenced by maternal ideals and new secular technologies of reform, complemented the diminished but nonetheless crucial role of evangelical maternalists, who continued to strive for the salvation of fallen women. Some men supported the view that women were innately qualified to work in and administer women's prisons; however, many were unwilling to grant women authority over these new institutions (Freedman 1981: 61).

In the second half of the nineteenth century, matrons were qualitatively different from their earlier counterparts (Rafter 1992). The newer matrons were more carefully selected and trained than their predecessors. Ironically, the new matron was expected to exhibit the characteristics of a middle-class homemaker and to inspire prisoners to become respectable, in spite of her own role outside of the home.[3] The use of prison matrons became commonplace in most penal institutions, when the number of female convicts permitted. The hiring of matrons seems to have been more closely regulated and scrutinized after the mid-1800s. Lists of criteria for matrons begin to appear in Prison Association records and reports around that time.[4] While it was preferable to have virtuous women working in prisons, it was difficult to attract them to this stigmatized and low-paying work.

By 1867, some prison associations had established a set of criteria for hiring matrons. For example, a report on prisons in the United States and Canada assembled by the Prison Association of New York (PANY) noted that while in many respects the qualifications for female officers were the same as those for male officers,[5] it was especially important that female officers be 'distinguished for modesty and demeanour, and the exercise of domestic virtues, and that they possess an intimate knowledge of household employment, which will enable them to teach the ignorant and neglected female prisoner how to economize her means, so as to guard her from the temptations caused by waste and extravagance' (PANY 1867: 125). Besides providing an interesting description of the required qualifications of matrons, this passage illustrates a shift in thinking about the responsibility of matrons (and the prison administration more generally) to protect women prisoners from the risks of 'temptation and extravagance.' By the mid-nineteenth century, sensibilities and mentalities governing the administration of women prisoners had shifted: they were no longer regarded as a moral menace to society, and were perceived to be *at risk* if not properly guided and encouraged.

Creating a 'Reformable Subject'

Central to the maternal penal strategy was the existence of a dutiful and daughterly subject who would be amenable to, or at least tolerant of, this new penal environment. The public image of convicts as first redeemable and later treatable was critical to the legitimacy of reformers. Accordingly, new conceptions of the female criminal, women's expertise, and the reformatory model evolved together (Rafter 1992). Drawing on their experiences working with women prisoners and their children, leaders of the movement began by challenging existing impressions of criminal women as wretched, depraved, and unreformable savages. They challenged the 'archetype of the Dark Lady, a woman of uncommon strength, seductive power, and evil inclination' and instead promoted a 'new concept of the female offender as childlike, wayward and redeemable, a fallen woman that [sic] was more sinned against than a sinner herself' (Rafter 1992: 49). Enthusiastic reformers suggested that the female criminal was a 'fragile vessel,' neglected and ill advised in her choices, a woman who could be redeemed through proper instruction and guidance. Reformers steadfastly maintained that women would remain criminal unless they received a new form of maternal treatment, one that provided 'healthier surroundings' within and after prison and allowed for a 'metamorphosis from depravity to true womanhood' (Freedman 1981: 53). They challenged the stigma associated with criminal women, substituting an indictment of society and, particularly, of men for causing the fall of such convicts (Hawkes 1994: 4). For example, in 1844 Margaret Fuller, a prominent maternalist, argued that women prisoners were victims who needed help to overcome the circumstances that led them to crime: 'Born of unfortunate marriages, inheriting dangerous inclinations, neglected in childhood, with bad habits and associates, as certainly must be the case of some of you, how terrible will be the struggle when you leave this shelter' (Chevigny 1976; cited in Freedman 1981: 30). Furthermore, Fuller and others questioned the predominant belief that these women were hopelessly fallen: 'How many there are in whom the feelings of innocent childhood are not dead, who need only good influences and steady aid to raise them from the pit of infamy into which they have fallen' (Fuller 1845; cited in Freedman 1981: 30–1).

These comments illustrate one of several attempts by maternalists to create and promote an image of criminal women as reformable and to place their crimes in a broader social and economic context. Following closely the principles of reform advocated by Elizabeth Fry in Britain, Fuller advocated maternal instruction, proper sanitation, and appropriate systems of classification (Freedman 1981: 31). The efforts of reformers were to a large extent successful, in that they were able to offer a competing image of the woman offender and to improve the conditions of confinement for some women. While the image of the 'Dark Lady' still held some sway, reform narratives now offered a counterimage which, although not congruent with the archetype of a 'Fair Lady,' did offer a new image of the female criminal as '*potentially* chaste, domestic and girlish' (Rafter 1992: 49). The image of the female criminal was pivotal to the self-image of the reformers because if she was not a 'victimized sister' but rather 'an autonomous, deliberately sexual being,' then 'the *raison d'être* of social feminists – their concept of womanliness and with it, the justification for their work – was built on air' (Rafter 1992: 51). This construction of a reformable and socially tolerable female criminal became an essential strategy of reform. This new image played a vital role in efforts by maternalists to secure the support of the state and civil society for their initiatives. Reform narratives simultaneously reflected maternal logics of separate spheres – both penal and civic – and a feminist concern for protecting women from exploitation and victimization by men. Reformers' feminist concerns were premised not on equality but rather on sexual difference. While these reformers did exhibit the kinds of feminist sensibilities that post–Second World War maternal feminists would demonstrate, in their analyses of the social causes of women's crime they did not necessarily seek to expand women's rights; rather, they were seeking to institutionalize what they presumed were innate sexual differences. Their reforms led to the development of sex-stereotyped programs and techniques of reform that feminist advocates and researchers would later criticize. Concerns about the treatment of women in state institutions, such as prisons, also inspired the development of independent women's prison reform associations.[6]

While many institutions set out initially to reform all women who came through their doors, these regimes were quickly modified to reflect the material reality that all women were not equally suitable for or willing to participate in reformatory regimes. This realization prompted the development of a complex classification schema that used clearly defined selection criteria to screen admissions and hand-pick the 'most appropriate' candidates. Reformers and administrators attempted to recruit young white women who were, by and large, first offenders convicted of relatively minor offences. Women perceived as 'unreformable' were given less attention and were more likely to remain in local jails or be sent to penitentiaries if their sentence permitted. This led to a bifurcated system of corrections: over time, a residual category of female convicts classified by reformers as beyond hope became a necessary evil. Rather than admitting that maternal strategies failed with some convicts, reformers defined certain 'experienced' women as unwilling and unable to reform. Thus, limitations and barriers to reform were blamed on the individual rather than on maternal strategies. In the United States there was a clear bifurcation in the women's prison system, based in part on the belief that 'some' women were reformable whereas others were not. In Canada, this bifurcation was not always so clear, but it is visible in the way that provincial reformatories were separated from the federal Prison for Women in Kingston.[7]

The Andrew Mercer Reformatory and the Reformatory Ideal

The American women's prison reform movement and its logic of separate spheres had a profound impact on how women's crime was interpreted and managed in other Western countries. That being said, the evolution of separate institutions for women in the late nineteenth century occurred under different circumstances in Canada than in the United States. American reformatories emerged from a particular set of historical circumstances[8] and were designed to deal with a specific type of offender – 'the reformable woman.' American efforts to construct women's prisons were stimulated and supported by an organized and powerful women's reformatory movement that existed long before Canadian women were actively engaged in penal reform. In Canada, the reform movement was less organized and more fragmented. Several concerned individuals visited women in gaols, prisons, and penitentiaries, and offered released prisoners financial and emotional support, but it is difficult to establish whether these efforts were coordinated, and whether they affected specific state policies.[9]

In Canada, separate reformatories for women were not developed through feminist lobbying; rather, they were a state-generated project. State reformers influenced by American penality, such as J.W. Langmuir (Ontario Prison Inspector, 1868), encouraged the state to adopt a maternal penal reform strategy predicated on the belief that virtuous women could uplift their fallen sisters.[10] Langmuir was disturbed by the lack of classification[11] and idleness of inmates in local jails. Based on evidence of American experts, he concluded that women were 'able to exercise great power and influence, in practical ways towards reclaiming the criminal and fallen of their sex' (Oliver 1994: 524). Langmuir advocated the construction of a distinct and potentially less expensive women's reformatory, wherein women could receive 'the great moral benefits of the separate principle' (Strange 1983: 10). Central to these assertions was a new image of the female criminal as impressionable and daughterly. Langmuir mobilized this image and a faith in moral reform, to convince a sympathetic government of the advantages of a facility that would reform female convicts.

Langmuir's successful use of a maternal logic secured support for the construction of the Mercer Reformatory. In 1874, the Mercer opened its doors under the supervision of Mrs O'Reilly. The Mercer[12] signified the institutionalization of this new form of women's governance, which drew on a variety of rationalities and technologies to justify and promote a specific women-centred strategy. While Christianity remained central to the new reformatory regime, pivotal was the belief that strict prison discipline could be tempered by and combined with maternal guidance in a homelike atmosphere. The distinctly feminine disciplinary methods resulted in the creation of an environment that was distinct from comparable men's facilities. Institutional rhetoric stressed a language of domesticity and informality, as Berkovits notes: 'The building itself was not referred to as a prison, but as a "house," the all female corps of guards were called "attendants," and the prisoners themselves, "residents." Superintendent O'Sullivan [who succeeded O'Reilly] often quite overtly referred to the prisoners as her "daughters" and herself as their "mother." Staff members were referred to by first name (Mr. John, or Miss Margaret, for example), and were collectively described as "the family." O'Sullivan's own relatives mixed freely with the inmates, and they were well known to each other' (1995: 3–4).

This informality and familial atmosphere can be contrasted to the environment in custodial institutions, which tended to be more formal. The integration of maternal metaphors and images led to the reconstruction of penal settings. Maternally based prisons were no longer simply places of confinement: they were now expected to fulfil their legal obligations in a homelike atmosphere.

In many respects, the construction of the prison as a home ignored material and legal realities that reflected the ultimately repressive aspects of a court-imposed custodial sentence. Women's behaviour in the Mercer was constantly monitored, and mobility was severely limited. Most of the women sent to the Mercer were unwilling participants. As such, they were not always receptive to maternal reform strategies. I return to this point in chapter 5.

Maternally Based Programs of Prisoner Reform

Specialized programming for women prisoners was one innovation of the Mercer regime. Part of the Mercer's public appeal lay in its claim to reform fallen women through a strict gender-specific regime of hard labour, moral and religious training, and after-care. Norms of domesticity and the ideal of true womanhood were central to the Mercer's programming strategy; however, administrators also relied on the same technologies promoted in early penitentiaries. The programs offered combined basic education with religious, moral and domestic training. They also taught obedience, servility, and the importance of knowing one's place in society (Ruemper 1994: 372). These programs included the Clean Speech Society (a modified Swearer's Anonymous), hard labour to instil discipline, and vocational training to prepare women for careers in domestic service.

Industrial training played a significant role in offender reform. According to Oliver (1994: 540–1), Inspector Langmuir 'habitually referred to the Mercer as an Industrial Reformatory.' Similarly, Superintendent O'Reilly regarded the work program as central to the institutional maternal regime. Her acceptance of the conventional Protestant wisdom about the relationship between idleness and crime is illustrated in the following passage: 'Of all wretched women the idle are the most wretched. We try to impress upon them the importance of labour, and we look upon this as one of the great means of their reformation' (Ontario Prison Inspector, Annual Reports 1881; cited in Oliver 1994: 541).

This commitment to labour was extended to sentencing practices. Langmuir tried hard to convince Premier Mowat to educate sentencing authorities about the importance of industrial training at the Mercer, and the need for sentences long enough to ensure an appropriate training regime (Oliver 1994: 541). While the training received by women was gender specific (laundering, sewing, knitting, and domestic service), the Mercer's emphasis on labour was not unique: the ideal of productive labour was central to most Canadian penitentiary and reformatory regimes. While Langmuir and O'Reilly were campaigning for industrial training in the 1880s, concerns were repeatedly being raised about the absence of productive training for women inmates at Kingston Penitentiary, where women had been incarcerated since 1835. These concerns about idleness and productive training for women prisoners continued to be voiced throughout the late nineteenth century and into the twentieth.

The normative regulation of women prisoners continued after they were released from the Mercer. For instance, the scheme for parole was designed to reinforce the importance of proper womanly conduct, which, when exhibited, allowed prisoners to earn marks toward the rebate of their sentences (Strange 1983). Mercer officials arranged employment for women on release; on some occasions, members of Superintendent O'Sullivan's own family hired prisoners as domestics to satisfy their parole. This seemingly well-intentioned practice served to regulate women's compliance with parole regulations; it also ensured continued surveillance of female prisoners after release. The regulation of women through the parole process began with ensuring that female prisoners were 'appropriately employed upon release.' Most women were employed as domestic servants. Factory jobs and other types of employment in the city were dismissed as inappropriate because of the temptations of city life. This was consistent with early beliefs that women's crime was a result of exposure to negative influences and, in particular, the absence of 'good' maternal and domestic influences. Community strategies of surveillance and regulation were an integral component of newly emerging after-care services. In the twentieth century, well-intentioned women became involved in the policing and normalization of ex-convicts by hiring them as domestic servants and befriending them upon release.[13] Once the Mercer opened, more and more Canadian reformers found another outlet for their talents. Consistent with the objectives of evangelical maternal logic, reformers from the Upper Canadian Bible Society sent female prisoners bibles; at the same time, the Tract Society, the YMCA, and the Committee of the Hospital for Sick Children supplied religious literature (Ruemper 1994: 361). Representatives from local churches, the Prisoners' Aid Society, the Salvation Army, and the Women's Christian Temperance Union visited the women and provided a variety of religious services, such as preaching, bible reading, praying, and counselling. Organizations such as the Salvation Army and the Prisoners' Aid Society also aided the women's reintegration into the community by providing them with monetary, spiritual, and emotional support.[14]

While these organizations had benevolent intentions, they also provided an important regulatory function consistent with the wider maternal logic informing the Mercer. Reformers ensured that once individuals were released from the Mercer they continued to conform to the ideals of domesticity and 'true womanhood' taught at the reformatory. Their main objective was to ensure that these women did not fall back into their old habits. For example, reformers often met women at the door of the prison on the morning of their discharge to ensure they had appropriate clothing, lodgings, and employment (generally in domestic service). If a woman was not prepared for release, she could choose to go to a home of refuge, such as a Magdalene Asylum, a Salvation Army Prison Gate Home, or a Rescue Home. These homes were often extensions of institutional regimes.

The women released from the Mercer were encouraged to keep in touch and reassured that they would always be welcome 'home.' Letter writing was a common way of continuing to regulate of women after their release. Oliver (1994) and Berkovits (1995) suggest that the correspondence between superintendent and ex-prisoners was a testament to the maternal success of the Mercer; in contrast, Strange (1983) shows that maternalism had marked regulatory effects. O'Sullivan's diligent correspondence with some inmates revealed to her certain details of their private lives that she might not have learned otherwise. By gaining the confidence of inmates, O'Sullivan was able to use her maternal position to offer advice and encourage future moral behaviour. One former inmate wrote to her about missing her 'mentor' and feeling lonely. She also mentioned her financial difficulties and requested job references. In response, O'Sullivan reassured the woman, telling her that she 'will find good friends in Montreal' and updating her with news about her family, weddings, and staff members. She ended by noting: 'I sincerely trust that you are keeping your good resolutions and no taste of liquor passes your lips' (cited in Berkovits 1995: 11). Another inmate wrote to O'Sullivan to apologize for breaking her parole conditions by taking an unauthorized vacation. In her return letter, O'Sullivan tried to persuade her to return to the prison: 'My little cottage up North is nearly finished and I shall be sorry indeed if you are not here to go up again with me to Lafontaine ... I shall expect to hear from you shortly – don't think that I am angry with you; I am grieved and sorry that you did as you have. But I want you to begin once more and be the *good little girl we all liked so well here*' (emphasis added; cited in Berkovits 1995: 12).

These letters show how benevolent techniques were used to manage women prisoners in accordance with certain normative standards. Berkovits (1995: 11) notes that 'throughout these letters there was not one trace of bitterness or blame on either side,' but he fails to acknowledge how seemingly benevolent maternal techniques were being used as forms of positive discipline (cf. Foucault 1977).

Maternally minded reformers joined forces with prison officials to continue to govern women even when the reformatory had no legal authority to regulate their behaviour (Wetherell, 1979). Images of a mother raising her child to observe the proper manners and habits of bourgeois society dominate the narratives of the Mercer. The propensity of the staff to check up on and maintain contact with released inmates extends this metaphor by suggesting that children require constant supervision, support, and guidance – even throughout their adult lives. The task of 'post-adolescent mothering' was bureaucratized through the development of formal release mechanisms, the hiring of social workers, and the development of state-sponsored after-care services. At the same time, initiatives similar to those of the Mercer staff illustrate an extension of the state's obligation to not only punish but also rehabilitate prisoners through techniques of maternal governance.

'Daughterly Subjects'

Consistent with the Mercer's familial emphasis, the reformatory selected matrons by stressing the importance of 'loving but demanding mothers who forgave past errors but insisted on obedience'; to complement this role, penal administrators preferred to deal with 'daughterly subjects' (Strange 1983: 20). Although reformers often professed that *all* women could benefit from maternal guidance, Mercer officials preferred women who had been classified as 'reformable.'[15] Neither Langmuir nor Mercer officials deviated from this preference, and they assumed that sentencing authorities would send only the 'most suitable persons for reformatory discipline and treatment' (Strange 1983). A 'suitable' Mercer candidate was a young first offender who had not yet been corrupted by the evils of incarcerations and seduced by a criminal lifestyle – a woman who epitomized the naïveté and deference of an immature child, and who conformed with the ideals of middle-class reformers such as the Women's Christian Temperance Union. There was a preference for young, single, white females who were Protestant, Canadian-born, literate, and temperate and who had some experience in domestic and personal service (Ruemper 1994: 371). However, the women incarcerated at the Mercer did not conform to these ideals.[16]

Brothel keepers, prostitutes, unwed mothers with illegitimate children, and women infected with venereal diseases were regularly incarcerated at the Mercer. Oliver (1994: 542–3) notes that in the early years of the Mercer, while over half the prisoners were classified under the occupational category 'domestic' (which included homemakers, maids, cooks, laundresses, and servants), over one-quarter of the remaining population was classified as 'prostitutes.' Although there appears to have been a sharp decline in the number of prostitutes who were sent to the Mercer between 1891 and 1900, and an increase in the number of domestics, Oliver (1994: 543) suggests that these shifts were more likely a result of changes in policing strategies and classification procedures, and did not reflect a radical shift in inmate characteristics. Whether the changes in occupational classifications were made by institutional officials or by police, they are instructive for two reasons. First, they demonstrate the inconsistency between 'ideal' and 'real' subjects of maternal reform campaigns: in practice, Mercer officials were obligated to accept all prisoners sent to the Mercer by sentencing authorities (Oliver 1994: 537). Second, the stigmatization of women by labelling them as prostitutes is inconsistent with a benevolent maternal desire to redeem basically innocent women. Seen in this light, the overrepresentation of women prisoners in the category 'domestic,' provided a convenient rationale for domestic training programs and wider maternal reform strategies.

The antithesis of the maternal ideal is the unco-operative and recalcitrant woman. Some accounts of the Mercer's regime suggest that there were serious difficulties in managing certain prisoners through maternal strategies. Both Berkovits (1995) and Strange (1983) describe several occasions when maternal strategies failed to break the spirit of certain prisoners. Berkovits's (1995) analysis of women prisoners' resistance to maternal strategies is theoretically limited; even so, he does offer some interesting examples of the tensions that existed between prison officials and their charges. For example, he indicates that institutional officials observed the following behaviours: inmates quarrelling among themselves in nurseries, fighting, throwing dishes, stealing tools to make weapons, tearing their clothing, breaking furniture, assaulting staff members, and swearing and uttering threats (1995: 5). There were also some serious incidents between staff and inmates, as well as group protests. Some staff members were singled out for their punitive techniques and subjected to physical attacks. On one occasion, a laundry attendant, M. Mick, was attacked with a pair of scissors (1995: 5). Other examples of prisoner resistance included assaults, riots, escapes, pilfering, smoking illicit cigarettes, smuggling contraband in and out of the institution, using the telephone without permission, altering their appearance (perming their hair), and making a general mockery of the rules of silence by passing notes and singing or speaking loudly in the cell block. Clearly, some of the women at the Mercer defied conventional stereotypes of the 'reformable woman' or 'daughterly subject.'

Attempts were made to segregate these women from the rest of the population so that criminally experienced women, such as a brothel keepers, could not corrupt apparently naïve women. These women's actions often led to some form of institutional discipline. These 'unreformable' women tended to be subjected to punitive techniques designed to physically compel submission (such as cold baths or a 'good spanking') or to be segregated and confined in 'punishment rooms,' in which they received few benefits of the 'loving home' to which they were confined.[17] The following points to some of the techniques used by Mercer officials to regulate and discipline women deemed 'difficult to manage': 'One prisoner, being punished in the dungeon, was forced by the Surgeon to eat discarded bread that she claimed was not thrown out of her cell by her, as he claimed, but carried through her cell grates by rats. The Surgeon decreed that she was not to receive fresh bread until all of the previous bread had been eaten' (Berkovits 1995: 7).

Mercer officials also used more invasive physical techniques of restraint and corporal punishment, such as whipping and the use of handcuffs. When one inmate serving an indefinite sentence went on a hunger strike after being placed in segregation for threatening to kill Attendant Mick, Superintendent O'Sullivan, on the advice of the surgeon, advocated the use of a 'cold bath' to encourage her to behave.[18] When entire cell blocks disobeyed institutional rules and regulations, forms of mass punishment, such as deprivation of lighting and prolonged periods of being locked in a cell, were used to encourage conformity. However, some of the more severe corporal punishments used in the 'maternal regime' at the Mercer to deal with recalcitrant inmates were formally discouraged by penitentiary officials. The rules and regulations of penitentiary discipline in the late 1800s formally discouraged corporal punishments, segregation on a diet of bread and water beyond six consecutive meals, and segregation beyond six nights.

The Mercer's male surgeon, Dr King, played an important paternal role in disciplining inmates, and the superintendent often deferred to Dr King in disciplinary matters. His 'diagnosis' often resulted in cures that were not easily distinguishable from typical means of punishing inmates. Berkovits (1995: 9) notes that some of Dr King's techniques bordered on cruelty and were consistent with the beliefs of the surgeon at the 'more strict' central prison for men. For example, the 'cold bath,' which required 'plunging a refractory inmate into a cold bath then briefly strangling her under water until she submitted' to the wishes of prison officials (Strange 1983: 53), was a medically sanctioned treatment. The 'cold water treatment,' a similar procedure, was described by Superintendent O'Sullivan as follows: 'Shutting a woman in an empty cell properly equipped for the purpose and ... as I have explained before to you, turning the hose not directly upon the woman but upon the walls of her cell; Dr King states that this has usually been found effective, and one three minute application is sufficient' (cited in Berkovits 1995: 8).

Dr King was described by prisoners as a 'son of a bitch' and an 'old fool,' partially for his excessive clinical examinations for 'malingering' and 'self abuse' (Berkovits 1995: 9). Sometimes prisoners withheld medical information and refused to speak to the doctor about their concerns (Berkovits 1995). These descriptions of penal discipline seem inconsistent with the image of a loving mother, but they do conform to a particular image of familial relations of power in which the father figure plays the role of disciplinarian. Clearly, nonmaternal methods of prisoner management were often used, as were scientific technologies of reform, which became increasingly popular after the turn of the century. New scientific methods of discipline such as hypnosis, and older techniques such as the cold bath and segregation (legitimated with a medical logic), were combined with more maternal forms of discipline, such as eliciting promises to behave and minor suspensions of privileges.

The use of physical discipline shows how maternal strategies can easily be integrated with and used to legitimate more overtly repressive forms of penal discipline. Repeated altercations with unreformable women created serious problems of order, and as a result, these women were more frequently punished than 'lovingly mothered.' However, despite the propensity of some of the Mercer's administrators to resort to punitive techniques, Oliver (1994: 558) claims that Superintendent O'Reilly's approach tended to be kind and humane, and that she appreciated the limited value of strict punishments, which she believed undermined the prospect of winning the inmates' co-operation. Strange (1983: 39) indicates that O'Sullivan often complained that certain inmates were unsuitable for reform. The presence of women who resisted the motherly approach to reform, in an environment that did not allow for adequate classification, meant that O'Sullivan found herself exerting 'more energy in punishing than reforming the unfortunates sent to the prison' (39).

Persistent defiance by an incorrigible few led to requests for alternative arrangements for recalcitrant women.[19] Women who presented persistent management problems were sometimes transferred to the Female Unit in Kingston Penitentiary (Berkovits 1995: 6). Some early failed attempts to reform women subjected to this new regime were blamed in part on sentencing officials, who sent inappropriate women to the Mercer, and on the women themselves, who were labelled incorrigible and stubborn and thus unreformable. According to Ruemper (1994: 362), between 1899 and 1917 a large number of women were confined at the Mercer on drunk and disorderly charges, and were considered by the institution to be unreformable. There were also some specific concerns about brothel keepers; prison officials believed that these women were undermining their efforts by attempting to lure inexperienced women into a life of prostitution.

There is little evidence to support the contention that perception of a woman's potential for reform informed the placement of women in reformatories as opposed to prisons or the federal penitentiary. While the woman's history was likely considered at the time of sentencing, the decision whether to send a woman to a reformatory instead of the penitentiary was usually governed by the length of her sentence, not necessarily her character, notwithstanding that the two were related. After Confederation (1867), a woman who received a custodial sentence of less than two years was usually sent to a prison or reformatory. If her sentence was greater than two years, she was sent to one of the federal institutions that accepted female inmates. In general, the institution where a woman served her sentence was governed by her proximity to that institution at the time of sentencing. Women do not seem to have been uniformly classified and sent to the 'most appropriate institution.' Before the Mercer opened, little thought was given to the character of the offender and her potential for reform. While the degree of judicial concern about a woman's reformability is unclear, we do know that officials at the Mercer were becoming increasingly concerned about the reformability of their clientele (Strange 1983).

Although the limitations of the maternal logic were profound, maternal penal reformers continued to resort to domestic metaphors and to support the creation of separate institutions for female prisoners. Admittedly, the role and status of certain women was threatened by the perceived limitation of regimes predicated on the innate abilities of women; but at the same time, links between maternal logic and modern scientific logic created new opportunities. The integration of maternal and scientific ideals resulted in a new type of maternalism that advocated new rehabilitation programs administered by professionally 'trained' women. Even though the main weakness of the Mercer and other reformatories was that it was impossible to turn a prison into a home, future generations of penal reformers would resurrect the metaphor of motherhood and the ideal of 'a home.' The absence of 'good mothering' would continue to be perceived as a cause of crime, and a maternally tempered prison environment would continue to play an important role in attempts to resocialize and normalize women. The instruction and training of inmates advocated by reformers from the early twentieth century on would emphasize sociological, psychological, and medical interventions that retained many elements of the ideology of separate spheres. The relationship between maternal logic and a scientific logic of rehabilitation and professional expertise are examined in detail in the next chapter.

Conclusions: Maternal Success or Failure?

Was the Mercer a success? Feminist historians and Oliver (1994) make competing claims. They all agree that the Mercer provided an alternative to the neglect that women suffered in prisons and custodial regimes, but they differ in their evaluations of the regime's 'administrative' success. Strange (1983) notes that after a concentrated attempt to institute a regime of kind discipline, it became evident that maternalistic efforts could not fulfil the lofty and unrealistic goal of reform. The common opinion among feminist historians is that despite the best intentions of maternal reformers, these icons of motherly discipline were undermined by the material realities of imprisonment. For example, Freedman (1981: 105–6) argues that 'power triumphed over sisterhood not because they were single sex institutions, but because they were prisons.' The concrete womb that emerged was quite unlike what had been anticipated by benevolent and well-intentioned reformers. To varying degrees, Freedman (1981, 1996), Strange (1983), and Rafter (1992) provide evidence of an important struggle between different groups of women (reformers, administrators, matrons, and inmates) within a social, political, and economic context wider than that of the prison. They use a feminist historical analysis to illustrate not only the perpetuation of punitive and coercive disciplinary power, but also the reproduction of certain configurations of power among and between class, race, and gender.

Rafter (1992) notes that the reformatory model was in certain ways harsher and 'less just' than previous custodial models that did not recognize gender, precisely because of the double standard it invoked. She argues that the reformatory model was fundamentally unjust because it ignored liberal notions of penality, which stressed the importance of the proportionality principle – a principle that was cherished by many of the founding 'fathers' of the penitentiary model (e.g., Bentham). According to this principle, the punishment should fit the crime. Rafter (1992: 41) and Strange (1983) both argue that reformatory officials in general, and specifically women's reformatory officials and maternalists who advocated the use of indeterminate and indefinite sentences, did not adhere to the principle of proportionality. Rafter notes that 'those who lobbied for reformatories maintained that it was quite proper to ignore the rule of proportionality because their aim was not to punish but to treat – to retrain and reform, processes that required time. But in light of the concept of proportionality the up-to-three (or however many) years was a high price to pay for minor offenses' (41).

Furthermore, Rafter (1992) argues that the punishment of men was qualitatively different from that of women because it was based on behavioural standards that were not necessarily comparable to standards imposed on men in reformatories and on both men and women in custodial regimes.[20] For Rafter, the harshness of the reformatory lay in its tendency toward 'partial justice,' in that it sought to remold the prisoner instead of punishing by denying certain fundamental liberal principles of justice.

Oliver (1994: 520), on the other hand, is critical of what he claims is an attempt by feminist historians to interpret the history of the Mercer (Strange 1983), and women's reformatories more generally (Freedman 1981; Rafter 1992), as a page in the history of women, thus emphasizing gender while neglecting correctional history. His argument disregards the influence of gender on the history of corrections. This is problematic, given the relevance of masculine and feminine stereotypes to the composition of a variety of correctional regimes informed by a diverse array of rationalities at different historical junctures. However, Oliver (1994) adds that it is not surprising to find that the maternal feminist regime embodied cultural and class limitations as identified by feminist historians. Relying on Rothman (1990), he also indicates that it is not surprising that this regime reproduced the power relations of a penal institution, and thereby undermined the progressive ideals of the reformers. Yet, in his subsequent analysis of the Mercer he seems to ignore Rothman's observations. Oliver claims that it is difficult to measure the success of this program using contemporary feminist criteria, and that instead of being subjected to a feminist critique, the Mercer should be evaluated from the perspective of the success or failure of a women's prison in Ontario between 1880 and 1900. In that regard, he argues that the distinctly feminine regime of the Mercer and the maternalistic qualities of its superintendent, which created an environment where 'the front door was always open,' made this institution unique compared to men's facilities, such as the Central Prison in Ontario and Kingston Penitentiary. Likewise, he notes that 'men were sent to the Central Prison for punishment and women to the Mercer for, as O'Reilly explained it, discipline in the context of kindness, friendship and support' (1994: 550). However, Oliver does not adequately address the less benevolent and more regulatory aspects of this maternal strategy of 'punishment,' which in effect resulted in a more extensive and prolonged period of state and nonstate supervision. The evidence provided by Berkovits (1995) seems to contradict Oliver's claim about the benevolence of Mercer officials with respect to certain inmates. Nonetheless, Oliver (566) notes that with regard to the administration, the Mercer was a success and that the more problematic issue was the failure of male bureaucrats to appreciate the wider social significance of the Mercer's accomplishments.

It is perhaps this very unwillingness to appreciate the maternal contribution of the Mercer to women's penality, and penality more generally, that led to a renewed apathy in women's corrections during the first half of the twentieth century. Oliver relies heavily, and selectively, on institutional reports and on superintendents' and inspectors' annual accounts of prison activities to evaluate the administrative success of the Mercer. He argues that because 'O'Reilly was able to run the facility without resort to frequent punishments or other harsh disciplinary tools,' and because she was able to avoid 'scandals, riots, charges of brutality or other incidents characteristic of punitive prisons everywhere,' the Mercer was 'an exceptional administrative success' (1994: 550–1).

Not only does Oliver compare the regimes in men's facilities to those at the Mercer, but he also compares accounts of the regime at the Mercer to reports from the Female Unit in Kingston Penitentiary. From this comparison, he notes that 'the contrast between the ambience of the Mercer and the unruly, often violent behaviour which Kingston Penitentiary officials complained had characterized the female behaviour in that institution in the 1840s and early 1850s is striking' (551). In making this claim, Oliver overlooks three important points. *First*, given the tradition out of which the maternal regime at the Mercer emerged and the grandiose expectations placed on a newly appointed female prison governess in an era when few women worked in prisons, it is reasonable to assume that this institution had a vested interest in presenting the regime in a positive light. By revealing a litany of failures or construing the women in their charge as unreformable, Mercer officials would have been undermining their own maternal philosophy. In other words, they had a strong incentive to present themselves as a progressive alternative to more punitive forms of punishment. *Second*, Oliver's comparison of the Mercer regime to accounts of 'unruly women' at Kingston Penitentiary overlooks a wider political context, as well as accounts of the Female Unit during a comparable time period. It is important to remember that unlike the Mercer, Kingston Penitentiary was not designed with female prisoners' reform in mind. There is a long history of officials at Kingston Penitentiary complaining that female convicts were an inconvenience. In general, officials at Kingston did not want female convicts in their prison, and for the most part they did not have a meaningful strategy for managing the women in their charge, whom they basically neglected. Furthermore, it is not surprising that the apathy, neglect, and abuse experienced by female convicts created a response that was regarded by administrators as 'unruly.' Once Kingston Penitentiary hired a matron and gave her the authority and resources to run the Female Unit, reports of female prisoners' activities were less sensational.

Third, Oliver's account of the Mercer's 'success' assumes that discipline that occurs within a 'context of kindness, friendship, and support' is less invasive and repressive than discipline in a more punitive setting. This assumption overlooks a vast literature on the regulatory and repressive aspects of therapeutic and benevolent regimes (Dobash, Dobash, and Gutteridge 1986; Garland 1985; Rose 1989). Most importantly, Oliver disregards the evidence of riots, escapes, extreme punitive measures, and assaults on staff, which are revealed in institutional records (Berkovits 1995; Strange 1983). While these incidents may have been less frequent and less severe than those in other institutions, they clearly run counter to the image of a 'happy home.'

The Mercer is an important page in both the history of Canadian imprisonment and the genealogy of maternal logics. When we place this experience in a 'wider correctional context,' it becomes apparent that the problems encountered in attempts to institute a maternal regime in many ways epitomize the contradictory nature of the correctional enterprise – a contradiction that Ekstedt and Griffiths (1988) and other Canadian correctional historians have characterized as 'the split personality of corrections.' Rather than a 'split personality,' it is perhaps more appropriate to think about the *multiple* personalities of women's penality. Prisons, penitentiaries, and reformatories have adopted two fundamentally contradictory objectives: to punish and to reform. At different historical junctures, these contradictions are evident in political and administrative reform discourse. The failures of the silent system, the rehabilitative model, and the maternal strategy had a common basis. While new technologies often emerge promising something new, better, and more humane, they are ultimately compromised by the existing institutional culture. Oliver seems to ignore this. While the Mercer may very well have differed from other institutions of the time by virtue of its feminine ethos, it is problematic, as Rothman suggests, to assume that this regime was an inevitable and sure step in the progress of humanity. Perhaps what is most interesting about these projects is how they contributed to a particular history of the governance of women by women under a rubric of motherhood that legitimated a variety of techniques. The Mercer was a historically specific attempt by women to govern women prisoners as women. Opinions remain divided on whether the maternal ideal of a caring but strict home was accomplished.

Chapter Three

Finding a New Home: From Kingston Penitentiary to the Prison for Women

The previous two chapters argued that international women's prison reform and the administration of women's prisons exhibit multiple logics. They showed how pastoral and disciplinary forms of governance were central to the reform strategies mobilized by Elizabeth Fry, American women prison reformers, and the state officials who envisioned and administered the Andrew Mercer Reformatory. The disciplinary governance of women prisoners has both coercive and productive capacities, and this approach to governing is gendered. Maternal logics have a flexible and eclectic quality that allows them to be fused with different penal logics under different circumstances. Prior to the emergence of liberal equality strategies of governance in the late 1960s, maternal forms of discipline tended to dominate women's penality. However, this maternal logic was more apparent in early American and British reform campaigns and in the administration of the Mercer than in the Female Unit at Kingston Penitentiary (1834–1934). While traces of a maternal logic can be found in the existing records of this regime, the governance of women in this facility was considerably less maternal than at the Mercer. Our knowledge of this regime is limited; however, it appears that while maternal reform logics also operated in the federal system, they were less pronounced. Unlike the Mercer and many American reformatories, the Prison for Women (P4W) was not deliberately designed or premised on a maternal model of reform.

This chapter explores the role of maternal and other logics in the governance of women in the Female Unit at Kingston Penitentiary and later at the legendary P4W, opened in 1934. Many have suggested that the dominant theme in the history of federal female offenders is 'the juxtaposition of paternalism and neglect' (Cooper 1993: 46). I disagree with this characterization and argue that while early custodial regimes for women were in fact a low priority for penal administrators, this was not because women were 'insignificant' and 'too few to count.' From the point of view of governance, small numbers are not insignificant if those small populations become the objects of novel forms of governance.

The first section of this chapter focuses on early conditions of penal discipline, the perceived importance of female matrons, and the struggle to build a separate federal prison for women. The second part of the chapter analyses the multiple logics informing reform practices at P4W, from its beginnings in 1934 through to the 1950s.

Warehousing Women: The Female Unit at Kingston Penitentiary

The experiences of women prisoners in penitentiaries and prisons vary considerably, depending on where the institution is located and on the spatial, fiscal, and human resources available to the administrators. In the nineteenth century, women were theoretically subject to the same treatment as men. Like men, women were expected to conform to a strict regime of silence, religious training, and hard labour. Once incarcerated, women performed hard labour, which for women prisoners could mean anything from washing, scrubbing, and sewing to picking oakum (Backhouse 1991: 230). Gosselin (1982: 72) indicates that in the Provincial Penitentiary in 1846, 'men and women worked together during scheduled periods of labour, their work being to break rocks – to be used for the construction of a church.' Many officials believed that they were simply warehousing women who were beyond reform and difficult to manage.

The care received by most women prisoners was inferior to that received by their male counterparts. Women prisoners were subject to abusive treatment and deplorable living conditions. Even when they were not subject to physical discipline, they were often sexually exploited by jailers and male convicts. This exploitation ranged from various types of sexual assault and harassment to expectations that women prisoners' labour (laundry, sewing, cooking, and so on) could be used to meet the needs of the wider male population. While the treatment of women convicts varied over time, this is likely indicative of different administrative approaches; most studies agree that women convicts often experienced unduly harsh conditions. Typically, women convicts depended heavily on the good will of the jailers, other prisoners, visitors, and outside charities. In many of the new penitentiaries and existing prisons in Canada and the United States, the management of women epitomized the neglect and disorder witnessed by early American and British reformers.

Prison regulations rarely distinguished between male and female offenders. Stewart's (1993) accounts of Oakalla prison in British Columbia as 'rat-infested and draughty' reflect similar conditions evident well into the mid-twentieth century. The conditions in early American custodial institutions prompted the Auburn prison chaplain to note: 'To be a male convict in this prison would be quite tolerable; but to be a female convict, for any protracted period would be a fate worse than death' (Freedman 1981: 16). The fact that women were more commonly held in local jails or prisons, as opposed to the penitentiary system – which seems to have been reserved for the most incorrigible and dangerous prisoners – was of little consolation to women convicts, for living conditions in these prisons were equally appalling. Repeat offenders and women who committed particularly serious crimes were sent to the Kingston Penitentiary (Oliver 1994: 521).

To most early penitentiary administrators, the gender of the inmates was incidental and at best acknowledged as inconvenient. John Macaulay, president of the Canadian Penitentiary Board of Inspectors, noted that the sentencing of women to the penitentiary interfered with the administration of discipline and caused some inconvenience for administrators: 'Though their labour as seamstresses can always be turned to good account, they cannot be effectually subjected to the peculiar discipline of the prison until a separate place of confinement suggested for them by the plans and the report of the recent Commissioner shall have been prepared for their reception.'[1]

The status of women in Canadian penitentiaries as 'inconvenient' created the conditions for serious forms of abuse and administrative apathy. Several commissions and annual reports documented overcrowded, unsanitary, and generally intolerable conditions in the Female Unit at Kingston. For example: 'The sleeping cells were frightfully over-run with bugs, especially in the spring of 1846; the women used to sweep them out with a broom. It was so very bad, that on one occasion it was suggested to the warden to let the women sleep in the day room and [the matron] would sit up all night with them, and be responsible for them; the warden would not consent. The women suffered very much, their bodies were blistered with the bugs; and they often tore themselves with scratching' (Canada – Brown Commission 1849: 16).

Penitentiaries were criticized for abusing inmates (in particular flogging women and young children) and for their extensive use of corporal punishment for relatively minor offences, such as swearing, insulting the staff, refusing to wear shoes, and general incorrigibility (Canada – Brown Commission 1849). Even after the public condemnation that followed this report, women continued to be punished for offences such as 'making a disturbance,' 'abusive language,' calling a guard an 'old fagot,' 'disobedience,' 'threatening another convict,' and 'talking in the work room.' The typical punishment for these offences was three or four days in an empty, darkened cell. If the prisoner's behaviour did not warrant a dark cell, she was locked in a solitary confinement cell that had some light and meagre furnishings. Segregated women were placed on a bread-and-water diet; on rare occasions, food was prohibited.[2]

It is reported that women prisoners were punished more frequently than men, but less severely (Oliver 1994). The rules for punishment in the late nineteenth century reflect some discrepancies in how male and female convicts were treated. Men appear to have been subject to longer and more severe punishment. For example, the published rules and regulations for Kingston Penitentiary in the 1890s contain separate sets of instructions and options for male and female prisoners. The most significant differences between the two sets of rules were that dietary punishments of bread and water could not exceed twenty-one meals for men, and six meals for women; confinement in a cell with a 'hard bed, with or without a blanket' could not exceed one month for men, and six nights for women; and while both men and women were potentially subject to solitary confinement and 'forfeiture of remission of sentence,' only men could officially receive the punishments of 'flogging with a leather paddle' and 'the application of water from a hose in the presence of a warden.'[3] The Female Convicts Punishment Book, 1850–1856, reveals that women were generally subjected to solitary confinement and placed on diets of bread and water. However, it is difficult to ascertain whether other, undocumented punishments were used to discipline refractory convicts.

In practice, the normative and corrective techniques of penitentiary discipline (rules of silence, continuous surveillance, hard labour, and religious instruction) were rarely used with female populations. When I claim that the penitentiary discipline of women was ineffective, it is not to suggest that these technologies of discipline were consistently and effectively applied to men.

An 'Insignificant' Population?

Explanations for the adminstrative apathy that historically has surrounded the treatment of women in penitentiaries have tended to stress the small size of the female population. On a larger national scale, the population of women prisoners tended to be smaller than the men's population; but on an institutional level, the number of women incarcerated at Kingston Penitentiary throughout the nineteenth and early twentieth centuries was not insignificant, even if it was still *significantly* smaller than the number of men (see Table 3.1).[4]

Most female offenders were housed in the Female Unit of the Kingston facility; however, a few inmates from the Maritimes were shuffled back and forth between the existing unit in eastern Canada (Dorchester Penitentiary) and Kingston Penitentiary, whichever was most politically convenient. The Saint John and Halifax penitentiaries usually held a few female convicts; when Dorchester Penitentiary was built to replace these two institutions in 1880, a small female ward was built in its west wing. This unit was used until 1885, when its women prisoners were transferred to Kingston.[5] Between 1894 and 1917, women prisoners were retained at Dorchester, where the female population rose to a peak of seventeen women in the fiscal year 1908–9.[6] In 1923 the Dorchester unit was finally closed, and the remaining three inmates were transferred to Kingston, pending the building of a new women's prison.[7] Shortly after this transfer, administrators argued that the women prisoners should be returned to Dorchester because of the inadequacy of Kingston's sixty-year-old 'wretched' and 'makeshift' cells and the absence of productive labour in the Female Unit.[8]

The highest number of women prisoners received at Kingston Penitentiary in one year was thirty-four in both 1858 and 1863. Because there were so few women prisoners, they were thought to be unworthy of scarce resources. Even so, their conditions were by no means forgotten. Comments made by the warden and matron at Kingston in 1868 indicate that they were concerned about the inadequate accommodations for female prisoners.[9] Also, in the early 1900s, penitentiary administrators repeatedly reported overcrowding problems in the Female Unit.[10] The initial architectural plans for Kingston Penitentiary (1835) included a separate prison and yard for women prisoners, but these

TABLE 3.1
Average and highest number of male and female prisoners received (per year) at Kingston Penitentiary (1835–1934).

					YEARS					
	1835–44	1845–54*	1855–64	1865–74	1875–84	1885–94	1895–1904	1905–14	1915–24*	1925–34*
Women										
Average	7.2	9.5*	23.5	15.4	9.1	9.5	6.3	5.6	17.2*	15.5*
Highest	11	14	34	24	14	21	12	16	21	21
Total	72	95*	235	154	91	95	63	56	103*	124*
Men										
Average	83.4	107.1*	220.7	200.8	205.4	159.8	160.8	176.5	292*	355*
Highest	142	150*	274	277	345	207	221	239	390*	477*
Total	834	964*	2207	2008	2054	1598	1608	1765	1752*	2838*
Total	906	1059	2442	2162	2145	1693	1671	1821	1855*	2962*

*Denotes missing data

plans were not realized until 1912. There were no separate prisons for women in either Quebec or Ontario until 1874. In the meantime, women prisoners at Kingston were housed in less than adequate conditions, but by no means were they entirely ignored. Women prisoners were not 'invisible' to male administrators, and the fact that matrons were hired bears this out.

Moral Matrons: Governing by Example

Shortly after Kingston Penitentiary opened, warden Henry Smith expressed that a female matron needed to be hired to govern the women prisoners. In 1836 he noted: 'As it was found impossible to employ the female convicts with any advantage to the institution under the direction of the keepers, a matron was by order of the Board engaged in the month of October last, under whose care their labours have been beneficially applied in making and mending the bedding and clothing for prisoners.'[11]

The hiring of matrons to govern the female population meant that women prisoners were subject to more surveillance than before. Matrons were responsible for the moral reform of women prisoners and for the development of disciplinary programs. As the size of the female population expanded, prison administrations began reluctantly to employ additional matrons and nurses specifically to care for women prisoners. As well, in 1844 'nursing' and 'hospital' staff were added to the roster of paid employees. Mrs Elmherst (1835–40) seems to have been the first matron employed in Kingston Penitentiary;[12] however, the first recorded matron's report did not appear until 1852.[13] Elizabeth Smith was hired in 1844 to work in the hospital, and Ellen McGarvey was hired in 1845 as a nurse. Thereafter, nurses were regularly employed.[14]

These occupations were not rewarding, and few women aspired to become matrons or prison nurses. Unlike the British and American 'ladies' involved in penal reform movements, the women who chose this type of employment were often impoverished and desperate, with limited legitimate options for survival. Matrons tended to receive lower rates of pay and to have less authority than male guards in similar positions (Oliver 1994: 521). Rarely they were provided with the necessary resources to reform female convicts efficiently and effectively. Eventually, matrons would play a critical role in the normalization of convicts and in the creation and maintenance of penal discipline. Although Kingston matrons were not hired for the specific purpose of creating a maternal program of discipline (as was the case at the Mercer), the presence of women penal officials altered the custodial environment. Even though matrons were hired to alleviate managerial difficulties associated with an integrated prison population (such as physical and sexual abuse, communication, and inadequate classification and programming), prison administrators expected these women to play an important role in the reform of offenders. The maternal significance of their role is reinforced by the comments of the Protestant Prison Chaplain in 1852: 'The Female Superintendent should bear a relative position to the Warden himself, since much must necessarily depend on her, in which, even that superior Officer cannot, with propriety, be consulted. The Female Superintendent, according to my opinion, should, both in moral and social deportment, and in religious and secular education, be raised to such eminence, as that the unhappy convict may look up to her as an example; and command obedience by moral influence, rather than physical force.'[15]

Over time, selection criteria for matrons would emerge; but at first the job was given to anyone who was willing to live in the prison and supervise women convicts. Simply being female qualified a woman for this undesirable occupation. A few years later, the importance of hiring a 'religious' matron to instruct Catholic female convicts in their prayers and catechism was reinforced by the Roman Catholic chaplain.[16]

In the mid-1850s, Martha Walker, an English widow, became a matron at Kingston. She seems to have been paid and treated better than her predecessors. According to Oliver (1994: 521), Walker had a great deal of authority and autonomy. She was responsible for managing the Female Unit, and in this capacity she designed an education program and a set of rules to address the specific needs of the female population. The employment of Walker as matron had a profound impact on how the public perceived women convicts. Penitentiary staff stopped regarding them as 'the most refractory and unmanageable prisoners in the penitentiary.'[17] Through her efforts in the Female Unit, the charismatic Walker eventually won the respect and admiration of male administrators and chaplains. She came to advocate using virtuous women to rehabilitate and train their misguided sisters. However, the independent efforts of Walker and a few middle-class reformers did not fundamentally challenge the conditions under which women were confined in Canadian institutions.

By the mid-nineteenth century, matrons were fairly commonplace in most prisons. Official narratives suggest that matrons were good role models and teachers, and able to discipline misguided convicts. It was accepted that their role was important, given the widespread concerns about the sexual abuse and moral contagion that were so often the results of poor methods for classifying and separating the prison population. The hiring of matrons to discipline women and to administer gender-specific programs meant that penal administrators could publicly claim that they were trying to reform women in gender-specific ways. However, penal officials rarely expended valued resources on the female population. They sympathized with the matrons charged with governing a population of convicts often regarded as 'unreformable,' but they rarely gave matrons the resources or support necessary to carry out the task of moral reform.

In 1869, Matron Belinda Plees expressed concern about overcrowding, the greater number of women coming to the penitentiary, and the refractory nature of 'two or three exceedingly bad and turbulent women who take delight in disturbing the prison.' She noted that in general, things had been 'going on satisfactorily,' but added, 'There are serious drawbacks for want of proper cells, where lazy, worthless, characters could be isolated, and their day's work extracted from them. Such a system I believe would tend much more to subduing and reforming them than the present way I am now obliged to adopt, viz. – putting them in a dark cell on bread and water where they can sleep all day and, in the night, sing and hammer so as to disturb the whole establishment.'[18]

In the same annual report, the warden acknowledged that although the Female Unit was inadequate, it had some positive aspects. For example, the women convicts had been keeping the prison 'beautifully clean and neat,' and they were being reformed. He also commented on the improved quality of women's penal discipline: 'The poor unfortunate creatures, who are sent here, are generally of the unfortunate classes and of the worst temperament. They are, here, taught the usefulness of labour, and those, well disposed, are allowed to learn the working of a sewing machine, so that, on their release, they may be enabled to obtain a livelihood.'[19]

Even though this warden did not appear to concur with the negative portrayal of women prisoners submitted by the matron, his comments echoed her frustrations with the accommodations available to women prisoners. Prison administrators at Kingston continued to struggle with the challenge of managing women convicts in a wholly inadequate regime of penitentiary discipline. Until separate reformatories (1874) and penitentiaries (1934) were built, few changes were made to the conditions of women's confinement. The regime seems to have been altered only slightly by changes in administrative staff. The hiring of women to govern other women was a typical maternal strategy, yet the matrons at Kingston were not provided with the resources to implement maternalist programs.

The Struggle for a Separate Female Unit

The inadequate living conditions, the extreme punitiveness, the absence of penitentiary discipline, and the inability to occupy women with profitable labour, led the Brown Commission in 1849 to recommend that a separate building be erected for women prisoners. It was hoped that once it was constructed, the reforming of women could be attempted. This recommendation prompted what became a ninety-year administrative struggle to build a separate and autonomous federal penitentiary for women. In 1846, makeshift cells were constructed and the twenty-six women were confined in cells measuring 8 feet 4 inches long, 7 feet 6 inches high, and 30 inches wide.[20] A few years later, a separate unit for women prisoners was opened in what is now the north wing of Kingston Penitentiary. At the time of Confederation, the warden's report strongly advocated that a proper female prison be built outside the penitentiary walls. Similar recommendations were repeated by Moylan, the Inspector of Penitentiaries, between 1885 and 1890.

The petitions to build a separate women's prison were strongly predicated on the ideal of separation/classification. Penitentiary officials repeatedly expressed their concern about interactions between male and female convicts, and between female convicts and male prison staff. For example, in one of his reports Inspector Moylan noted: 'I have always considered this portion of the penitentiary [the female unit] unfit for the use that is made of it. Apart from its objectionable proximity to the male prison, the cells being underground in a gloomy and dismal compartment, is sufficient cause for recommending change.'[21]

After Moylan filed his report in 1893, a blueprint for a proposed prison for women outside the walls of Kingston Penitentiary was drawn by the architect and chief trade instructor of Kingston Penitentiary. Although this facility was never built, the blueprints bear a striking resemblance to the existing P4W, built some thirty years later.[22] Despite numerous requests and recommendations by administrators, wardens, and commissioners, separate quarters for women prisoners were not built until 1910, when a separate cell block was opened with accommodations for thirty-four women. In February 1909, Warden Platt wrote an 'unofficial letter' to the Inspector of Penitentiaries, speculating on what to do about the Female Prison, the Keeper's Hall, and the Roman Catholic chapel while the north wing of the penitentiary was being rebuilt. The outcome was that a new women's prison was built on the penitentiary grounds, surrounded by a seven-foot stone wall.[23] Shortly after the new unit opened, it was overcrowded, and women were made to sleep in the corridors of what was now called the Female Department.[24]

The 1914 Royal Commission on Penitentiaries commented on the new women's prison inside Kingston Penitentiary. It noted that while the new building was an acceptable alternative to Kingston Penitentiary, it would be in the women's best interests to transfer them either to an entirely separate women's prison or to provincial institutions.[25] By 1916, a population of some forty female prisoners was placing a strain on the Kingston facilities, which included only thirty-two regular and two double sick-bay cells. To relieve this overcrowding, the Female Department at Dorchester Penitentiary was reopened in 1919–20, and thirteen women prisoners from the Maritimes were transferred to the east coast.[26] By 1927, overcrowding was so severe that prisoners were again sleeping in the corridors of the Female Department.[27]

Beyond fleeting concerns about the separation of women prisoners from their families and children and the hiring of additional female staff, there were few significant efforts to reform the Female Unit at Kingston (constructed in 1910) until September 1920, when the Biggar-Nickle-Draper Committee on the Penitentiary Act and Regulations submitted a report. This committee was appointed by the Minister of Justice, Charles J. Doherty, to review and revise the penitentiary regulations and to advise the government on changes to the existing legislation. The committee was specifically directed to review the policies and procedures governing the reformation of convicts; 'the differential treatment of classes of convicts'; prison labour and the suitability of prison industries; staffing; prison discipline; remissions procedures; visits to and letters from convicts; and the facilities for 'self education of convicts and the provision of formal educational instruction' (Doherty 1920: 7, cited in Canada – Biggar-Nickle-Draper 1921). The committee's mandate was vast and was informed by a specific logic of correctional reform. Its report denounced past correctional practices based on retribution and argued strongly for more rehabilitative approaches to penal management: 'It is necessary to eliminate wholly the idea of vengeance, not on humanitarian grounds, or because of its painful consequences to the individual, but solely because of its stupidity and on grounds of common sense ... The system should be such as to constitute, in so far as possible, a training of the convicted person to retake, as he must, his position in society, to prevent his being deteriorated by the punishment he has undergone, and to enable him while undergoing it to fulfil his natural family obligations. (1921: 11)

Detailed recommendations for training female convicts were not outlined in this report, but the general philosophy of the report was meant to apply to both male and female convicts, and, of course, 'family obligations' were highly gendered.

The committee's denunciation of punitive correctional techniques was reaffirmed by its allegiance to a scientifically based rehabilitative model of correctional reform. This shift toward a rehabilitative ethos was linked to a wider ideological and political shift that resulted in the rise of criminology, and in particular biological, psychological, and social positivism.[28] This new ethos argued that the central administration of prisons should be based on 'development and cure' rather than on 'repression and restriction' (1920: 11). The committee also advocated the 'use of modern scientific resources for the examination and classification of convicts' to cure their physical and mental illnesses. Closely linked to these notions was the belief that meaningful instruction and the employment of convicts in remunerative and productive labour was essential to reform. The committee was quite critical of traditional prison labour programs, contending that repetitive and meaningless labour, such as stockpiling or breaking rocks ('hard labour'), did not promote the desired habits of industry.

These ideas were pivotal to the future direction of women's penality. Drawing on the principle of separation, the committee argued that women convicts should be held in a 'completely separate institution out of view of the penitentiary for male convicts': 'Notwithstanding what ... would be possible hardship to a very few women in their withdrawal from the neighbourhood of their friends outside, arrangements might perhaps be usefully made for the concentration of all female convicts at a single institution of which the head should be a woman warden.'[29]

The ideal of separation emerged as a key theme in the resulting campaign to build a separate penitentiary for women. Even though the Biggar-Nickle-Draper Commission recommended the development of a separate institution administered by a female warden, it did not recommend that women prisoners be subject to a special maternal or women-centred regime.

Rationale for a Separate Women's Penitentiary: The Nickle Commission, 1921

Unlike previous administrators, Nickle and his fellow commissioners faced little resistance to the idea of a separate federal prison for women. While there was strong support for hiring a female warden to manage the Prison for Women independently, when it opened in 1934 its administration was ultimately governed by the warden of Kingston Penitentiary, and then by the warden of Collins Bay Penitentiary until the mid-1960s.[30] A few days after the Biggar-Nickle-Draper Report was submitted in 1921, the Minister of Justice appointed the same W.F. Nickle to report on the management of the women in Kingston Penitentiary. The Nickle Commission of 1921 was the first federal commission report to address the specific issues of women prisoners and their treatment. In his report, Nickle strongly advised that the Female Unit be removed and that a new prison be built in keeping with 'the best judgement of those conversant with modern prison building.' He stipulated that there was no need for 'the erection of forbidding stone walls' of the sort that characterized most penitentiaries. Instead, he stressed the importance of putting minimal security measures in place to secure the institution from the intrusion of outsiders and to prevent escapes (Nickle Commission 1921a: 5). While Nickle made several other significant recommendations, such as for the hiring of a French-speaking matron and for programs for female convicts, the recommendation to close the existing female prison at Kingston Penitentiary and replace it with a new, centralized prison for women was the most significant.

Nickle, like earlier administrators and reformers, emphasized the importance of classification and of separate accommodations for women. In his view, it was important to build a new facility in order to ensure that female convicts would be adequately segregated from male convicts and male staff. Like many others, he was particularly concerned about the harmful effects of women convicts' 'innate' flirtatious habits and men's inability to resist this temptation:

> As would be expected, the natural happens, and certain classes of the convicts carry on, when chance permits, active or subdued flirtations with responsive officials or sympathetic male convicts. It is not to be assumed

that in all or perhaps in most cases the conduct of women is responsible, except in so far as it is a breach of regulations. Without doubt some of the *women, more particularly at certain periods, are thrown into a violent state of sexual excitement by the mere sight of men,* more often by their being or working contiguously to the female quarters and my attention was called to one instance of this group of cases where a sedative had to be given to soothe desire. Certain objectionable notes were found in the yard of the Female Prison [inside Kingston Penitentiary] to indicate that to some of the men the proximity of the women is equally harmful. (Emphasis added; 1921a: 3)

This discussion, and the description that followed of the different types of women confined at the prison (mildly flirtatious or violently sexual), are consistent with earlier themes of the fallen woman versus the reformable woman. It was implied that the 'bad' women prisoners were to some extent responsible for the sexual abuse that happened at the prison. Only rarely was the conduct of the male guards toward 'decent' women viewed as a problem; the frailties of men were usually explained as arising from the sexual power of women convicts.

Nothing did more in recent years to disorganize discipline in the Female Prison than the improper conduct of male officials with the female convicts. Jealousies that still exist; decent women were offended by gross misconduct and a feeling of gross resentment aroused against the administration that will take some time to quiet ... While the disclosures of the past year have shown how unscrupulous officers have taken unfair advantage of the opportunities for flirtations, improprieties and indecencies that presented themselves, yet it can be truthfully contradicted that many decent officers are fearful, knowing that a few designing and crafty women might ruin a well earned reputation. (1921a: 4–5)

These moral concerns, as well as frustrations with the inadequacy of programming, informed his recommendation for an entirely autonomous female prison staffed solely by women. Nickle was also appalled by the filthiness of the female prison, the inadequacy of medical care, the use of convict labour to wash, mend, and launder the personal clothing of staff, and the appropriation and sale of convicts' handiwork.

Nickle anticipated that the new prison and its incumbent regime could govern prisoners through 'building female character.' Better selection and training processes were presented as possible solutions to past staff negligence, and to what he perceived was a lack of initiative in attempts to prepare convicts for the responsibilities of citizenship on release. He expressed his frustration with penal regimes that rely on 'repression, rather than reintegration and make no effort to develop latent benevolent inclinations but tend to accentuate the least attractive qualities of human nature' (1921a: 34). His criticisms were not new; in his narratives he was relying on evangelical and social scientific analyses of observable problems. This approach was in marked contrast to the maternalist agenda of Inspector Langmuir, who fifty years earlier resorted to domestic metaphors when calling for the establishment of a separate reformatory. Nickle did not rely as heavily on maternalism to justify the construction of a centralized federal penitentiary. Rather, he embraced a more scientific rehabilitative approach that would stress 'curing' the female offender. However, his emphasis on 'curing,' was not based on the psychiatric ideals of 'curing the criminal mind,' but rather on the evangelical goal of 'curing the soul' of the offender. In his view, matrons, everyday, nonscientific knowledge, and not scientific experts, had a central role to play in the rehabilitation of women prisoners. He argued that the prison offered women administrators 'a great opportunity to do something worthwhile,' and that their success in this institution would contribute to the 'curing of souls and bodies' (1921a: 21).

Nickle's approach reflects a combination of evangelical, rehabilitative, and maternal logics. The following passage demonstrates these logics in the context of his concerns about the prison's potential for doing harm:

So many people seem to forget that human nature in the convict does not differ from that of the person outside the walls, and that most of those within will some day be again without. You have not accomplished much if, after years in the prison, you send the unfortunate back to a life either only broken in spirit or filled with bitterness and resentment against her fate and society. Offenders are sent to prison ... as a punishment and not to be punished; the function of those in charge should not be to repress but to stimulate their charges with fresh hope for better days and better things. (1921a: 16)

He also advocated limiting the use of techniques that have little psychological benefit:

Individuality is lost through convicts being addressed by number and not by name. Nothing as far as I can see, is gained by this practise, while much is lost: self respect and esteem is destroyed. The individual becomes a non-entity. This practice should be stopped. Little effort as far as I could see, to appeal to a woman through her emotions or religious tendencies; even in the House of the Lord she is made to feel that she is a convict. (1921a: 17)

Here, Nickle was expressing an allegiance to a rehabilitative mentality that was consistent with the views of several 'nonexpert' religious reform groups, such as the Prisoners' Aid Association[31] and the Salvation Army, which also stressed the importance of supportive relationships with inmates and discharged prisoners.[32] Nickle ardently supported the involvement of nonstate reformers or 'friends on discharge,' who would help the women become law-abiding citizens. Typical of many reformers in this period, he advocated increased state involvement in and support of after-care services and discharge planning. Like many early-twentieth-century penologists, Nickle was quickly losing faith in the nineteenth-century penitentiary ideal. Although he supported the ideal of rehabilitation, he did not consider rehabilitation to be synonymous with scientific expertise.

Institutionalization of Women's Knowledges: The Prison for Women, 1934–50

Construction of the Prison for Women began in the spring of 1925. Surviving accounts of its construction indicate that the project was characterized not only by delays but also by 'quite unnecessary structural changes and alterations' that greatly inflated the cost of the prison. While inmate work gangs[33] from Kingston Penitentiary were used to build the prison, it is quite likely that a number of local contractors supplied the project with both materials and services.[34] The change in architectural plans, and the eventual building of a congregate-style as opposed to a cottage-style prison (the latter more commonly associated with maternal discipline), was perhaps simply a matter of economics and of the practicalities of supervising a large number of inmates. In many American states, this rationale had been used to justify changes in women's prison designs (Freedman 1981). The new women's prison was a T-shaped complex surrounded by an imposing sixteen-foot limestone wall. Inspector Moylan's reports in 1892 and 1893 indicate that a large portion of the P4W's boundary wall had already been constructed for the purpose of enclosing one of two planned additions to Kingston Penitentiary (namely, the new women's prison and a Criminal Lunatic

Asylum). There is little reason to doubt that the existence of this wall dictated the placement of the present P4W.[35] While no towers were constructed in the wall, the exterior wall was topped by ten feet of wire fabric and six lines of barbed wire to add height. The front section of the wall contained living quarters for the matrons, a chapel, and an administrative area. Besides single-cell accommodations for one hundred inmates, the rear of the institution contained a laundry room and sewing room.[36]

In spite of its antiquated design (strikingly similar to that of an 1883 blueprint mentioned earlier), some reformers expected this new federal prison to accomplish goals similar to those of earlier American reformatories. After P4W was completed in 1932, its first occupants were not women, but rather one hundred male inmates temporarily transferred from the corridors and prison isolation unit of Kingston Penitentiary. This transfer was necessary because of severe overcrowding, and because of damage to Kingston Penitentiary arising from a major riot.[37] These men were eventually removed from P4W, and in January 1934 approximately forty female convicts were transferred to their new location.[38]

It is difficult to determine the extent to which a maternal ethic of care and the scientific project of rehabilitation influenced the first few years of P4W. It is also difficult to ascertain from surviving records the extent to which Nickle's recommendations were implemented.[39] There are few accounts of 'rehabilitative programs' at P4W in its first few years of operation. For the most part, rehabilitative programming at P4W between 1934 and 1970 consisted of educational, vocational, and leisure programs aimed at structuring inmates' 'free time.' These programs reinforced conventional gender stereotypes. However, unlike the regime at the Mercer, maternal discipline was at the discretion of a handful of well-intentioned staff members. Some psychologists and psychiatrists were hired on contract in the 1960s.

The personal recollections of one early staff member, Mrs Vera Cherry, a nurse who lived and worked in the P4W for over two decades, indicate that maternal guidance and kindness informed administrative strategies more than scientific techniques of rehabilitation.[40] Mrs Cherry began working in Kingston Penitentiary in the late 1920s and was transferred to P4W with the women prisoners. She was one of many prison staff who had devoted their lives to caring for marginalized women. While her decision to work in the penitentiary was based largely on her financial needs as a young single woman during the difficult years of the Great Depression, once employed she devoted herself to the women. She presented herself as a surrogate mother to the women, and affectionately recalled stories of teaching prisoners domestic skills such as knitting, sewing, cooking, and housekeeping, and of times spent talking to the women about their problems. Mrs Cherry remembered a few meaningful moments during her career, including the day several women helped her make her wedding dress and plan her wedding. She referred to the prison as 'just like a nice big home.' She recalled bringing her own children into the institutions to be cared for by the prisoners during summer holidays. Mrs Cherry believed firmly that many of the women incarcerated at the prison had made mistakes resulting from poor judgment, but that they were not inherently bad people. She used her observations of the inmates' behaviour around her own children to validate this opinion: 'They were not terribly dangerous convicts or even mean women, many of them were mothers in difficult circumstances. I remember the days when I used to bring my children to the institution in the morning and fetch them in the evening after the women had played with them and cleaned them up like they were their own.'[41]

Mrs Cherry relied heavily on benevolent maternal techniques. When a prisoner was angry or upset, she would not punish her; rather she would put her arms around her and hug her, or place her in a bathtub and talk to her the whole time she was in the tub until she cooled off.[42] However, Cherry also recalled the use of segregation to control angry or disruptive prisoners. She attempted to govern women through kindness and to nurture them as if they were her own children. Ironically, in her spare time she learned domestic skills like sewing from women prisoners while encouraging them to engage in gender-appropriate activities.

The dark side of this 'happy home' was evident in her recollection of experiences with alcoholics, drug addicts, recidivists, and political prisoners (Doukhobors),[43] who were segregated in the 'basement' because of their noncompliance and disruptive behaviour. These same women were also actively excluded from certain programs because of their past offending behaviours. For example, prison records from the early 1950s indicate that women with substance abuse problems were not accepted into home grooming courses because they were deemed 'unsuitable candidates.'[44]

At P4W, just as at the Mercer Reformatory, some offenders were considered unreformable. Problems at the P4W were documented in the Annual Report of 1950–1, in which it was noted that 'the type of inmate being admitted has increased difficulties' and that the presence of Doukhobor women 'has had a most disturbing effect on the balance of the population.'[45] Many Doukhobor women were incarcerated as a result of their involvement in political protests against the Canadian state, which were an effort to preserve their unique cultural, religious, and philosophical heritage (Yerbury and Griffiths 1991). These protests often involved nudity and arson. Once incarcerated, they continued to engage in such behaviours; thus, they were defined as 'difficult to manage.' When the Doukhobor women were released from P4W in 1952, the Annual Report noted that 'this removed a most difficult nerve-racking problem.'[46] Problems with this population were also reported by a retired correctional officer, who recounted how Doukhobor prisoners on hunger strikes were forcefed by strapping them to a table and inserting a tube down their throats. During the Second World War, several 'aliens' ('internment prisoners') were held at P4W.

Records indicate that in some instances these women received differential treatment, and that they placed an additional strain on an already overburdened staff.[47] Despite maternal narratives and a formal state commitment to improving women's penal conditions, the use of overt forms of coercion continued. Women prisoners were subject to harsh and sometimes cruel forms of treatment that were inconsistent with the wider logic of welfare-based governance.

A few years after women moved into P4W, the Archambault Commission (1938) condemned the institution and strongly recommended that it be closed and that its inmates be transferred to provincial facilities. The Archambault Commission was established after a series of disturbances in federal institutions and on the recommendation of the Canadian Penal Congress. Archambault believed firmly in the principles of reform on which the penitentiary had been founded. He argued that 'the task of the prison should be, not merely the temporary protection of society through the incarceration of captured offenders, but the transformation of reformable criminals into law-abiding citizens' (1938: 9). He argued that over the last hundred years the state had failed to carry out its duty and responsibility to reform and rehabilitate offenders. He sharply criticized the current Superintendent of Penitentiaries for being 'arrogant' and 'neglectful' and for using 'extreme dictatorial methods' to manage the penitentiary system (Adamson 1983, cited in Ekstedt and Griffiths 1988: 51). This report made several general recommendations about the administration of penitentiaries. It also addressed the specific issue of P4W and, more generally, women's criminality.

> The general conclusion to be drawn from women's relative place in crime is that, as a separate problem, it is comparatively unimportant, and that custodial care should be delegated to properly constituted and properly managed reformatories, and that no woman should be confined in penitentiaries. *There is no justification for the erection of and maintenance of a costly penitentiary for women alone, nor is it desirable that they should be confined, either in the same institution as men, or in one central institution far from their place of residence and their friends and relations.* (Emphasis added; 1938: 148)

The 1947 Gibson Report restated Archambault's recommendations. Even so, the state made few concrete efforts to alter the conditions or circumstances of women's confinement. Minor cosmetic improvements were made (including the construction of tennis courts and gardens), and a few additional privileges, such as radio reception, were extended to women prisoners in an effort to improve conditions and address some of the adminstrative problems.

Despite the best of intentions, Mrs Cherry and other staff and matrons had difficulty disciplining the women because of staffing limitations. However, the warden was reluctant to hire additional matrons because of the small number of incarcerated women.[48] Over the next twenty years, with the 1941 addition of a poultry farm for egg production, and the securing of naval contracts for producing pillow slips, the institutional employment opportunities for prisoners improved. The women at P4W manufactured several items for the Army and Navy (surgical dressings, clothing, and bedding) in the industrial sewing rooms.[49] In the late 1940s, women volunteers from the Kingston area began to play a more active role in the delivery of educational and recreational activities.

Conclusions

Informed by the notion of separate spheres, maternal reformers and state officials at the turn of the century argued in favour of all-female institutions, 'prisons uncontaminated by male influence, in which criminal women would receive sympathetic care from members of their own sex' (Rafter 1992: 46). In many ways, the development of separate prisons for women marked the institutionalization of differential treatment for women prisoners. Facilities such as P4W featured some remnants of early maternal strategies, but by and large they were a regime designed for women who were perceived to be beyond hope of maternal and spiritual redemption. It was not until the early 1950s that expert-based rehabilitative strategies emerged. These strategies are discussed in more detail in the following chapter.

The programs and techniques of reform that emerged at P4W in the postwar period reflected both 'everyday,' nonexpert forms of governance, such as the encouragement of feminine appearance, and new psychiatric and social work technologies. The operationalization of new penal logics and their integration into pre-existing regimes was erratic and unpredictable. Programs emerge when they are politically expedient, and to a degree they depend on the leadership of charismatic figures, who are essential to the development and design of rehabilitative programs for women.

Many are still inclined to read the history of women's imprisonment as a series of techniques of governing that neatly and easily replace one another over time. Likewise, it is argued that disciplinary power is connected to expert knowledges that replace nonexpert knowledges. This chapter showed how a range of knowledges, forms of power, and technologies of governing can exist simultaneously and shape the regime of a particular institution. The following chapter will extend this theme and show how nonstate agents and volunteers play an equally important role in the governance of women prisoners, and how 'everyday,' nonscientific maternal knowledge of women is blended with expert systems such as domestic science, social work, and psychology.

Chapter Four

Laywomen's Expertise: Women's Prison Reform, 1945–70

Scholars interested in the therapeutic regulation of women prisoners have focused on state agents of social control, and on how these agents construct and respond to the 'disturbed' or 'maladjusted' female offender using medical or psychiatric definitions of women's deviance (Edwards 1981; Dobash, Dobash, and Gutteridge 1986; Allen 1987a, 1987b; Carlen and Worrall 1987; Sim 1990; Chunn and Menzies 1990; Kendall 1993b; Faith 1993; Smart 1995). In contrast, the activities of women penal reformers and their role in the governance of incarcerated women through nonmedical and pseudo-scientific knowledges are largely unexplored. The rehabilitation of prisoners is usually considered to be a function of the state and male experts.

This chapter examines two issues. *First*, I argue that rehabilitation is a flexible and enabling logic that can be used to describe and legitimate a wide range of expert and nonexpert interventions and reforms, from hiring psychologists to providing lessons in domestic science and social etiquette. Like other current terms such as 'maternalism' and 'empowerment,' rehabilitation is vague enough to be perceived as compatible with and facilitated by a diverse range of programs and interventions. And, like 'maternalism,' rehabilitation has always been gendered, with existing gender ideologies being deployed to give specific content to vocational and leisure programs for women prisoners.

Second, I argue that discipline is not driven solely by experts: it also relies on nonscientific relations of power/knowledge. In women's prisons, these nonscientific knowledges are often based on women's knowledge of everyday techniques of mothering and household management. This maternal knowledge and related relations of power are present in penal programs commonly described as rehabilitative. Reformers and prison staff use this nonscientific expertise to govern the habits and conduct of prisoners to produce a particular type of normative subject.

Valverde (1996, 1998) has shown that there are everyday forms of ethical governance that are not the same as expert-based disciplinary governance and that persist into the present day. An example is the regulation of an individual's habits. In contrast to Dobash, Dobash, and Gutteridge (1986), Sim (1990), and other studies, I argue that the disciplinary governance at the Prison for Women (and possibly in some men's prisons and juvenile facilities) is also to some extent based on everyday knowledge. I show how the logic of 'rehabilitation' used at P4W includes both scientific *and* nonexpert, everyday knowledges of women's experiences and needs, and how women reformers combined these knowledges to normalize and regulate the female offender through their own 'feminized' view of 'rehabilitation.'

I analyse how reformers and prison staff helped promote a gender-specific ideal of rehabilitation based on their knowledge of the female offender. Here, I am concerned with three wider questions: What constitutes expertise? How is women's nonscientific knowledge or 'expertise' used in the design and delivery of 'rehabilitative programs'? And how does the social construction of women reformers as 'experts' legitimate the reformers' role in women's penality?

The type of 'rehabilitation' applied at P4W is to a large extent organized around everyday knowledges (Smith 1987) that reinforce certain expectations about appropriate feminine conduct. Volunteerism, in particular women's volunteer labour, played a critical role in shaping Canadian penality (cf Whittingham 1984). Although policy documents as early as the 1920s called for a more 'rehabilitative' penal logic, there are no records of expert-based psychiatric and psychological rehabilitative programs at P4W until the late 1950s. However, that does not mean that women administrators and employees of P4W were not using knowledge generated by experts to define and govern women prisoners. It is likely that prison staff combined everyday and expert knowledges in their efforts to manage female offenders.

New Forms of Governing: Rehabilitation and the Woman Prisoner

At P4W, women's everyday knowledge was gradually professionalized (cf Kunzel 1993) and used by reformers and prison staff in the governance of women prisoners. At the turn of the century, women reformers were considered to be 'experts on their sex.' Reformers, including early prison staff, used 'everyday' knowledge to govern women's leisure habits and create 'ladylike' subjects. The lay knowledges of women like Elizabeth Fry were incorporated into many penal regimes; however, in the mid-twentieth century, with the rise of professional expert knowledges such as psychiatry and psychology, this knowledge was marginalized. This competing notion of expertise was associated with formal training and qualifications. Forms of prisoner training that previously relied on women's everyday maternal knowledge – house cleaning, cooking, child rearing and so on – became the subject of formal university courses such as domestic science: being a well-intentioned, virtuous woman and a good mother no longer qualified a woman as an expert on her own sex.

By the mid-1940s, several women reformers had acquired various bachelors' degrees from universities; but rather than acknowledging themselves as experts on female crime, well-meaning volunteers used their status in university women's clubs and in the community to advocate the hiring of professionally trained psychiatrists in women's prisons. While women reformers trained in social work and domestic science actively participated in the reform of women prisoners, they were not given the same professional expert status as male psychiatrists and psychologists.

Before discussing the specific programs at P4W, it is important to discuss briefly a few of the wider transformations in penality at the turn of the century. These transformations had a profound impact on Canadian corrections between 1940 and 1970, and form the basis of the common understanding that rehabilitation is a form of 'expert' intervention based on a scientific understanding of the criminal mind. For many, the rehabilitative ideal, when mixed with punishment, produced 'the notion that the primary purpose of penal treatment is to effect changes in the character, attitudes, and behaviour of convicted offenders, so as to strengthen the social defense against unwanted behaviour, but also to contribute to the welfare and satisfaction of offenders' (Allen 1981: 2, cited in Cullen and Gilbert 1982). Thus, the objective of the 'benevolent state' was to use forms of social control, such as penal institutions, to help the offender change his or her character and thereby achieve rehabilitation. As Marshall (1981: 23, cited in Cullen and Gilbert 1982) notes, after the rehabilitation model was introduced in corrections, 'virtually everything done with, for or to the offender after conviction was labeled *treatment* ... A wide variety of programs and correctional measures have been included under the catch-all term *treatment*, ranging from teaching an inmate how to make a license plate to solitary confinement to intensive forms of individual psychotherapy.' Throughout the past century, virtually every penal regime has employed the rationality of rehabilitation[1] and justified penal technologies on the basis of this ideal.

Most of the postwar advocacy surrounding the training of female offenders stressed the importance of rehabilitation. Given this emphasis, the most appropriate candidates to train female offenders were thought to be social workers or individuals with professional training in modern penology. Professionally trained men and women began to replace matrons, who often had little or no formal training. This increased reliance on professionally trained social workers, psychologists, and psychiatrists was reflected in institutional practices. The Archambault Commission (1938) identified the reform of offenders as a key objective; however, the first classification officers (typically professionally trained psychologists) were not employed by the Penitentiary Service until after the war (Watkins 1992: 11). In 1957, Mrs M.E. Batstone became the first social worker officially appointed to the staff of P4W.[2] She was responsible for rehabilitating prisoners, and worked closely with local Elizabeth Fry Societies, the Salvation Army, and Children's Aid Societies.

In the United Kingdom after the war, it seems that women's prison programs were largely run by experts. Sim (1990: 157) notes that scientific experts and the research conducted by prison medical staff, academics, and other medical workers helped set the rigid parameters within which women's actions were explained. These experts legitimatized individualized and often painful interventions into prisoners' lives. In contrast, in the Canadian Penitentiary Service psychology was not part of the medical or psychiatric component of the penal regime; instead, it was organizationally related to inmate classification services (Watkins 1992: 11). Watkins (10) indicates that the first evidence of psychological involvement in corrections appears in Ontario in the early 1950s: there was one psychologist for 115 girls at the Ontario Training School for Girls (Karrys 1952). The first full-time psychologist was employed in 1951, and the first full-time psychiatrist in 1959 (Joliffe 1984; Watkins 1992; Kendall 2000). Kendall (2000) notes that a central psychiatric facility with nine cells was established in Kingston Penitentiary in 1948, and that by 1949 electroconvulsive therapy had begun in

Canadian penitentiaries. By the 1960s, the Penitentiary Service employed seven psychologists, each of these with a potential caseload of 800 inmates (Faguy 1973; Watkins 1992). The medical model of punishment that emerged in the 1960s in Canadian penitentiaries evolved out of the 1956 Fauteux Report, which stressed treatment and an increase in psychological and psychiatric services. Given the absence or inaccessibility of medical and psychiatric records and program descriptions, the level of 'expert intervention' into the lives of women at P4W is difficult to ascertain. However, one would expect that if a comprehensive scientific rehabilitative regime arose at P4W in the postwar era, records would exist. There are few accessible records which suggest that such a regime existed; however, the recent lawsuit filed by a former inmate, Dorothy Mills Proctor, indicates that some psychiatric experimentation occurred at P4W during the 1960s (this will be discussed later).[3]

Most criminologists assume that rehabilitation programs are designed and delivered by trained professionals such as psychiatrists and psychologists. Foucauldian studies of women's penality (Dobash, Dobash, and Gutteridge 1986; Sim 1990) tend to assume that rehabilitation programs are always run by male experts. Sim (1990: 129), for instance, states:

> Criminal women have been a central concern for prison managers and medical and psychiatric professionals since the emergence of the modern prison system at the end of the eighteenth century. They have been studied, probed and tested not only because of their supposed uniqueness but also because of the threat they posed to the social order of stable family relationships. As with male prisoners, regulation, discipline and normalization were key weapons in the prison's struggle with imprisoned women ... And at the centre of this iron therapy stood the figure of a medical man.

Many contend that around this time, scientific theories became the backbone of many techniques of governing citizens. For example, Sumner (1990: 29) notes, 'broad images of disease, the devil, crime and treason had been intellectually converted by the, mainly American, sociology of deviance between 1937 and 1968, into neutral sounding deviations, allegedly curable by psychiatry, social work and social policy.' These expert knowledges contributed to the development of new techniques and strategies of governing institutionalized and marginalized populations. The earlier development of national and international congresses and the organization of conferences and associations eventually 'pressed the claims of criminology upon the legislatures and penal institutions of virtually every western nation' (Garland 1985: 77). Penal administrators began to gather at international conferences, where some of the more outspoken advocates of the new penology stressed the importance and value of reform for individuals, and for society more generally. Debates about the causes of crime and the most appropriate techniques of reform dominated the penal culture. Traditional notions of motherhood, and evangelical or utilitarian ideals and techniques of reform, were being challenged by scientific experts. According to the new understanding of crime, criminality was caused by an aberration or abnormality in the individual – it was not a sin or the end result of faulty reasoning. While various modes of penal 'care' already existed as a result of the integration of pastoral and maternal techniques of managing prisoners, turn-of-the-century penality was influenced by a new mode of caring founded on the scientific principle of rehabilitation. This new reliance on science necessitated a corresponding reliance on various medical and social scientific experts. In many American institutions, scientific reform programs that encouraged inmates to develop self-esteem and independence began to overshadow more traditional attempts at redemption through motherly example (Freedman 1981; Strange 1983; Rafter 1992; Ruemper 1994).

According to Ruemper (1994: 352), some women's penal regimes in Ontario followed a similar pattern. Thus, while early-nineteenth-century state penal policy emphasized individualism and the 're-moralization' of deviant and dependent subjects through technologies (such as discipline, segregation, hard labour, and moral and religious training) designed to train the deviant to exercise reason, welfare state penal policy emphasized the diagnosis of deviance by experts and the normalization of individuals through the use of curative techniques and specialized experts (353–4). Under this new welfare regime, the state assumed responsibility for reforming the offender, and to that end recruited experts who relied on new scientific technologies of reform. Ruemper (354) argues that at the Mercer Reformatory, 'experts' were used by the state to aid in the reform of criminal women: 'the doctor who took charge of the woman's sexual morality as well as her health; the ministers and their assistants who looked after the woman's spiritual morality; the teachers who taught them obedience as well as reading and writing; the matrons who trained them in humility and the domestic arts; and other community agencies, such as the Prisoners'

Aid Society, whose members helped the women re-enter society in their proper sphere.'

The strategies of normalization that emerged with this scientific penality developed a new range of methods for sanctioning that were not restricted to the task of punishing (Foucault 1977). This quotation from Ruemper shows how women were governed both by medical experts and by nonexperts – such as matrons, volunteers, and ministers – rather than by one form of power/knowledge. Given the claim that expert knowledge such as psychiatry, and related techniques of thera-peutic discipline, replaced everyday knowledges and nonexpert tech-niques of Christian and maternal governance, one would expect to see more evidence of scientific expertise at P4W in the form of therapeutic programs and psychiatric reports. Yet a number of histories of this prison and commissions of inquiry have shown the opposite (Canada – Nickle 1921a; Canada – Archambault 1938; Canada – Fauteux 1956; Canadian Committee on Corrections – Ouimet 1969; Royal Commis-sion on the Status of Women 1970; Canada – Clark 1977a; Berzins and Cooper 1982; Axon 1989; Task Force on Federally Sentenced Women 1990; Shaw 1991a; Cooper 1993). I argue that the absence of such scientific programming tells us something important about the largely unexplored role of nonexpert knowledges and technologies in the gov-ernance of women prisoners.

Penality relies on a combination of expert and nonexpert forms of knowledge. The rise of welfare-based penality led to the coexistence of multiple knowledges and techniques of governing; some of these existed previously, and others were new. In the mid-twentieth-century regimes at P4W, a nonscientific logic of rehabilitation was used to legitimate moral reform projects geared toward the domestication of female prisoners. Programs such as domestic science did not rely on traditional scientific knowledges or even on medical expertise; instead, they emphasized an everyday maternal 'expertise.' What was new, however, was that in the mid-twentieth century women were now seen as requiring professional training in maternal and domestic skills – skills that previously where regarded as routine everyday skills passed on through generations by female relatives.

The Persistence of Maternal Discipline:
Household Management at P4W

In the late 1950s, the practice of having the supervising matron and other members of P4W staff reside in small apartments inside the main

institution was discontinued. The elimination of the positions of matron and supervising matron was significant, because it fundamentally
altered the implied maternal organization of the prison. The removal of
matrons' living quarters fractured a common bond of institutional
living, and thereby compromised the illusion of a 'homelike' atmosphere. This professional distance was in keeping with the new therapeutic model, but it directly undermined the homelike atmosphere
that earlier administrators had attempted to foster. At the same time
(1960), the supervising matron's position was abolished with the appointment of Isabel Macneill, a wartime commander of the Women's
Royal Naval Service (WRENS), as P4W's first superintendent.[4] Most
observers acknowledged that she was the best thing that ever happened to the prison (McNeil and Vance 1978: 81). In spite of her
unconventional career choices, she firmly believed that domestic training could provide skills that were important for women who were
likely to spend much of their everyday lives in the kitchen or doing
household chores.[5] Superintendent Macneill was directly responsible
to the Commissioner of Penitentiaries for the treatment and training
of prisoners and for the direction and disciplining of staff. For these
purposes, she was given all the disciplinary powers of a warden, and
certain other powers necessary for her to discharge her responsibilities effectively.[6]

Macneill believed that putting women in prison was a waste of time
and resources, and she attempted to feminize the overtly harsh and
masculine prison environment. She tried to improve both the physical
environment and the level of training and programs offered to prisoners, over strong resistance from male bureaucrats at the newly established Regional Headquarters (RHQ) of the Correctional Service of
Canada. Although she was officially in charge of P4W, senior male
bureaucrats often questioned her decisions regarding daily operations.
For example, she attempted to personalize the prison environment by
allowing women to put curtains over their cell bars to create a small
degree of privacy, and she stressed the importance of 'meaningful
programs.' Her attempts to create a 'freer and more normal environment' were scrutinized because they were inconsistent with wider
correctional objectives of formal discipline and surveillance. She described her conflict with RHQ over the curtains in the following passage: 'The women hang curtains over those horrible bars (at their cell
doors) because they tried to feminize and make the place a little more
humane. The regional director came and said those must be removed
because the staff cannot see what is going on in the cells. I said we

should let them have some privacy in their lives and he said: "no, you must put up polyurethane curtains and I will order them." So I said he could order them but I would not put them up. So we had a conflict this over this sort of thing.'[7]

Few male administrators perceived her feminine approach to prisoner reform to be a 'legitimate' form of discipline. As a result, struggles over trivial matters shaped the daily administration of P4W; Macneill had to fight for nearly every program and concession. She was the first woman to govern a federal penitentiary, and her ideal of discipline was somewhat different from that of her male counterparts. Her feminized but nonetheless militaristic style received mixed reviews. Although she was before her time in advocating rehabilitation programs and alternatives to custody, for Macneill, rehabilitation meant providing education, and training women in necessary and 'appropriate' vocational skills. She supported programs that was geared towards this, such as domestic science.

Specialized Penal Training in Household Management

Reform narratives of this time repeatedly highlight the importance in women's prisons of appropriate demeanour, and cleanliness, neatness, and order. These things were seen as the key measure of the effectiveness of a prison's administration and management. Advocates of domestic reform techniques at P4W had three objectives: to train women prisoners in household management; to promote self-improvement; and to reintegrate women into proper roles in the community. While there is some evidence that matrons at P4W had been informally involved in this type of training since the facility was opened in 1934, maternal reformers reaffirmed the importance of these objectives in the 1950s. Descriptions of the domestic science program at P4W in the mid-1960s identify it as a rehabilitative program. However, this program resembled several earlier maternal reform strategies used by early penal reformers and administrators.

Macneill viewed home economics courses as integral to the training of women prisoners who were considered 'potential home-makers.' To implement this technology, she hired a professionally trained domestic science instructor in 1962, and secured the funds to build a fully equipped home inside the walls of the prison. This small bungalow home, better known as 'the little house,'[8] is described by Webb (1965: 2) as follows:

The house is surrounded by flower beds, trees and shrubs, and a small vegetable garden. Once the last barrier of the institution closes behind you, you step into the front entrance hall of the bungalow, you are mesmerized by the complete change in atmosphere. You literally become part of the warm odours of baking, mingled with the clean smell of soap suds from the laundry room, which permeate the house. Each room is immaculate, kept that way by the girls as much through pride in surroundings as from the inevitable chastisement untidy house-keeping brings from Mrs. Hof.

The house training program was governed by Mrs Betty Hof, the prison's qualified domestic science instructor, who apparently controlled and disciplined 'her brood like a mother hen.'[9]

Descriptions of Mrs Hof's management of the prisoners in her charge evoke an image of a caring but firm mother who endeavoured to create a supportive, homelike environment. The women temporarily residing in this house followed a ten-week regime that included instruction in meal preparation, home care, and personal grooming. The meal preparation component taught women skills in home baking and an appreciation for thriftiness and budgeting. This program, like several others designed to regulate the conduct of women prisoners, focused on training women in 'proper habits.' The following description of 'waste' (Webb 1965: 3) evokes a number of familiar images of mothering and of the disciplining of children to instil certain habits: 'Waste is not allowed, and while the trainees are allowed to eat as much as they wish during the noon meal, once the food is on their plates, it must be eaten. They learn that while certain dishes are more appealing than others, a variety of food is essential, and the palate of everyone eating the meal must be taken into consideration.'

Mrs Hof's regime was further praised for its 'emphasis on economy in meal planning' and for 'periodic lectures about the hungry people in the world.' Women were also provided with maternal guidance as they learned some of the finer skills in keeping a house in 'orderly shape.' Every woman was expected to participate in a weekly regime of heavy cleaning that included washing and waxing floors and furniture, scrubbing cupboards and appliances, cleaning silverware, and doing laundry. Prospective homemakers were also taught how to prepare for company: how to set a table, serve tea, say grace before meals, and so on. The professionalization of Mrs Hof's role (i.e., as a domestic science instructor rather than a mother) shows how women's maternal knowledges were still part of 'scientific rehabilitation.'

This emphasis on social and personal habits was a popular technique of penal governance that was often legitimated through a rehabilitative narrative. The premise behind many of these strategies was that the women prisoners had not been trained by their biological mothers to govern themselves properly. Habit-based training stressed particular racialized and gendered middle-class norms. For example, prisoners' grooming habits were highly regulated. They were required to maintain a 'pleasing' appearance and were instructed in personal hygiene. Personal grooming was considered important because 'most [of the prisoners in the program] are not married, and while the way to a man's heart is through his stomach, the old adage tells us, he must first be lured by a pleasing appearance' (Webb 1965: 3).

Advocates of this type of habit training emphasized the 'healthy' benefits of proper grooming. Concerns about 'healthy' relationships and grooming were further institutionalized in vocational programs, such as hairdressing and cosmetics. This emphasis on personal appearance developed into a wider strategy to morally regulate the prisoners by creating 'marriageable women.' It was believed that if a woman was pleasurable to the eye, then despite her criminal record she would be able to attract a suitable mate and regain some of her respectability in the law-abiding community. However, her ability to achieve these middle-class ideals of womanhood was limited by her low social status as an ex-prisoner.

In extreme cases, women participated in forms of experimental cosmetic surgery in order to improve their appearance or to remove tattoos and other blemishes (Chandler 1973; Mitford 1973; Richmond 1975). Plastic surgery was one of the 'new treatment techniques' introduced at Oakalla in 1953 to correct 'any disability which might have contributed towards delinquency, such as scars, squints, unsightly or obscene tattoos' (Richmond 1975: 48).

This normative emphasis on feminine appearance and social habits continued well into the 1970s at P4W. Prisoners were encouraged to dress neatly and wear makeup. Eventually, clothing regulations were relaxed: instead of wearing institutionally manufactured and issued clothing, women were now permitted to wear their own clothing and jewellery and to wear clothing ordered from department store catalogues. In the 1970s, administrators at P4W attempted to reinforce heterosexuality, monogamy, and femininity among the women prisoners by sponsoring weekly Saturday night dances with students from Queen's University Law School.[10] These dances were a direct outcome of homophobic concerns about lesbian activity in the prison. Additional concerns about an 'unnatural' all-female environment led to the reintroduction of male correctional staff. The dances were a source of concern for the guards' union for two main reasons: affectionate relations might develop between male law students and women prisoners; and the women might use their 'charm' to convince visitors to bring contraband (i.e., drugs) into the institution.[11]

Scientific Interventions

Women also participated in aversion therapy; in behaviour modification programs, including electroconvulsive therapy; in group therapy; in biochemical restraint; and in other modern techniques of psychological treatment popular in the 1950s (Ekstedt and Griffiths 1988: 54). While these techniques were most commonly used in provincial reformatories, they were also used at P4W in combination with more maternal technologies of physical, spiritual, and emotional improvement. The 1998 statement of claim (pending law suit) filed by Dorothy Proctor verifies that experiments were conducted at P4W in the early 1960s that involved administering mind-altering drugs – primarily lysergic acid diethylamide (LSD-25) in conjunction with other potent drugs – and administering electrical currents to the brain (ECT, EST, and SEDAC, hereafter collectively called 'electroshock'). One of the purposes of this experimentation was to modify the behaviour of prisoners – in particular, to 'alter the criminal disposition of offenders' and reduce recidivism.[12] Approximately thirty female inmates were involved in these experiments. Some of the results of the were reported in an academic journal, along with references to other psychological studies conducted at P4W (Eveson 1964).

Seventeen-year-old Ms Proctor was serving a three-year sentence at P4W when she was identified to be a participant in this experiment. According to court records, during the first year of her incarceration she was placed in solitary confinement for lengthy periods of time as punishment for breaches of various prison rules. While incarcerated, she was compelled to undergo experiments under the direction of Gerald Wilson, a contract psychiatrist, which involved the administration of mind-altering drugs in conjunction with electroshock. These experiments continued throughout the second and third years of

Proctor's incarceration at P4W and while she stayed at the Institute of Psychotherapy. This series of experiments shows an extreme exercise of disciplinary power and a flagrant abuse of individual rights, which coexisted with the more subtle maternal regime at P4W. This same case also illustrates the vulnerability of offenders to penal regimes. I am not suggesting that the prisoners lack power or agency, but rather that prisoners are not voluntary participants in these therapeutic regimes, and the relationship between the prisoner patient is different from the therapist/patient outside the prison. This is in part the basis of Ms Proctor's lawsuit. She claims that while she was an inmate at P4W, 'she was in no position at any time to refuse to participate in these experiments, given the coercion and duress inherent in being a prisoner [and teenager] at the Prison for Women at that time' (Ontario Court – General Division, Statement of Claim 1998: 7). In March 1997, after several denials of any wrongdoing in this case, the Commission of the Correctional Service of Canada ordered a Board of Investigation under sec. 20 of the Correctional and Conditional Release Act to investigate and report on Ms Proctors's allegations. Even though this board was not able to obtain several relevant Correctional Service of Canada records, it did produce a final report, which found, among other things, that Ms Proctor was administered, without her informed consent,[13] LSD-25 while in solitary confinement, and that she had sustained long-term negative effects as a result, including brain damage. The board recommended compensation and an apology for Ms Proctor and the other unnamed inmates involved in the experiments. As of September 2000, the lawsuit is still pending. To date, only Ms Proctor has been willing to be identified. The other women involved in the experiments wish anonymity, as their families are often not aware that they were incarcerated. Some are now grandmothers, and some have died (CAEFS 1999a: 17). Rather than implementing the recommendations of the Board of Investigation, CSC appointed the McGill University Centre for Medicine, Ethics and Law Division, 'to obtain independent advice concerning the long term effects of LSD, and to develop guidelines, or protocols, for addressing each individual case' (CAEFS 1999a:17).

Notwithstanding the presence of scientific and (sometimes abusive) 'rehabilitative' techniques, such as cosmetic surgery, behaviour modification programs, chemical therapy, and electroshock, women prisoners' behaviours and habits were more often governed through informal processes. Domestic science training and personal grooming programs in prisons capitalized on everyday processes of producing and shaping normative behaviour to rehabilitate or reform prisoners. Valverde (1996) argues that 'habit' is a technology for governing citizens without elaborate expert discourses or technologies. Contrary to most studies of welfare penality, my research shows that psychiatry, psychology, and social work, while present at P4W as early as the mid-1950s, were not the primary mechanisms for governing women prisoners. Psychology and psychiatry play a more significant role in *current* correctional interventions (Kendall 2000). Programs run by institutional staff, such as domestic science, industrial sewing, and hairdressing, all focused on the production of 'good' citizens who understood their place in the social hierarchy; but these programs did not deploy quantitative or scientific studies, and were not staffed by psychiatric social workers or other 'experts.' Also, volunteer visitors to the prison contributed to the governance of women's habits. Although they seemed simply to offer women prisoners 'fun' programs that broke up the idleness and tedium of incarceration, they made an important contribution to the governance of women's work and leisure habits.

The Professionalization of Prison Staff

The domestic science program established at P4W after the war shows how a term like 'rehabilitation' can be used to describe a variety of distinct programs of governance. However, this program also illustrated a wider trend: the professionalization of women's penality. The shift toward scientific rehabilitation affected the governance of women prisoners in two ways. *First*, on a policy level there were increased calls for the hiring of professionally trained female staff. Changes in penality and maternal logics coincided with white middle-class women's interest in penal reform. An emphasis on 'training' women for a variety of criminal justice positions was an important element of early women's reform platforms, and it led to the professionalization of past maternal strategies. The commitment and voluntarism of benevolent mother figures was no longer deemed sufficient for managing women in conflict with the law. There was an increased reliance on professional women trained in modern methods of treating and governing women criminals. While maternal rationalities influenced the training of women professionals (nurses, social workers, teachers, matrons, and others), the training these women received was also heavily influenced by scientific and, in particular, medical and psychiatric interpretations of women's crime.

Second, laywomen volunteers became increasingly involved in the maternal governance of women prisoners' habits. The interest of laywomen in the rehabilitation of women prisoners, and their concerns about the absence of official data on the needs and experiences of these women, contributed to the development of Canada's largest prisoners' rights organization for women: the Canadian Association of Elizabeth Fry Societies (CAEFS). The second half of this chapter outlines these two developments in Canadian penality.

In the mid-twentieth century, the University Women's Club was one of several organizations that stressed the importance of technologies of training. This group's emphasis on training was linked to a wider political agenda that called for an increase in the number of trained women working in state institutions. Rather than evolving simply out of a concern for the welfare of women prisoners, most of the prison reform initiatives supported by this club were related to its wider interest in promoting educational and vocational opportunities for women. The records of the Toronto University Women's Club show that its members were actively engaged in penal reform politics in Ontario between 1949 and 1958, during which time the Group for the Study of Penal Reform was formed. Initially, this group expressed an interest in juvenile training schools and courts; however, its interest quickly shifted to 'women and girl offenders.'[14]

Through a longstanding guest speaker series, the club exposed its members to a wide variety of speakers with a variety of views on criminal justice issues. The organization of the speaker series was motivated by the club's desire to keep its members up to date on current issues, and to become more active in social reform. One of the lectures attended by club members was delivered by Major Gibson, Commissioner of Penitentiaries, who spoke about the aims and principles of penology. In a 1948 speech to the School of Social Work at the University of Toronto, Major Gibson noted: 'For penology is a new science, as yet hardly recognized by the public as a profession, but nevertheless one that deals with the problems of human behaviour and treatment that have most important economic and social implications. I say it is a new science because it is only in the last hundred years or so that mankind has begun to deal with crime and criminals on the basis of treatment rather than mere punishment ... One of the aims of penology then is the scientific solution of that problem.'[15]

He also noted that the 'basic philosophy of modern penology' was to use 'constructive efforts to bring about change in the anti-social atti-

tudes' that led to the offender's incarceration. Besides advocating rehabilitative penology, Gibson stressed the importance of community participation in and support of the correctional process. He claimed that
prison reform had always suffered from a general lack of public interest
in and knowledge of the problems in prisons.

Although there was little consensus on the role of women volunteers
in the penal sphere in the late 1940s, these women felt strongly about
increasing the number of trained women working in penal settings. In
the late 1940s the Toronto Study Group began to lobby actively for
penal reform, in collaboration with the Canadian Federation of University Women (CFUW) and other local clubs.[16] They contacted the provincial Department of Reform Institutions[17] and informed it that 'there
was a group of women with a sympathetic interest in their work, eager
to encourage improvement.'[18] While some of their ideas were welcomed by the government, the study group grew frustrated with the
government's reluctance to implement those ideas. Their early efforts
included lobbying the government to implement the recommendations
of the Archambault Report (1938), and passing relevant resolutions. For
example, the Group for the Study of Penal Reform presented a resolution at the February 1949 business meeting that encouraged all University Women's Clubs to write to the Minister of Justice to commend
officials at the Penitentiaries Branch for recent reforms. In particular,
the club supported proposals made by Major Gibson to train correctional personnel. One of his most influential proposals was for the
establishment of a 'training school' for penitentiary officers.[19] Gibson
argued that officers' training should be designed to 'deal not only with
the practical matters of duty and discipline, but to give our officers an
insight into and understanding of the principles of modern penology
and the factors that play a part in the making of the criminal, so that
they may return to their duties with an intelligent understanding of the
requirements of modern penological treatment, and apply those principles in their dealings with prisoners in their charge.'[20] The commissioner's advocacy for training in modern penology was consistent with the
aims of women reformers, who equally believed that a properly trained
staff was essential to a successful rehabilitation program.

All local University Women's Clubs encouraged their members to
lobby the provincial government to provide funding for the recruitment and training of female probation officers and social workers.
Where there was an absence of trained social workers, club members
lobbied the Department of Health and Welfare in Ottawa for more

federal grants to schools of social work. In May 1949 the Toronto Study Group on Penal Reform recommended at an annual meeting that the club 'continue to study the problem of women and girl offenders' and to lobby for the appointment of a female Assistant Minister of Reform Institutions. Through this advocacy work, the University Women's Club was able to forge links with other like-minded organizations and women such as the Business and Professional Women's Study Group.

The club's main interest was in promoting employment opportunities for women, which reflected their views that women were the most appropriate candidates for certain jobs. Its advocacy for women parole officers was a way of suggesting that women were best suited to hear and deliberate on the cases of women prisoners:[21] 'the considerably higher percentage of failures among women parolees than among men parolees [was] attributed to this lack [of female parole officers].'[22] Whatever the motivation, the club's efforts were successful, and by September 1953 three women probation officers had been appointed to newly established posts in Ontario to work primarily with women offenders.

The hiring of female staff and efforts to professionalize women's involvement in penal reform were also supported by the emerging John Howard Society of Ontario (1929), an organization that specialized in male prisoners. The University Women's Club and Local Councils of Women[23] reportedly sent representatives to meetings of the John Howard Society to keep apprised of their work. The penal reform efforts of the British Columbia University Women's Club were eventually filtered through representatives at John Howard Society meetings (Stewart 1993: 19). In Ontario, women's organizations such as the University Women's Club and the Elizabeth Fry Society acted quite independently of the John Howard Society. However, the like-minded John Howard Society often supported the efforts of women volunteers in communities that did not have established Elizabeth Fry Societies.

The Growth of Elizabeth Fry Societies

Elizabeth Fry Societies are autonomous agencies that work with and on behalf of women involved with the justice system. These societies are 'community based agencies dedicated to offering services and programs to women in need, advocating for reforms and offering fora within which the public may be informed about, and participate in, all aspects of the justice system as it affects women.'[24] Today these organizations reflect a wide range of views, from radical feminism to conservative maternalism. There are twenty-one member agencies across the country registered with the Canadian Association of Elizabeth Fry Societies (CAEFS), which is a national federation of the local societies. This chapter focuses on some of the activities of the Toronto, Ottawa, and Kingston Elizabeth Fry Societies between 1950 and 1970.

The goals of Elizabeth Fry Societies were threefold: to rehabilitate women prisoners; to educate the public to support penal reforms; and to promote the scientific study of women's crime.[25] The activities of some members of this organization are an excellent example of the hybrid governance of women's habits through everyday maternal techniques and knowledges on the one hand, and professional scientific knowledges and techniques of social work on the other. This organization mobilized a variety of knowledges to rationalize its programs of governing; it also produced some of the first official data about female offenders. Today, members and staff of Elizabeth Fry Societies across Canada are perceived as 'experts' on the female offender.

The Elizabeth Fry Societies of the early 1950s were a product of their time, and most societies advocated a postwar maternal logic. The founding mothers of Canadian Elizabeth Fry Societies came from a diverse array of backgrounds in philanthropy, politics, and social reform. In Ontario, the Elizabeth Fry Society grew out of the passionate commitment of prominent women such as Agnes Macphail,[26] Margaret McClelland, Dr Margaret Maclean, Flora Macdonald, Muriel Fergusson,[27] and many others involved in the National Council of Women of Canada and University Women's Clubs. The first Elizabeth Fry Society was established in British Columbia in 1939. Elizabeth Fry Societies later emerged in Kingston (1949), Toronto (1950), and Ottawa (1951) with the mandate to serve women in conflict with the law. They have since grown to establish a monopoly in this area. Each local society has its own separate history and personality; however, all of them follow the spirit and legacy of the eighteenth-century Quaker reformer, Elizabeth Fry. Unlike Elizabeth Fry herself, the women reformers who organized under her name in the mid-twentieth century did not subscribe strictly to the ideal of religious training. Elizabeth Fry Societies were actively involved in providing multidenominational chaplaincy services for incarcerated women, and they advised their members against using their visits to proselytize. Although agency volunteers and staff have tended to be white middle-class Christian women, some agencies, such as the Toronto Elizabeth Fry Society, have made a point of including individuals from a wide variety of backgrounds on their boards of directors.

Local societies often began with informal monthly meetings in women's homes and church basements. At these meetings, women discussed how they could help women in jail, and how to improve rehabilitative opportunities for women prisoners recently released from jail.[28] For example, the Toronto society was started in 1950 by a small group of women in the First Unitarian Congregation of Toronto, who believed that social action was needed to improve conditions in prisons and to ensure that the recommendations of the 1938 Archambault Report were implemented. These women (known as the Alice Huston Alliance) invited Agnes Macphail, a Member of Parliament who was interested in penal reform, to a spring meeting to seek advice on how to proceed.[29] Macphail informed the group that there was an absence of services for women comparable to those offered to men through the John Howard Society. She encouraged them to 'lay the foundations of the first female after care agency in Toronto.' Thus, on 13 May 1952, with Agnes Macphail as their honorary president, the Elizabeth Fry Society of Toronto was publicly recognized as an aftercare agency for women in conflict with the law (Cowley 1978: 8).

Benevolent Discipline: Lay Reformers and Pseudoscientific Rehabilitation

Elizabeth Fry Society representatives lobbied for the hiring of professionally trained staff in women's prisons; they also actively involved themselves in the moral governance of women's habits and in the delivery of community-based rehabilitation programs. They regularly visited local jails, P4W, the Mercer (which was replaced in 1969 by the Vanier Centre for Women in Brampton, Ontario), and several juvenile detention centres. During these visits they observed that there were few amenities, meaningful programs, or recreational opportunities for women prisoners.[30] At first, the women visitors worked on solving basic problems and deficiencies. For instance, in the early 1950s, Ottawa Elizabeth Fry volunteers collected odd pieces of used furniture to furnish a common room in the women's section of the Carleton County Jail. They also started a sewing program and provided women prisoners with materials and tools to make clothing and stuffed animals, which the society later sold to raise money to help improve prison conditions. Volunteers also provided women with basic amenities such as soap, hair combs, pens, and paper.[31] Similar activities were conducted at P4W in Kingston.

However, the emerging Elizabeth Fry Societies were interested mainly in rehabilitating women prisoners and in providing community after-care services to support women released from penal settings. For example, the general mandate of the Toronto Elizabeth Fry Society was 'to act in all areas which can contribute to the effective rehabilitation of the offender. These areas include the laws under which the offender is charged, the jails in which she is held, the courts in which she is tried, the kind of sentence she receives, the design, program, personnel of the prison in which she serves her sentence, the use of probation and parole and access to bail, and the attitude of the community to which she returns after her sentence' (Cowley 1978: 12).

'Rehabilitation' was quite broadly defined by the Elizabeth Fry Societies. Their mandate was quite consistent with the wider ideals of the federal Penitentiary Branch and the provincial correctional bureacracies, which also strongly supported offender 'rehabilitation.' With rehabilitation as their goal, Elizabeth Fry members advocated practical interventions combined with modern techniques of social work (Stewart 1993: 25). In effect, the societies advised their volunteers to adopt the same strategies as professional social work 'experts' in their attempts to rehabilitate women prisoners.

To fulfil their mandate, Elizabeth Fry workers and volunteers designed institutional and community interventions that they believed targeted the causes of women's crime. Volunteers engaged themselves in regulating the habits of women prisoners, and later parolees. They believed that one of their main tasks was to reinforce appropriate behaviours through role modelling, and through mothering and befriending women. In light of all this, many Elizabeth Fry Societies established rehabilitation committees that focused on developing normalization strategies appropriate to the needs of women offenders. These strategies targeted women in prison and in the community, and stressed the importance of professional and nonprofessional interventions. Elizabeth Fry members, like the Salvation Army and other penal reformers, believed that education and vocational training were vital to rehabilitation, and that redirecting women to embrace these 'useful tasks' would discourage them from pursuing unhealthy interests such as drinking, taking drugs, and engaging in sex with men or with other female convicts.

The Elizabeth Fry Society helped institutional officials find suitable employment for women prisoners about to be released from custody. In 1956 the Elizabeth Fry Society of Kingston participated in one of the first prerelease programs designed to help women reintegrate into the community.[32] These early forms of release were often used to help women prepare for re-entry into society. Sometimes, women were released to the homes of reformers to perform domestic duties; on other occasions, women were employed by private companies. It was believed that this employment reinforced the rehabilitative programs in the prison.[33] Many reformers and administrators believed that community resources were essential if the normalization process that began in the institution was to continue (Cheriton 1957). Elizabeth Fry staff and volunteers made a point of being available to listen to women's problems and providing them with various forms of sisterly and motherly guidance.

A 1964 letter written to the government by members of the Kingston Elizabeth Fry Society Rehabilitation Committee noted that to enhance the rehabilitation of women prisoners, prison officials should 'draw on interested groups of professional people who come into the prison to provide activities for leisure time.'[34] Elizabeth Fry reformers contended that these activities kept inmates in contact with individuals outside the prison and gave them an 'opportunity for constructive thinking rather than the spending of free time in idle gossip.'[35] Along with an active program of prison visiting, volunteers provided women with various forms of entertainment, and taught them middle-class domestic skills such as serving tea. Beginning in 1949 the Kingston Elizabeth Fry Society regularly visited P4W to provide educational and recreational services. These activities included French and English classes, leather hobby craft and art classes, physical education programs, sports tournaments, special events and concerts, and folk dancing.[36] Most of these early interventions focused on creating 'legitimate' and 'socially useful' leisure options for women both inside and outside prisons. Elizabeth Fry workers quickly gained the respect of prisoners (Hart 1959: 24). These subtle encouragements to adopt socially acceptable habits were extended into the community by volunteers who advocated early release programs. Elizabeth Fry Societies claimed that community outings were necessary to prepare women for release and to ease the difficult transition from prison to community living.[37] These views were shared by the Toronto and Ottawa agencies, which also supported prerelease programs and community supervision programs. Once prisoners were released into the community, well-intentioned volunteers escorted women on outings, and subtly monitored their behaviour and associations.

In the mid-1950s the Toronto agency also established a 'rehabilitation committee' to 'take a personal interest in the rehabilitation of girls and women in prison.'[38] The main activities of this nine-member committee were institutional visits and aftercare, which involved maintaining contact with women upon their release from prison through letters and visits. Like the superintendents at the Mercer, Elizabeth Fry Society volunteers used a variety of seemingly kind, nonintrusive techniques to continue to govern the habits and conduct of released prisoners. While the agency was becoming increasingly concerned about the rehabilitation of offenders, its definition of a 'rehabilitated' woman continued to conform to the traditional middle-class morality upheld by early maternalists. For instance, in one of the annual reports of the Toronto Elizabeth Fry Society, the Rehabilitation Committee provided the following success story: 'Last year I told you about a young girl who had held her first job ever and lost it. This girl now seems to have settled down. She married a man who knew her background and accepted her, and in January of this year they had their first baby. One can't say: "And so they lived happily ever afterwards" because that does not happen too often in actual life, but after being out of the Mercer for nearly two years, she seems to be fitting into a good life pattern.'[39]

The same annual report also noted that 'in nearly every case, the attitude of a girl who is being visited by an Elizabeth Fry Society member, changes – sometimes rapidly, sometimes imperceptibly, because she feels that someone cares.'[40] Inspirational stories such as these reinforced traditional maternal and domestic images of the 'happy family' and the 'reformed woman,' and the agency used them to promote its work and to recruit new volunteers and sources of funding.

In the late 1950s, certain intrusive state surveillance activities – especially parole supervision, counselling, and treatment program delivery – were taken over by some local Elizabeth Fry Societies, which argued that they had a specialized expertise. Federal and provincial governments supported the work of local agencies through contracts for parole supervision and program development. This financial relationship entailed a series of legal obligations – for example, agency staff were now required to monitor paroled offenders' behaviour and report any infractions to state officials. The agency's accountability to the state in this area altered its relationship with prisoners. Volunteers had been regulating the conduct of offenders on an informal level; now they had a wide range of formal mechanisms of social and legal control to fall back on if informal techniques failed to produce the desired results. Many agencies entered into these supervisory relationships only reluc-

tantly, and continuing to believe that relationships between ex-offend-
ers/parolees and agency staff should not be based on coercion. Several
agencies rationalized their involvement in formal state processes by
arguing that they best understood the needs of women in conflict with
the law and that they could offer a unique range of services that were
sensitive to the needs and experiences of their clientele. Elizabeth Fry
Societies believed that their 'policing' of paroled women's conduct was
preferable (because gentler and more humane) to state interventions.

Besides using the ideal of rehabilitation to promote proper leisure
habits, Elizabeth Fry volunteers lobbied correctional officials, government representatives, and judges, and networked with other social
agencies, to promote their reform agenda and to create an 'expert
identity' for themselves. Elizabeth Fry volunteers and staff successfully
lobbied the government to hire prison social workers, psychologists,
and a part-time psychiatrist, and to appoint women to national and
provincial parole boards, and eventually to award them government
contracts and private funding so that they could operate transition
homes for women being released from prison.

With the introduction of scientific experts and professional social
workers who determined the nature and extent of treatment required
by women prisoners, the role of volunteer visitors was redefined. Stewart
(1993: 33) notes that after professionals were introduced in the penal
sphere, voluntarism came to be regarded with suspicion by the professional workers, who perhaps needed to establish their own credibility
and justify their specialized training and expertise. In the mid-1950s,
fears of being displaced led the president of the British Columbia
Elizabeth Fry Society to encourage members to 'look for new ways to
be useful' (cited in Stewart 1993: 33). This comment reflected a growing
trend for paid state experts (i.e., not volunteers) to determine the direction and philosophy of rehabilitation programs. More and more often,
women hired to work for Elizabeth Fry Societies were professionally
trained in social work or a related field. By hiring their own 'experts,'
Elizabeth Fry Societies were able to promote their own philosophy of
rehabilitation, which focused more on the specific needs of women in
conflict with the law than on a gender-neutral ideal of rehabilitation.

Reformers devised new strategies for contributing to the rehabilitative network. These new strategies included expanding the society
across the country, developing comprehensive public education campaigns, and forging new links with 'experts.' For example, in the 1950s
the Ottawa agency began negotiations with the Ottawa Welfare Bureau

and the Catholic Family Bureau, in the hope that both bureaux would appoint staff to liaise with incarcerated women and aid in their rehabilitation.[41] Also, links were established with schools of social work through guest lectures and by offering field placements for students who were interested in corrections work. For example, Dr C.W. Topping, an active patron of the British Columbia Elizabeth Fry Society as well as a faculty member at the School of Social Work at UBC, extended members of the Elizabeth Fry Society an open invitation to visit his classes, in return for the agency's support of his students in field placements (Stewart 1993: 34). In the same vein, the Toronto Elizabeth Fry Society promoted the development of trained social workers by establishing the Agnes Macphail Fund at the School of Social Work, University of Toronto, for students wanting to work in the field of prisoner rehabilitation (Cowley 1978: 8). The social workers hired by the Toronto society worked in the Mercer Reformatory and the Don Jail, counselling women before release and aiding them in the community. This involvement is notable because prior to the Toronto society's involvement, no formally trained social workers had been attached to either the Mercer or the women's section of the Don.[42] This early intervention led to the development of a comprehensive volunteer visiting program, wherein 'non-expert' volunteers belonging to the Elizabeth Fry Society were trained in some basic social work skills of listening and supporting women prisoners. This agency and several others continue to send trained social workers into most jails, prisons, and penitentiaries across the country with the goal of helping women make the transition from prison to the community.

The emphasis on scientific rehabilitation continued into the early 1960s. Inspired by the 1956 Fauteux Report, which strongly recommended a philosophy of rehabilitation, the Kingston Elizabeth Fry Society drafted a series of recommendations for 'the reorganization and revitalization of Prison for Women.'[43] In this report, they proposed that 'the purpose of Prison for Women be clearly and firmly stated to be rehabilitation of its inmates.'[44] The recommendations of this document are quite consistent with several years of women's advocacy for professionally trained staff and for the administrative autonomy of P4W. The report encouraged the prison to establish new and higher-paying positions that would attract 'qualified and competent personnel.' It added that these individuals should be hired by a 'staff selection committee' consisting of the warden, the deputy warden, a psychologist, a social worker, the National Employment Services Special Placements Officer, and 'a layman of experience' in personnel selection. The inclusion of the category 'layman of experience' was a direct attempt by the society to reaffirm the importance of their 'nonexpert, everyday' knowledge of women prisoners to formal program development. At the time, the staff of several Elizabeth Fry Societies were not professionally trained and had a vested interest in creating a formal institutional space for their experiential knowledge of female offenders.

With the goal of formalizing hiring and training processes and raising the level of staff training, the report suggested the following projects: ongoing evaluations of staff performance, staff training, staff meetings, and participation in conferences. The Kingston Elizabeth Fry Society report also contained a 'job breakdown' for the position of psychologist, along with an outline of treatment expectations. Here, 'treatment' was defined extremely broadly as 'the total of all influences brought to bear on the inmate during her stay at the institution. It may be positive or negative, and result in behaviour changes for the better or worse. The *ultimate* purpose of positive institutional treatment is to gain greater inmate acceptance of society's rules which regulate the behaviour of every individual in society.'[45] According to the authors of this report, the best way to deliver treatment in the prison setting was to 'provide an environment which encourages the growth of the inner resources of every inmate – so that self-respect and self-confidence are increased.'[46]

It is worth noting carefully here how involved this lay organization was (or how involved it was perceived to be) in defining the roles to be played by social workers, psychologists, psychiatrists, and a vast number of formally trained penal professionals. The Kingston society's 1960 report represented an interesting shift in relations of power. Laywomen played an active role in defining the position of staff psychologist at P4W. The part of the report titled 'Job Breakdown – Psychologist' (see p. 127) suggested that the psychologist should perform the following tasks: initial reception (including intelligence testing, personality testing, and vocational testing); retesting (on the basis that it was 'advisable to retest individuals at frequent intervals'); group therapy; individual therapy; research projects; and further group testing. A similar lay advisory role was outlined in the part of the same report titled 'Reception and Treatment' (see p. 128). Here, the reformers' role was formally integrated into a proposed treatment process. For instance, Section IV of the treatment and reception plan outlined the role and significance of scientific testing and program ascription, while simultaneously ensuring that the largely nonprofessional role of an Elizabeth Fry representative would be institutionalized. Experts would not simply displace lay visitors; rather, the role of lay visitors would evolve to accommodate the demands of an increasingly professionalized penal sphere. Women reformers were using their own brand of expert knowledge to make a unique contribution to a setting more commonly associated with male professionals. In the 1960s, women reformers played an active role in carving out a space for male psychiatrists and psychologists at P4W. What remains uncertain is the extent to which these reformers supported the medical and therapeutic interventions and experiments carried out by those psychiatrists and psychologists, whose hiring they had urged.

Promoting and Policing Women's Needs: Reformers' Role in Knowledge Production

Elizabeth Fry Societies were also quite involved in promoting the development of a gender-specific knowledge of social problems such as alcoholism and addictions. Elizabeth Fry members recognized that many of the women they worked with had drug and/or alcohol problems. To secure services for women with addictions, the Toronto and Ottawa agencies began working with the Alcohol Research Foundation.[47] Local agencies began to form advisory boards composed of representatives from various mental health, social services, and governmental bodies. Reformers also lobbied for formal access to specialized treatment programs. For example, in their 1957 study of the 'chronic petty offender' the Toronto Elizabeth Fry Society recommended that chronic alcoholics be treated in clinics and in extreme cases provided with supervised residential accommodation. At the time, 'the addict' and 'the alcoholic' were generally portrayed as male deviants.[48] The Elizabeth Fry Society played an important role in having addiction and alcoholism recognized among women. In the 1960s it urged the Ontario Minister of Health to establish a narcotics research foundation, and enlisted public support for this idea by writing letters to other organizations and to members of the provincial legislature. Shortly thereafter, the Alcoholism and Drug Addiction Research Foundation expanded its research to include narcotics.[49] This concern about addictions evolved into a gender-sensitive addiction program, designed and delivered by Elizabeth Fry Society staff.

Despite growing international interest in prisoner rehabilitation in the scientific community, and despite academic interest in the causes of

crime, few scientific studies of crime have focused on the female offender. Most early data on female offenders in Canada were collected
and interpreted by women reformers, not by state experts or academics. Reformers – mainly those associated with Elizabeth Fry Societies –
played a key role in the production of knowledge about women and
crime. They believed that one of their primary responsibilities was to
educate the public on women in conflict with the law. To this end, they
collected data and anecdotal stories about women offenders. Some
agencies participated in activities typically associated with the activities of experts, such as record keeping and information gathering.
Members of Elizabeth Fry Societies contended that because there was
very little hard information on women in conflict with the law and
their needs, it was important for them to keep accurate statistics and
gather information about the clients they served whenever possible.
This information-gathering process often resulted in conference presentations and lectures on women's criminality. Once representatives
of local agencies had gathered enough information about their clients,
they began to produce information pamphlets, and to lecture on the
causes of women's crime and on the rehabilitative needs of their
clients.

This concern for expanding the educational role of the Elizabeth Fry
Societies led to the development of Public Action Committees, permanent speaker bureaux, active research programs, and monthly newslet-
ters for mailing to members and interested groups. Independently or
collaboratively, agencies began to prepare and publish a wide variety of
position papers on issues facing women in conflict with the law. The
topics of these papers included the following: prostitution, co-correc-
tions, juvenile delinquency, 'native affairs,' employment opportunities,
incarcerated mothers, solitary confinement, and visiting hours. Various
briefs were also written on proposed legislative changes (such as the
Female Refuges Act, the Bill of Rights, vagrancy laws, and various
amendments to the Criminal Code).[50] Between 1957 and 1963, the
Public Action Committee of the Toronto Elizabeth Fry Society also
concerned itself with mental health issues, institutional rehabilitation
programs, and drug and alcohol addiction research.[51] In 1955 the Toronto society's annual report noted that 'a fair portion of staff time is
going into the collection of statistical information which we hope will
form the basis of material for research work; for it is evident that until
some research is carried on in this field, the measure of effectiveness of
any program is limited.'[52]

These education campaigns generally took the form of public lectures and lobbying through the media. They served two important functions. *First*, since local societies relied on charitable donations, these programs were a valuable source of revenue. *Second*, they helped create a social climate amenable to the idea that treatment and not punishment should inform penal institutions (Stewart 1993: 29). The themes of rehabilitation and community responsibility were central to most educational campaigns and lobbying efforts. Canadian reformers – like their predecessors in the American women's reform movement – were flexible and creative in their efforts to present the dilemmas and experiences of women in conflict with the law. They often used storytelling techniques to teach lessons on social responsibility and to motivate citizens to take responsibility for the social conditions that lead to crime.

By the late 1960s, the Elizabeth Fry Societies were beginning to exhibit a more politicized understanding of women's crime, and to promote more professional and expert strategies of rehabilitation. To legitimate these strategies and to secure funding for a relatively small population of federally sentenced women, they began to informally study the social and psychological causes of women's crime. Many believed that research would lead to the development of programs to address the causes of women's crime. Reformers gave speeches and wrote articles and pamphlets to demystify women's crime and to expand society's awareness of the needs and experiences of female offenders.

These reformers played a central role in promoting scientific rehabilitation strategies and collecting data on female offenders. Throughout the 1950s and 1960s, reformers located outside the state, such as social worker Phyllis Haslam, were collecting data and studying the needs and experiences of female offenders. But it was not until the mid-1970s and early 1980s that the Correctional Service of Canada began to research the needs of women prisoners with the goal of developing programs designed specifically to meet their needs. Before that, state officials had relied on the knowledge and experience of nonprofessional and professional women outside the state when developing programs.[53] Haslam in particular was often invited to write articles and to speak at correctional conferences about the needs and management of female offenders. The information she collected was used to train probation/parole and correctional officers working with female offenders.[54] In the mid-1970s, Haslam was a member of the National Advisory

Committee on the Female Offender (see chapter 5). Many of today's knowledges about women in conflict with the law were generated not by male criminologists or medical experts, but rather by women reformers intent on doing good.

Phyllis Haslam,[55] the Executive Director of the Toronto Elizabeth Fry Society from 1953 to 1978,[56] was one of the most outspoken and prominent advocates for research on women's crime, for the hiring of professional staff, and for the development of suitable rehabilitative programs, although she has not been mentioned in the literature on women's penality. Haslam and women like her in other agencies were important because they secured the resources and promoted the logic that provided a foundation for many contemporary programs and policies of Elizabeth Fry Societies across Ontario. She is remembered for her role in 'pushing the provincial and federal governments to stop ignoring the program and resettlement needs of women in conflict with the law.'[57] William T. McGrath of the Canadian Corrections Association felt that 'she played an important leadership role in informing national correctional authorities about the female offender.'[58]

Haslam, a professionally trained social worker, used her expertise to advocate on behalf of women in conflict with the law and to secure a position for her agency in the correction of women offenders. She took every available opportunity to expound on the importance of rehabilitating offenders and to encourage community participation in the rehabilitative process. She tried to increase public awareness of the social and political dimensions of women's crime by arguing that criminal women were the inevitable consequence of a 'deteriorating social fabric.' Her advocacy and writings show how a variety of reform strategies and logics coexist. Perhaps surprisingly, her writings – in particular a chapter that she wrote for McGrath's popular text *Crime and Its Treatment in Canada* – were used to train policymakers and correctional workers.[59]

In one of her articles, 'The Damaged Girl in a Distorted Society,' Haslam contended that women criminals are harmed by society's reactions to their behaviour. She suggested that women's crime is a product of wider social problems such as poverty, abuse, and familial breakdown. To impress on her readers the gravity of these problems, she recounted the tragic stories of four women: an unmarried mother, a thief, a prostitute, and 'a dull girl.' While these tales emphasized different problems, they shared common themes. Each story described in detail how women are cast aside and ridiculed by society. Haslam challenged conventional stereotypes and argued that the community is often judgmental, and too reluctant to help women in trouble.

Haslam refused to blame women for their own misfortunes, and stressed the importance of treatment and rehabilitation. She believed that sexism further complicated and magnified women's problems (Haslam 1970: 2). Unlike earlier reformers, Haslam avoided making overt claims about moral aspects of women's conduct. In her categorization of women's deviance, she eschewed traditional moral condemnations of prostitution and unwed motherhood. Instead, she focused on the moral obligations of society and more specifically the family. For instance, she categorized the tragic circumstances of the prostitute and the unmarried mother as 'two manifestations of the deprivation of love' (1969: 3). Rather than reviling women for becoming prostitutes or for becoming pregnant out of wedlock, she encouraged society to try to understand women's circumstances and history. Although Haslam believed that offenders must be held accountable for their actions, she also maintained that society had 'its own part in crimes.' Her emphasis on forgiveness, love, and community support for women offenders has evangelical overtones. In some ways, her writings were comparable to those of Elizabeth Fry and the Salvation Army. However, her concern about family breakdown and social deterioration was more consistent with postwar maternalism and scientific rehabilitation than with nineteenth-century evangelicalism, in that it placed less emphasis on spiritual salvation.

Despite increased liberal feminist influences in the late 1960s, many reformers, Haslam included, continued to promote traditional postwar maternal logics of reform. Like earlier reformers and scientific experts, Haslam connected a girl's need for maternal love to healthy childhood development. She argued that the shelter and security of a stable and loving home were essential to crime prevention, rehabilitation, and community reintegration. She often attributed women's criminality to childhood neglect or being 'unloved by her family.' Although she clearly identified social responsibilities, she also individualized and pathologized women's criminality by focusing on women's deficiencies. The supposed absence of maternal love was thus pathologized and used to legitimate therapeutic interventions aimed at restoring women's self-worth. For instance, Haslam (1970: 2) said that a factor

which has direct bearing on women not turning so readily to crime has to do with the relationship of the girl to her home. As a child she will mimic her mother as she goes about her work. To the extent that she has an adequate mother, she will learn her potential role of being a good wife and mother ... Having learned these and many other strengths from being part of a home – she does not have the same pressures on her to achieve status by more aggressive methods. But once more we note that a negative experience in the home may well plant the seeds which flower into criminal behaviour.

Haslam further claimed that older women sometimes resort to crime when they lose the stabilizing influence of a home after the loss or death of a parent or husband. According to Haslam (1970: 5) these losses caused women to lose their sense of 'purpose in life because there is no one who needs them or loves them or cares what happens to them.' The image of a stable home is pervasive in Haslam's writings. She believed that a stable home life is essential to the normalization of women and the prevention of delinquency.

Haslam's views on crime tended to construct women as victims of wider social evils, and thus denied women agency and the power of resistance. Haslam constructed the offender as unable to care for herself and contended that society had a moral obligation to care for unfortunate citizens. While she tried to politicize the social structures that affect women's offending, she invariably attributed women's crime to maternal neglect. (The relationship between crime and maternal neglect was often raised in postwar psychiatric discourses. See Parr 1995 and Valverde 1995.) Haslam's beliefs about the moral duty of the community to care for the offender were a form of maternalism; for example, she claimed that society must 'do some thinking on behalf of inadequate and damaged people.' She denied women's power to change their own circumstances and to act on their own behalf. Her uncritical embrace of the home as a technique of governance clearly aligned her logic of reform with that of early reformers, who reinforced the importance of maternal guidance in eliciting conformity. Her maternal vision of reform was in conflict with growing feminist criticisms of 'the home,' which Haslam acknowledged but did not politicize. The next generation of reformers would reveal the dangers of the home for women prisoners and women in general in terms of the high incidence of physical, sexual, and emotional abuse that occurs in this 'private' space.

Her emphasis on a 'stable' and 'suitable' home was critical in advancing the wider political and practical interests of Elizabeth Fry Societies. Societies that operated community-based halfway houses and community programs contended that they were providing women with much-needed maternal guidance and that they were offering healthy role models and training in desirable social skills. They had the added advantage of providing a regulatory regime for women released into the community after prison. Implicit in Haslam's writings was the suggestion that women can be rehabilitated if they are brought under the wing of a caring and loving maternal role model in a pseudo-familial environment or 'stable home.' In this light, the halfway houses operated by Elizabeth Fry staff were appropriate and constructive rehabilitative options that should be taken seriously by judges, paroling authorities, and correctional administrators.

Unlike her predecessors and many state reformers, Haslam believed that therapy should take place in the community and that programs should be run by individuals who were trained in social work and had a 'capacity for disciplined sympathy' (Haslam 1969: 9). While she did not reject the notion of institutional programing, she favoured community options run by community-based experts such as the staff of Elizabeth Fry Societies – herself included. She was quite critical of the intrusive and punitive measures commonly associated with state-run custodial institutions. For example, she noted: 'We push people who commit offences out of sight into prisons where for the most part the emphasis is on custody, not treatment' (1969: 9). Somewhat predictably, she argued that community-based treatment administered by trained professionals was more likely to rehabilitate 'damaged girls.'

Haslam used the state's past failure to rehabilitate women, and the ideal of community, when she lobbied for state funding for community programs. In particular, she contended that Elizabeth Fry Societies should be funded to design and administer programs for women offenders. To legitimate her agency's expert status, she conducted a series of informal surveys of women offenders. Using these data, she argued that women's crime is different from men's. She noted that in general, women tend to commit minor property offences or to engage in 'self-destructive offences' involving alcohol, drugs, vagrancy, and attempted suicide. Based on these data, she argued that male and female criminals are different. On this basis, she contended that female offenders required different treatment and that Elizabeth Fry Societies had the expertise to meet women's needs.

Haslam's interpretation of women's needs was based on her personal knowledge of individual women offenders. Although she was a trained social worker, she had very little to say about therapeutic assessment techniques or the roles of psychiatry and social work. Nowadays, for assessments of women's needs to be seen as legitimate, those needs have to be defined and interpreted by experts using recognized assessment techniques. Haslam's methodology was much less scientific, but nonetheless influential.[60] It was not until the mid-1980s, following criticisms by the antipsychiatry and feminist movements, that reformers began to accept prisoners'/patients' own interpretations of their needs and experiences.

Near the end of her career, Haslam was nationally and internationally recognized as an expert on corrections, and more specifically on the female offender. In 1970 she was the first nongovernment Canadian delegate to the United Nations Congress of Corrections, held in Tokyo. She also became an active member of the Planning Committee of the United Nations Congress – one of the first and few women in the field of corrections to reach this stature (Cowley 1978: 17). In a newsletter prepared in honour of Haslam's retirement in 1978, Glenn Thompson, the Deputy Minister of Correctional Services, noted that 'the female offender has a good friend in Phyllis Haslam.'[61] Politically, Haslam was quite effective. She was highly regarded for her efforts in public education. She steadfastly believed in the rehabilitation of prisoners, and through her speeches, conference presentations, and involvement on commissions, she helped place the female offender on the public and political agenda. Her role in constructing the staff of Elizabeth Fry Societies as experts, in the production of knowledge about women offenders, contributed to the state's recognition of the legitimacy of this agency. She combined her vision with her research to further the public's understanding of female crime and to secure a position for Elizabeth Fry Societies in the wider correctional sphere.

Once Elizabeth Fry Societies were acknowledged by the state as having a particular expertise, they began to play a more complex role in the governance of women in conflict with the law. Not only were they governing the lifestyles of women through informal visits to the prison, but they were also playing a critical role in the legal and therapeutic regulation of women through parole supervision, halfway houses, and various individual and group counselling programs. Each society participated in challenging popular stereotypes about women's crime and in producing a new image of women in conflict with the law. This collective action increased the prestige, authority, and power of the organization as an agent of social change (Cowley 1978: 14).

Building of Prison for Women, Kingston, Ontario, October 1931. Courtesy of the Correctional Service of Canada Museum, Kingston.

Building of Prison for Women. Inmate workmen and officers from Kingston Penitentiary, c. 1928–9. Courtesy of the Correctional Service of Canada Museum, Kingston.

Prison for Women, Kingston, Ontario. Courtesy of Margaret Shaw.

The main gate of Prison for Women, Kingston, Ontario. Courtesy of the Correctional Service of Canada Museum, Kingston.

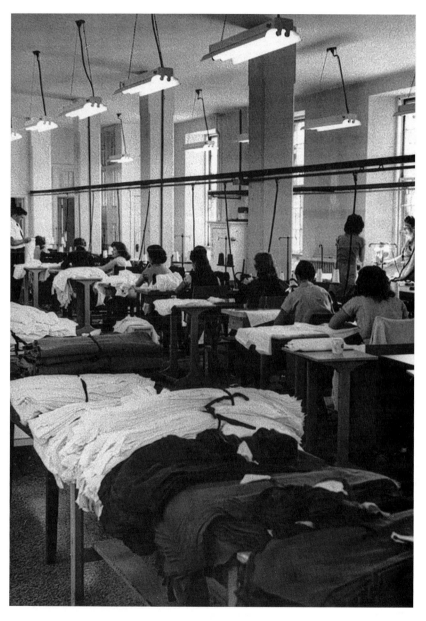

Female inmates making shirts in Prison for Women, 1962. Courtesy of the Correctional Service of Canada Museum, Kingston.

Planned site of the Grandvalley Institution for Women, Kitchener, Ontario. Courtesy of Sean Hannah.

Okimaw Ochi. Aboriginal Healing Lodge, Spiritual Lodge, Maple Creek, Saskatchewan. Courtesy of Margaret Shaw.

Okimaw Ochi. Aboriginal Healing Lodge, Administrative Building, Maple Creek, Saskatchewan. Courtesy of Margaret Shaw.

Joliette Institution for Women. Courtesy of the Correctional Service of Canada.

Some agencies established halfway houses run by residential staff who had degrees or training in the social sciences. In some cases, agencies actively policed the behaviour of offenders on parole who were enrolled in their programs. Women offenders using the services of the agencies were held accountable for their behaviour (i.e., for adhering to curfews and abstaining from alcohol and drugs), and were expected to abide by the rules and laws governing their release from prison and their residence in transitional homes. By the mid-1970s, Elizabeth Fry Societies had expanded their network, widened the meaning of penal reform, and developed a range of services and programs that their founders would scarcely have envisioned (see p. 130 for a list of services provided by Ontario Elizabeth Fry Societies as of 1996). As of the fall of 1996, there were twenty-four autonomous Elizabeth Fry Societies across Canada providing services and advocating for 'women in conflict with the law.'[62] Each individual agency, including the national Canadian Association of Elizabeth Fry Societies (CAEFS) and the regional Ontario Council of Elizabeth Fry Societies, continues to be governed by its own volunteer board of directors.[63] In many provinces, the Elizabeth Fry Society is synonymous with treatment and services for women in conflict with the law, and as such these agencies provide much-needed services to women in prison. Since the early 1970s, most Elizabeth Fry Societies across the country have promoted a feminist analysis of the problems facing women prisoners, and women more generally (see for instance Benson 1973). Several agencies have adopted feminist treatment models.[64] However, this has not ended their role in morally regulating women in conflict with the law, which they continue to play.

Equally important is the political role that Elizabeth Fry Societies play in Canadian penal reform through their national organization.[65] After CAEFS was established, Elizabeth Fry reformers gained greater political power and more access to government decision makers. CAEFS and most of its members do more than simply provide services for women in conflict or at risk of coming into conflict with the law; they pride themselves on their advocacy for the women they serve. CAEFS and its member societies receive their funding through voluntary donations, government grants, and fee-for-service contracts. This network plays a central role in correctional planning, in the policing of the state's treatment of women prisoners, and in promoting research agendas that are specific to women.

Conclusions

In the past century, penologists and social reformers have become more interested in the reform and 'healing' of women prisoners. Organizations such as Elizabeth Fry Societies, University Women's Clubs, and Local Councils of Women, and selected individuals, contended that women prisoners, like men, could be reformed through the application of appropriate technologies. Postwar ideals of rehabilitation influenced women's penality and played a critical role in the rhetorical legitimation of women's reform initiatives. The hegemonic status of motherhood was joined by another equally agile and persuasive ideal: rehabilitation. The ideal of correctional systems rehabilitating offenders led to a configuration of the state as caring (even while it was punishing its citizens). It was now perceived that the state, like a mother, had a duty, an obligation, and a responsibility to care and provide for its citizens. Early maternal penal strategies had been based mainly on an instinctual and intuitive knowledge about character reform; this new, caring state relied on expert and professionalized maternal knowledges.

At times, there were clashes between wider state agendas and those of maternal reformers, but eventually women prison reformers embraced new rehabilitative technologies of governing. By the mid-1960s, many women prison reformers had integrated a therapeutic approach into their own reform platforms. Women reformers quickly adapted to demands for expert (as opposed to innate) forms of knowledge. Some women trained as social workers used their training and knowledge to advocate more feminized and equitable models of care. In various ways, the emphasis on 'expert knowledge' offered women reformers a legitimate base of support for their entry into the workforce as 'experts on their own sex.' The hegemony of professional intervention often seems to threaten any reliance on the innate capacities of women and on amateur techniques; but at least in this era of reform, the threat turned out to be mostly hollow.

The belief held by reformers in the general principle of rehabilitation and in gender-specific programs shows how logics coexist and how governing occurs at multiple sites. The governance of women in conflict with the law extends beyond state institutions and into the community. This analysis of the activities of Elizabeth Fry reformers from 1950 to 1970 shows how the private sector, armed with an arsenal of technologies aimed at doing good, governed the behaviour and habits of women in collaboration with the state correctional institutions.

Job Breakdown – Psychologist, Prison for Women
Courtesy of National Archives (file 73-v56-1-6-40-v2).

Initial Reception   Hours per
(Approximately 7 inmates per month)   month

1. Intelligence Testing
2. Personality Testing } 6 hours per inmate = 42 hrs.
3. Vocational Testing

4. Appraisal for above   2 hours per inmate = 14 hrs.

5. Treatment Conference
   Classification Meetings } 2 hours per inmate = 14 hrs.
   Any further testing necessitated

Re-Testing
It is advisable to re-test individuals at frequent intervals (not
less than 6 months, not more than 1 year) to assess any change
in inmate's prognosis, or to assess suitability for parole. Also,
it is hoped to submit a report on each prisoner on her release.
(Assuming 7 inmates per month)   24 hrs.

Group Therapy
Possibly 2 sessions per week of 1½ hours per session   12 hrs.

Individual Therapy
Some more disturbed individuals stand more in need of
individual sessions than others.   20 hrs.

Research Projects and Further Group Testing
Sociometric testing and other such techniques can provide a
useful index on inmate's behaviour patterns, if administered
from time to time on a group basis. Further time for testing
for special purposes, e.g. research investigations, should also
be includes.   20 hrs.

Treatment Meetings
Meetings of treatment staff, committees for selection of staff,
and other administrative matters.   4 hrs.

Reception and Treatment
Courtesy of National Archives (file 73-v56-1-6-40-v2)

I. Reception
1. *Place* – Area below the administration offices. It is regretfully concluded that this is the only area available for the programme. It is
recommended that every effort be made to make the area attractive
and comfortable. It would need to include bedroom facilities in the
large unfinished room, a comfortably furnished sitting room in the
present matron's change room. The bathroom facilities are already
suitable.

2. *Time* – It is suggested that a period of 7 days on a trial basis be
instituted. It may require an extension for some or all inmates.

3. *Direction* – The programme would be under the direction of the
Clinical Team.

4. *Programme* –
   (a) Immediate –
   Bath in Reception Area
   Inventory of effects – by matron and inmate – the list to be
   signed by both.
   Assignment to a bed
   (b) Interpretation of the Reception Programme by the Deputy
   Warden or Social Worker.
   (c) Programme of Interviews to be arranged by the secretary of the
   Clinical Services, as follows:

   Warden – Interview
   Reception Card and Newcomer's Sheet,   – Secretary
       Social Background History
   Interpretation of the rules and routines   – Head Matron

   Interview with the Censor re correspondence and visits

   Medical Investigation – Nurse and Doctor

   Appraisal – Social Worker
   Appraisal – Psychologist

Educational and Vocational Interview   – Co-ordinator
   (where indicated)   – Teacher
                                            – Special Training
                                            – Supervisor.

Special visits when indicated to Social Worker, by a lawyer, C.A.S., etc.

Elizabeth Fry Representative – Re recreational auxiliary programme.

Regional Representative of National Parol Service

Chaplain

5. Evening programme of activity to be arranged with the cooperation of the Elizabeth Fry Society.

6. Conference – Inmate and key personnel – to chart plans for the inmate's stay in the Institution.

7. An interview with the Supervisor of the first work placement.

8. Tour of the building, if indicated.

Ontario Elizabeth Fry Society's Member Agency Programs

Member Agency Programs	Hamilton	Kingston	Ottawa	Peterborough	Peel	Simcoe	Sudbury	Toronto
Courts								
Court worker	✓	✓	✓	✓	✓	✓	✓	✓
Bail supervision				✓	✓	✓	✓	
Probation / parole supervision		✓		✓	✓	✓		
Community service orders	✓							✓
Local Jails and Detention Centres								
Visiting	✓	✓	✓	✓	✓	✓	✓	✓
Counselling / advocacy	✓	✓	✓	✓	✓	✓	✓	✓
Recreation	✓		✓	✓	✓		✓	✓
Temporary absence supervision	✓			✓	✓	✓	✓	✓
Release planning	✓	✓	✓	✓	✓	✓	✓	✓
Life skills	✓	✓	✓	✓			✓	✓
Vanier Centre for Women								
Visiting	✓		✓		✓	✓		✓
Counselling / advocacy	✓				✓	✓		✓
Temporary absence supervision	✓			✓	✓			✓
Release planning					✓			✓
Recreation					✓			
Prison for Women								
Visiting	✓	✓		✓	✓			✓
Counselling / advocacy	✓	✓		✓	✓			✓
Groupwork		✓			✓			
Recreation		✓				✓		
Temporary absence supervision		✓			✓			✓
Community assessments		✓		✓	✓		✓	✓
Release planning		✓	✓					✓
Residental services		✓	✓					✓

Post or Non-Institutional

Counselling / advocacy

Residence

Satellite housing

Second stage housing

Substance abuse

Parole supervision

Employment counselling

Shoplifting counselling

Incest counselling

Recreational / social

Employment training

Young Offenders

Shoplifting counselling

Residence

Community service orders

Youth crime prevention

Other

Drop in

Library

News bulletin

Speakers' bureau

Drivers

Sexual assault counselling

Courtesy of Ontario Council of Elizabeth Fry Societies, 1996.

Chapter Five

Breaking with Tradition: Feminist Reformers and the Empowerment of Women? 1970–96

Liberal Feminism and Women Prisoners' Rights Claims

In the 1970s, the women's movement in Canada and other Western countries launched ideological and political attacks on the historically entrenched notion of separate spheres that informed maternal and certain first-wave feminist strategies. In law reform, liberal feminist equal-rights strategies played a central role in improving the positions of some women. Legal struggles around abortion, labour law, family law, and criminal law led to an extension of legal rights and protections to women. These liberal feminist concerns about equality rights paralleled certain developments in Canadian penality. During the early 1970s, many Canadian and American prisons experienced riots and violent deaths of prisoners and staff, and faced serious allegations of abuse and misconduct. Public criticism and political pressure prompted several changes in penal administration, some of which reaffirmed the importance of inmates' rights. Rights-based strategies became an important tool for limiting the right of the 'benevolent state' to punish. At least theoretically, through these strategies governments were held responsible for their actions and were legally compelled to adhere to certain due-process requirements regarding inmate discipline, institutional release mechanisms, and therapeutic interventions. Prisoners' rights activists, such as Claire Culhane, sought to replace informal, arbitrary prison governance with formal, codified rules and regulations.[1] Rights-based advocacy emerged from a due process critique of rehabilitation and from increased political concern about conditions in Canadian prisons and penitentiaries.[2]

Criticisms of the rehabilitation movement dominated the correctional landscape. In political terms, these criticisms emerged from both the left and the right. On the political right, conservatives argued that rehabilitative technologies were 'too soft' on crime. The conservative emphasis on 'law and order' constructed rehabilitation as too lenient and as more concerned about the treatment of criminals than the victimization of law-abiding citizens. Based on the belief that offenders are rational actors, they argued that it was futile to try to rehabilitate offenders and that punitive approaches were preferable. On the political left, liberals who once supported rehabilitative policies became concerned about the abuses of rights taking place in the penal system – abuses that were being justified and legitimated through a rhetoric of rehabilitation (such as the Proctor case; see chapter 4).

The liberal feminist critique of penality identified several discrepancies in the treatment of men and women in state institutions. Equality concerns about women's prisons were a response to the conditions of women's confinement, the absence of programs and services, and the harassment of and discrimination against women staff and prisoners. Liberal feminists focused on opening *all* correctional jobs to women – a project that maternal reformers had begun several years earlier. The ideals of equal treatment and equal opportunity were essential elements in female correctional officers' struggle for acceptance in the wider male bureaucracy. Women correctional officers[3] used methods similar to those adopted by prisoners to secure equal employment opportunities in men's prisons (Feinman 1986; Zimmer 1986; Brown 1996; McMahon 1999). The recent Canadian literature illustrates that many female correctional officers are subject to harassment, abuse, and gender-based discrimination (McMahon 1999).

The main objective of liberal feminist reform was to eradicate gender bias so as to ensure that penal policies were gender-neutral. In a full narrative of Canadian women's penal reform, a considerable amount of space would have to be devoted to liberal feminist equality strategies: from the 1970 Royal Commission on the Status of Women, to the 1977 National Advisory Committee on the Female Offender and related reports, to the 1980 complaint by Women for Justice to the Canadian Human Rights Commission, to recent Charter of Rights and Freedoms Challenges sponsored by the Women's Legal and Education Action Fund, to the recent findings of Madame Justice Arbour in the 1996 Commission of Inquiry into Certain Events at the Prison for Women. But a detailed account of all the relevant legal battles is beyond the scope of this book.

In the early 1970s a new generation of liberal and radical feminist penal reformers began to actively pursue liberal, rights-based equality strategies to secure equal access to prison and community programs for female offenders and to improve their conditions of confinement. The 1970 Royal Commission on the Status of Women examined the lives of Canadian women generally; however, it was also the first feminist report to document the concerns of federally sentenced women specifically, and to place those concerns in a wider context of gender inequality. With respect to federal women's imprisonment, the commission recommended the following: the development of treatment facilities for female alcoholics to replace the detention of women in penal settings; the revision of the federal Prisons and Reformatories Act to eliminate all provisions that discriminate on the basis of sex or religion; the co-operation of the federal, provincial, and territorial governments in providing services and funding for rehabilitation services; co-operation with native communities; the development of halfway houses for women; co-operation between criminal justice officials and voluntary and/or community organizations; the use of female police officers for the supervision and management of women in custody; and the closure of P4W. The recommendations of this report sparked feminist reformers' interest in the plight of women in prison; they also helped reformers like Phyllis Haslam lobby the government for an investigation to document the situation of federal female offenders.

In the mid-1970s the federal government commissioned a series of research studies to further analyse the plight of federal female offenders. For example, in 1977 the National Advisory Committee on the Female Offender (NACFO) was established by the Solicitor General of Canada to 'study the needs of the federal female offenders, and to make specific recommendations to the Commissioner of Penitentiaries and the Executive Director of the Parole Service regarding the development of a comprehensive plan to provide adequate institutional and community services appropriate to her unique program and security needs' (Canada 1977a: 9). At the time of NACFO's inquiry into the conditions of women's imprisonment, the government was facing a great deal of pressure to provide women with *tangible* treatment options that addressed the 'special needs' of female offenders.[4] The recommendations of the NACFO report, and of those reports established in response to the NACFO report – the National Planning Committee on the Female Offender (NPFO), and the Joint Committee to Study Alternatives for the Housing of the Federal Female Offender – were supposed to provide women better access to programs and services offered in men's prisons. These committees officially recognized women's inequality and proposed strategies to improve women's access to institutional programs and services; yet few of these ideas were operationalized. Correctional Service employees were assigned to follow up on the recommendations of the NACFO report and to develop 'a master plan to sensitize bureaucrats to women's needs' (Berzins and Hayes 1987: 267). While government officials collected a great deal of information about the female offender and made recommendation for changes, the conditions of confinement for federally sentenced women did not improve, nor did their access to community resources. Nevertheless, the reports did raise social and political awareness of the oppression of women in prison.

Feminist reformers' frustration with this lack of progress and with the government's unwillingness to take the issue of women prisoners seriously led to a formal complaint to the Human Rights Commission on behalf of federally sentenced women. This complaint was launched by a group of feminist reformers called Women for Justice. The women involved in this rights group came from various factions of the women's community, and they were all deeply committed to the creation of a 'just' system of punishment for women. They included Maude Barlow, Lorraine Berzins, Claudia Currie, Sheelagh Dunn, Carol Faulkner, Bridgid Hayes, Christie Jefferson, Anne Marie Smart, and Denyse Stone. Some were active in corrections and related agencies; some were academics, interested lay people, and women's rights activists.

The founding of Women for Justice was a turning point in Canadian women's prison reform. This was the first time that women outside the field of corrections came together to fight for the rights of federally sentenced women. This organization, along with kindred groups like the Canadian Association of Elizabeth Fry Societies, set out to politicize and contextualize the discrimination faced by women, and to use the networking capabilities of the women's movement to lobby for changes on a national level. Women outside of the field of corrections, but deeply involved with women's issues, were encouraged to lobby for the rights of women in prisons within their own political and social networks. The plight of female offenders was thus constructed as 'a woman's issue.'

After a comprehensive, year-long investigation of the controversy surrounding P4W, the Canadian Human Rights Commission (CHRC) upheld the complaint by Women for Justice and declared that 'federal female offenders were discriminated against on the basis of sex, and that in virtually all programs and facility areas, the treatment of federal women inmates was inferior to that of men' (Cooper 1987: 139). The CHRC said that the state had a legal and moral obligation to provide women with programs and facilities 'substantively equivalent' to those provided to male inmates. The investigation also noted that few women were involved in the development of policies and in senior management of the prison, and suggested that increased involvement of women in this area could facilitate improvements. But the conciliation of the human rights complaint did not result in improved conditions for prisoners at P4W; in fact, conditions in the prison continued to deteriorate. In the late 1980s the same concerns were revisited in a Charter of Rights and Freedoms challenge sponsored by the Women's Legal Education and Action Fund (LEAF). LEAF was established in 1984 by a small group of influential Canadian women, almost all of them lawyers (including Shelagh Day, Mary Eberts, Nancy Jackman, Marilou McPhedran, and Kathleen O'Neil), who were concerned about the relevance of proposed Charter definitions of equality to women's lives (Razack 1991: 27). One of the main purposes of this organization was to engage in proactive equality litigation. The cases taken by lawyers working on behalf of LEAF 'had to concern equality rights that arise under the Charter of Rights and Freedoms or under Quebec's Charter; present strong facts; and be of importance to women' (1991: 48). LEAF declared that it was particularly interested in cases where women were doubly disadvantaged (i.e., subject to multiple forms of discrimination, for example, because of race or disability). In 1987, LEAF began to prepare a Charter case against the Correctional Service of Canada to challenge the social and material conditions of imprisonment at P4W. This Charter challenge was directed at the administration of the institution and focused on the paucity of programs and services and on the overwhelming hardships imposed by the policy of incarcerating federally sentenced women in one central location. LEAF and its supporters were confident that CSC's treatment of women at P4W would be seen to violate section 15 of the Charter on the grounds of sexual discrimination. But this case never reached the courts: it was postponed as a measure of 'good faith' pending the implementation of the recommendations of the 1990 report of the Task Force on Federally Sentenced Women (*Creating Choices*), which was designed to remedy the problem of women's imprisonment. The government firmly intended to implement the recommendations of this task force, which included closing the infamous P4W; thus, if the case had proceeded it would have been deemed moot. Many of the feminist reformers who supported the court challenge were participants on the task force, which acknowledged clearly the longstanding breach of women prisoners' rights by the correctional system.

Since 1934, eight major government commissions and task forces have investigated the problems of federally sentenced women and recommended that P4W be closed. There have also been several non-governmental reports urging the same thing.[5] The 1977 MacGuigan Report argued that P4W was 'unfit for bears, much less women.' Each successive report on federal women's incarceration has identified similar concerns and solutions. These concerns have included the neglect of women offenders because of their small numbers, the centralized housing of federally sentenced women at the P4W, the lack of appropriate programs for women offenders, and the overclassification of women, who regardless of the risk they pose are compelled to live in a maximum security prison. These reports have also noted concerns about the separation of women from their children and families, the absence of francophone and culturally appropriate programs, and the unavailability of community resources for women.

Although the P4W has been incessantly scrutinized and investigated, deplorable conditions continue there. This raises some concerns about the influence of liberal feminist reformers and the limits of feminist engagements with the state, and about the ability of reformers to fundamentally alter institutions like prisons. Rights-based arguments have not yielded much success for reformers concerned about the conditions of federally sentenced women. While there have been successes in some individual cases, neither threats of litigation nor CHRC rulings have resulted in practical changes. Reformers and federally sentenced women have discovered that when the state concedes a right, the structural arrangements required in order for women to exercise that right do not necessarily follow. Courts and tribunals have ruled that the state has an obligation to provide programs for women equal to those offered to men; however, they cannot compel the state to institute and fund such programs. As a result of these rulings, women have been offered access to the programs provided for men in men's penitentiaries. While this arrangement technically fulfils the legal requirement to provide comparable programs, offering women the *same* programs as men assumes that the programming needs of male and female offenders are the same (Moffat 1991). Also, there are practical difficulties in accommodating women who want to take vocational programs in men's institutions. Taking these women to programs often means assigning one or two staff to escort the offender out of P4W to a men's institution such as Collins Bay Penitentiary and return them at the end of the day. While the women are at the men's facility, there are additional concerns about security of women and their interactions with male offenders. Staff fear that women prisoners will engage in sexual relations with male prisoners, and this possibility creates additional security and supervision problems.

Women penal reformers used rights strategies to press for change; in contrast, radical nonstate reformers tended to downplay liberal equality as a rationality of reform, favouring instead the development of a women-centred approach to the punishment of women. In the early 1980s, reform groups such as Women for Justice, LEAF, and CAEFS, sought the expertise of women who were familiar with the prison system and those who worked with women in the community (Hayes 1983: 3). These reformers employed equality-based legal strategies (Baines 1981, 1988; Vickers 1986; Boyd and Sheehy 1989; Brodsky and Day 1989); but they also acknowledged that women offenders were not the same as male offenders. Alternatively, reformers made this argument:

> *The female offender had more in common with other women, particularly disad-*
> *vantaged women than they did with male inmates.* They are not on a whole
> dangerous or disruptive. Their crimes are often crimes of a woman trapped
> and unable to find options – the battered wife, the woman who sticks by
> her man, the woman sexually abused as a child who turns to prostitution
> or drugs, the woman who commits non-violent property crimes for money.
> They are often disadvantaged – without education, skills or employment
> and more often than not they are victims of racial prejudice. We realized
> that their crime could not be excused, *but that the key to prevention and to*
> *reducing the rate of recidivism lay in their affinity to other women.* (Emphasis
> added; Hayes 1983: 4)

This construction of the female offender was adopted in both state and nonstate reform narratives of the mid to late 1980s. Nonstate feminist reformers resorted to equality/rights-based strategies even while maintaining that they were more interested in developing strategies that focused on women's commonality with other women, and on differences between women and men in prison. This coexistence of equality and difference strategies of reform points out the complexity of reformers' efforts to alter women's penal regimes. Reformers did not advocate for equality in the naïve belief that it would satisfy the needs of women; rather, they believed that legal strategies and the threat of litigation might compel the state to address the longstanding concerns of women prisoners.

The Politics of Difference and the Ethic of Care

In the early 1980s there were debates at meetings of CAEFS on the future direction of the organization and its role in women's prison reform.[6] These debates marked a shift from a maternal reform logic to a feminist reform logic, as well as a generational shift. As one reformer notes, the changes in women's reform in the early 1980s could be conceptualized as a struggle between 'the blue hairs and the freaks.'[7] More radical feminist advocates were questioning the maternal and normative role of well-intentioned women reformers and challenging traditional maternal ideals about remaking prisoners into 'ladies.' Correctional reformers who advocated women-centred correctional strategies that celebrated feminist interpretations of women's difference used cultural feminist critiques of formal equality and arguments in favour of difference.

All of this took place in the context of a wider debate in radical and cultural feminist scholarship about women's difference and alternative visions of justice (MacKinnon 1982, 1983, 1986, 1987, 1990; Bacchi 1990; Freedman 1990; Jagger 1990; Rhode 1990; Pitch 1992). The ideas put forward in Carol Gilligan's (1982) book *In a Different Voice* were used by feminist legal scholars and reformers to promote an alternative, feminist vision of justice. Gilligan claims that the voices of law and legal practice are based on a 'male voice' or male norms and on values such as equality, rights, autonomy, and impartiality. She argues that the 'female voice' is different from the male voice in that it places more emphasis on values such as care, responsibility, and connectedness. Gilligan (1982) and others, including Frances Heidensohn (1986) and Kay Harris (1987), claim that the law and criminal justice institutions, although they are construed as operating from a gender-neutral stance, reflect a male voice. This argument is extended to the area of criminal justice and penal reform, where it is suggested that reform strategies need to emphasize the restructuring of law based on an 'ethic of care' (Heidensohn 1986; Harris 1987). For example, Heidensohn (1986) claims that the current model of criminal justice is based on a white, middle-class, male ethic of justice (which she calls the 'Portia model') in the sense that it embraces characteristics of men such as rationality, clear thinking, and procedural-mindedness. In this framework, 'justice' is secured through law reform and through litigation that focuses on legal equality. Heidensohn (1986) and others contend that liberal equality approaches are limited because they deny the structural inequality of women and more importantly, women's alternative visions of 'justice.' Heidensohn argues in favour of a more feminized version of justice based on an 'ethic of care' (which she calls the 'Persephone model'). A model of justice or reform based on an 'ethic of care' rejects liberal legal ideals of an 'ethic of justice' and instead advocates 'caring' reforms that focus on women's social, political, economic, and psychological differences.

Some cultural feminist scholars have argued that Gilligan's philosophy is important because it can be used to raise questions about the aims and purposes of penality (Daly 1989). It allows for a debate about the merits of a model based on an 'ethic of justice' (stressing a depersonalized response based on the wrongdoers' culpability and harm to others) versus one based on an 'ethic of care' (stressing a personalized response to offenders and their reintegration into the community). However, Daly also argues that Gilligan's model is limited. She claims that the problem with the treatment of women in the criminal justice system is not that a female voice is absent, but rather that certain relations of power are presupposed, maintained, and reproduced. She also challenges the concept of 'justice reasoning as male' and 'care reasoning as female' in the context of law and criminal justice. She suggests that such a bifurcation leads to the false assumption that justice for women can be achieved by simply adding women's voice to law or reconstituting the system along the lines of care. Daly's observation is particularly relevant in light of recent Canadian attempts to create a women-centred correctional alternative.

In practical terms, Heidensohn (1986) and others recognize that it would be difficult, if not impossible, to restructure the entire system of justice on the basis of gender-specific visions of justice. However, Heidensohn (1986: 292) adds that historically, women's prisons have been harsher and crueller for women than men's are for men, and that they can be reformed to reflect an 'ethic of care.' Likewise, Harris (1987) calls for a range of compassionate, constructive, and caring reforms to law and the criminal justice system. Daly (1989), on the other hand, is critical of the operational 'ethic of care models' promoted by Gilligan

(1982), Heidensohn (1986), and Harris (1987) because they tend to overlook the injustices and abuses associated with past individualized,
welfare-based models of justice (such as rehabilitation) that use the
ideal of 'caring' to justify a wide range of intrusive interventions into
the lives of both women and men. Notwithstanding feminist criticisms
of reforms predicated on an 'ethic of care,' this approach informs the
1990 Task Force on Federally Sentenced Women as well as some past
provincial initiatives in Ontario and Nova Scotia.[8] The difficulties associated with recent Canadian efforts to design and implement a 'women-
centred' model of punishment reinforce wider criticisms of an 'ethic of
care.'

Creating Choices, the Task Force on Federally Sentenced Women

By the late 1980s, reformers had come full circle in their narrative and
discursive approaches to the governance of women prisoners, to argue
once again that women prisoners must be governed through strategies
that recognize their difference from men. However, instead of relying
on maternal metaphors, reformers now relied on ideals of empowerment, healing, and choice supported by cultural feminism, aboriginal
culture, and other social movements. These ideals, which are congruent
with liberal feminist difference strategies, were used by reformers and
refashioned by the state to construct a new vision: women-centred
prisons. In this light, the tabling of *Creating Choices*, the 1990 Report of
the Task Force on Federally Sentenced Women, was a pivotal event, for
on this occasion feminist reformers participated in the evolution of a
neoliberal model of penal discipline that reconfigured the relationship
between state and community. The remainder of this chapter focuses
more narrowly on the 'co-operative effort' made by Corrections Canada,
aboriginal women, and feminist reformers – in particular CAEFS – to
create an alternative, 'women-centred' vision of punishment, and how
that effort was operationalized. Chapter 6 further will explore the shifts
in governing women in prison that have accompanied this reform
initiative.

The Task Force on Federally Sentenced Women was established nearly
ten years after the last committee specifically set up to 'settle' the issue
of federal women's imprisonment had faded into obscurity (Shaw 1993:
50). The task force's mandate was to examine the 'correctional management of federally sentenced women from the commencement of their
sentence to the date of final warrant expiry and to develop a plan which

would guide and direct this process in a manner that is responsive to the unique and special needs of this group' (TFFSW 1990: 1). There was no one specific event or organizational interest that led to the convening of the task force at this particular moment in time. Rather, the task force was established, and its recommendations were later implemented, as a result of a combination of factors. Mainly, the government was facing immense social and political pressure from reformers, feminists, aboriginal organizations, and the media, all of whom were berating the government for its long neglect of federally incarcerated women.[9]

As noted, in the early 1980s, politically active organizations such as CAEFS, LEAF, and Women for Justice were using litigation and the threat of Charter of Rights and Freedoms challenges to force the government to improve programs and services for federally sentenced women (LEAF 1991, 1993). As well, CAEFS was calling for a royal commission on women in federal prisons. Aboriginal organizations such as the Native Women's Association of Canada, and government and nongovernment reports (Proudfoot 1978; Jackson 1988; Task Force on Aboriginal Peoples in Corrections 1988), raised public awareness about discrimination against aboriginal people – in particular, the unequal treatment of aboriginal people in the criminal justice system.[10] Simultaneously, the Canadian government was struggling to address aboriginal peoples' demands for self-government and cultural autonomy.

All of this advocacy was reinforced by a series of prisoners' deaths at P4W. For many, these deaths underscored how our mental health system and penal institutions had failed to respond to the needs of incarcerated women. They made it clear that fundamental changes were needed in Corrections Canada's approach to managing federal female offenders. The coroner's inquest that followed (Ontario 1991) once again revealed the appalling conditions at P4W, the federal government's failure to develop programs appropriate to the needs of women prisoners, and the urgent need for change.[11] All of this exposed P4W and the government to increased public scrutiny (Moffat 1991: 191).

In March 1989 the government responded to the public's concerns and criticisms by setting up a joint community and government task force. A newly appointed, progressive Commissioner of Corrections, Ole Ingstrup, spearheaded this federal initiative. Ingstrup firmly supported the development of a new correctional vision. He was 'perceived by many to be an innovator, and someone sympathetic to the very real problems of imprisonment, which have built up in Canada' (Shaw 1992a: 442). The task force's recommendations for a new model of women's corrections were eventually accepted largely as a result of Ingstrup's support of them; however, it is questionable whether he should be seen as an innovator, given that those recommendations resulted in the expansion of prison capacity for women, a failure to expand community options and initiatives for women, the continued use of repressive incapacitative strategies, and an erosion of the ideals that informed this initiative.

From its inception, the forty-one-person task force committee[12] was unlike any previous government committee in Canada or elsewhere (Shaw 1993: 53). Its steering committee was co-chaired by Bonnie Diamond, at the time the Executive Director of the Canadian Association of Elizabeth Fry Societies, and James Phelps, a Deputy Commissioner of Programs and Operations at the Correctional Service of Canada. Two-thirds of the task force members were women. Two of these women had served federal sentences, and more than half the members were from nongovernment or volunteer organizations. No previous government inquiries into women's imprisonment had included so many imprisoned women or representatives from the volunteer sector and aboriginal and minority groups (1993: 53). Many of the task force members held a feminist perspective and a passionate commitment to change. The report adhered unequivocally to a feminist philosophy, and it clearly acknowledged the plight of aboriginal women prisoners. The task force's research was driven by a 'woman-centred approach' stressing 'that issues such as poverty, racism, wife battering, and sexual abuse are central to women's crime' (Task Force on Federally Sentenced Women – Creating Choices, hereafter TFFSW, 1990: 83).[13]

The Third National Workshop on Female Offenders (Pittsburgh, Pennsylvania, May 1989) had a strong influence on *Creating Choices*. That conference's theme, 'The Changing Needs of the Female Offender – A Challenge for the Future,' was generally interpreted as 'a call for the restructuring of corrections for women rather than the patch-working evident in so many correctional systems, which work against the objective of responsible self-sufficiency' (TFFSW 1990: 83). A second major influence on the task force was the aboriginal struggle for self-determination. The task force emphasized that the achievement of equality for aboriginal women in the correctional system was dependent on enhanced Aboriginal participation and increased aboriginal control over programs and services. Ironically, it was initially proposed that only one aboriginal woman sit on the task force's steering committee. The Native Women's Association of Canada rejected this marginalized role and argued for a stronger presence. Eventually, five aboriginal women would sit on the steering committee (Hayman 2000).

Task force participants engaged in a number of struggles and made a number of sacrifices in their efforts to co-operatively produce a vision for change. For example, many volunteer organizations expressed concerns about having to work within the existing legislative and penal structure when they believed that a community-based correctional approach was more appropriate (Shaw 1993: 54). There were also concerns about whether the voices of aboriginal women and prisoners would be heard and respected; after all, aboriginal women had had to struggle to be included on the task force. The Aboriginal Women's Caucus felt that while the government had an opportunity to make some meaningful choices, another task force was not needed since 'the government was always creating task forces, yet nothing changed' (Morin 1993:2). Aboriginal participants opposed the construction of additional prisons. In their view, prisons were part of the problem, not the solution. For example, Patricia Monture-Angus questioned how 'you become involved in a task force where you're recommending that you close one prison and just build more ... there is something about that that just fundamentally does not make sense' (Palumbo and Palumbo 1992: 5). Ultimately, many aboriginal women, and as well as reform groups like CAEFS, agreed to participate in the task force out of concern for women in prison. Notwithstanding the reservations held by the partners, the government and the community worked together to design a prototype for women-centred corrections. These reformers did not base their participation in this initiative on a naïve idealism regarding the possibility of change. They were sceptical, but they were also hopeful that an entrenched and punitive mode of governing could perhaps be altered.

The most significant long-term recommendation of the task force was for the closure of P4W and the construction of four small regional facilities and one aboriginal 'healing lodge.' Ideally, each regional facility would operate under a program philosophy that reflected community norms; all would make use of community services and expertise and be geared to the safe and earliest possible release of federally sentenced women. The primary programming would include health care, mental health services, addiction programs, family visits, mother-and-child programs, spirituality and religion, aboriginal programs, education, and vocational training (TFFSW 1990: 138–47). The Healing Lodge would allow federally sentenced aboriginal women to serve all or part of their sentences in a 'culturally sensitive' environment. This facility would address the needs of federally sentenced aboriginal women through native teachings, ceremonies, and contact with elders. Besides outlining a new, women-centred institutional model, *Creating Choices* also advocated improvments in community options for women. Corrections Canada was expected to play a leadership role in developing of women-centred community initiatives that facilitated the reintegration of federally sentenced women, and that expanded services and accommodation options for women, and that addressed the needs of women in minimum security, who were too often neglected. *Creating Choices* called for more community release centres, and for more halfway houses run by community-based agencies, and for aboriginal centres run by aboriginal groups or communities (1990: 126–8). It also proposed a series of more creative options in the community to address the needs of women who were not from large centres with community release centres or halfway houses for women, or who could not live in a group setting, or who had special concerns (i.e., children). These options would include satellite units, home placements, addiction treatment centres, multi-use women's Ccentres, mixed group housing and mother-child centres (1990: 128–9).[14] Unfortunately, to date few of these initiatives have been implemented, and in 1999 a halfway house for women in Ottawa was closed due to insufficient funds (CAEFS 1999a: 9).

Defining Women-Centredness

In April 1999 the recommendations[15] of the task force were presented in a report to the government, and in September of the same year the federal government announced that it would implement the task force's recommendations. The National Implementation Committee, in collaboration with the Construction Policy and Services Division of Corrections Canada, set about preparing a comprehensive operational plan for the four regional facilities. This plan was finalized in the fall of 1992. In October 1993, senior managers of CSC approved the design, operational plan, and staff training plan for the Healing Lodge (the development of the Healing Lodge took a different path, and will be discussed separately). In August 1993, a committee composed of the Federally Sentenced Women's Program Section at National Headquarters, the four wardens of the new prisons, and the Director of Burnaby Correctional Centre in British Columbia was convened to replace the National Implementation Committee. The *kikawinàw* (warden) for the Healing

Lodge joined this committee once she was hired. This group, known as the Federally Sentenced Women Committee, developed a coordinated approach to staffing,[16] program development,[17] and policy for the new institutions.[18]

The Federally Sentenced Women's Program of CSC and the wardens of the five 'new' institutions controlled the implementation process and selectively used 'volunteer' community resources to define the types and content of programming in the institutions. The involvement of communities in the planning process for the new prisons was left to the discretion of individual wardens. Organizations like CAEFS, which had co-chaired the task force, reported feeling excluded from the decision-making process. Despite its strong involvement in the task force, CAEFS was not given membership on the National Implementation Committee, which was made up mainly of civil servants. In June 1992, CAEFS withdrew its support for the implementation process because it felt that in operationalizing *Creating Choices*, the new committee had veered considerably from the original vision of the document. CAEFS was particularly concerned about the government's failure to develop and direct resources to the community strategies outlined in *Creating Choices*. In a 1997 press release, it noted that even though Canada had touted the task force report internationally as an example of progressive correctional reform, the principles and approaches envisioned by the task force were in serious danger of never being implemented.[19] CAEFS continues to support the principles and philosophy of *Creating Choices*.

Instead of embracing CAEFS's expertise and knowledge, CSC operated independently and sought the advice of outside 'experts' with limited experience in Canadian women's corrections. While CSC generally informs CAEFS and other 'stakeholders' of policy developments and research, they rarely work collaboratively. A somewhat adversarial relationship has been re-established between CAEFS, which speaks for and on behalf of women in conflict with the law, and CSC. By and large, feminists and activists have been only marginally included in the process of designing the new penal regimes. As a result, the possibilities for change have been restricted. By limiting the involvement of non-CSC partners in planning the new regional prisons and in operationalizing the vision of *Creating Choices*, CSC has reverted back to traditional bureaucratic correctional models. Yet CSC continues to maintain that it is adhering to a women-centred approach as defined by the task force. Activists continue to struggle for inclusion in the planning processes and to hold the government accountable for its treatment of federally sentenced women, by reminding CSC of its commitment to women-centeredness and to the recommendations of the task force (and, more recently, to the recommendations of the 1996 Arbour Commission). CAEFS's annual reports provide updates on the government's operationalization of *Creating Choices* and offer opinions as to the adequacy of the government's approach to managing women's corrections. These reports are in stark contrast to CSC's claims to be at the international 'cutting edge' of innovation and success (CAEFS 1994, 1995, 1996, 1997, 1998, 1999).

A New, Women-Centred Philosophy

The task force indicated that having rejected the traditional white male approach to correctional programming and management, it had to 'formulate a plan which would respond to the needs and risks represented by women themselves, which would respond in a way reflective of women's perceptions of, and interactions with, each other and society generally. However, it should be noted that the work to build a correctional system based on women's reality rather than sexual and racial stereotypes was made more difficult by the fact that a comprehensive, coherent female correctional model does not exist, particularly one that is also responsive to Aboriginal perceptions' (TFFSW 1990: 91).

Creating Choices envisions that the new, women-sensitive correctional model informing the regional facilities and the Healing Lodge will be characterized by these five guiding principles: 'empowerment, meaningful and responsible choices, respect and dignity, supportive environment, and shared responsibility.'[20] These principles are analysed below, one at a time.

In *Creating Choices*, **empowerment** is meant to highlight that the structural inequities experienced by women prisoners are similar to broader gender inequalities (1990: 105–6). It is noted that the 'research and the words of federally sentenced women have repeatedly stressed the connections between women's involvement in the criminal justice system and the inequalities, hardships, and suffering experienced by women in our society.' Empowerment is connected to the perception that women prisoners, like women generally, lack self-esteem and as a result believe they have little power to direct their lives: 'they feel disempowered, unable to create or make choices, unable to help create a more rewarding, productive future, even if realistic choices are presented to them' (1990: 105). The task force locates the disempowerment of women at two sites: in the structural arrangements of society, and in the woman herself, with an emphasis on the latter.

Meaningful choices is defined as the need to provide women with 'choices which relate to their needs and make sense in terms of their past experiences, their culture, their morality, their spirituality, their abilities or skills, and their future realities or possibilities' (1990: 108). The construction of meaningful choices in this report suggests that they are of two types: the choices offered to the prisoner by the institution in terms of programming, and the choices (or decisions) made by the woman while residing in the institution and on her release.

Respect and dignity is 'based on the assumption that mutuality of respect is needed among prisoners, among staff, and between prisoners and staff if women are to gain the self-respect and respect for others necessary to take responsibility for their futures' (1990: 109). The task force feels that this principle is important because Canadian correctional institutions 'have often been criticized for their tendency to encourage dependent and child-like behaviour among women' (1990: 109). Furthermore, many of the rules in the prison have been administered in an arbitrary and humiliating way, and this has contributed to the prisoners' sense of powerlessness (or disempowerment).

Supportive environment is understood in terms of the 'constellation of many types of environment ... political, physical, financial, emotional/psychological, and spiritual, especially for Aboriginal women' (1990: 110).

The final guiding principle of women-centred corrections outlined in the task force report is **shared responsibility**. Similar to the other principles, this concept emphasizes the responsibilities of the prisoner, the government, and the community:

> Governments at all levels, correctional workers, voluntary sector services, businesses, private sector services and community members generally must take responsibility as inter-related parts of society. This is essential in order to foster the independence and self-reliance among federally sentenced women to allow them to take responsibility for their past, present and future actions. To make sound choices, women must be supported by a coordinated comprehensive effort involving all elements in society. This, as Aboriginal teachings instruct us, is a holistic approach. (1990: 111)

Furthermore, this principle is important because 'the holistic programming and multifaceted opportunities, which support an environment, in which women can become empowered, can only be built on a foundation of responsibility among a broad range of community members. Currently, because the Correctional Service of Canada has legal obligations for federally sentenced women, *responsibility for federal women is too narrowly assigned to correctional systems*' (emphasis added; 1990: 111).

Under the heading 'supportive environment,' the task force emphasized the community's responsibility for empowering women prisoners, while simultaneously redefining CSC's responsibilities.

The 1992 Draft Operational Plan (CSC 1992a: 23–6) provided the following description, which was believed by CSC to 'capture the essence of operations' and to provide a framework for the planning and design of the new prisons.

DAY-IN-THE-LIFE SCENARIO

It's early morning when Anne wakes up. She knows there will be a formal count in half an hour at 7:00 a.m. so she spends the time in private musing. She has done a lot of this since she began her sentence two years ago.

'Two years ...,' Anne ponders 'so much has changed.' When she first arrived, she was scared, angry and separated from her family and friends and, worst of all, her three-year old daughter. Her recollections of admission were friendly staff ('Are they really like this?') and a houseful of strangers. Anne remembers her feelings of inadequacy, helplessness, fear and not being able to get ahead. Her case management officer, primary worker and her community worker helped her realize that there were positive things she could do to overcome these feelings. They helped her plan a strategy for what Anne calls 'successfully staying out.' She is now willing to accept responsibility for her criminal behavior and is learning to live an independent life.

At the very beginning, Anne's daughter was able to live with her thanks to the children's residency program. When Anne was first incarcerated, Katie was placed with her Aunt but she was experiencing emotional difficulties. She was acting out and social service workers felt that Katie would feel more secure if she could live with her mother. In a joint decision process between Anne, the social service worker and the caseworker, it was decided that it was in Katie's best interests to participate in the residency program at the facility.

Although Katie attended the on-site day care, Anne felt good about being able to be with her after work and at night. Sometimes during the day, if her schedule permitted, Anne used to take her lunch to the day care. But, when Katie reached pre-school age, Anne, her social service worker and the caseworker met and agreed that Katie should live in the community so she could attend community programs. It was difficult when Katie first moved out to live with Anne's mother and attend a pre-school program. However, Anne gives herself credit of 'letting go' – Katie, she feels, is having a more normal upbringing in the city with her own friends. Still, the weekends are wonderful when Katie stays with Anne. Anne is sure this has kept their relationship close.

It's 7:00 a.m., the correctional worker has arrived to take a formal count. Everyone is up, and having showers and getting dressed. The worker stays and chats with Anne and her house mates while they fix and eat their breakfasts. Anne and one of her house mates are in the same work program, business accounting. Today, there is a special session over lunch so both women pack bag lunches. Checking the house schedule, Anne confirms that it's her night to do dishes, and her closest friend in the house is to cook. Everyone pitches in for a quick kitchen clean-up.

By 8:00 a.m. it's off to work. The correctional worker is going with one of Anne's house mates to her dental appointment in town. Another house mate has elected to stay home with her baby, at least for a few months. Anne remembers those days, but is happy to be moving on. When Katie lived in, Anne was in school earning her high school equivalency. Since then she has taken two business courses, one at the local community college and one offered in-house. Some women are working in the town, but Anne felt that the on-site accounting work program was better suited to what she wants to do, giving her both the theory and the practical experience.

At 11:30 a.m., the instructor takes a formal count to ensure that everyone is accounted for. Anne slightly resents this, after all, she feels that she's a responsible person. However, she realizes that some other women do not have the same feelings and the counts are really no big deal.

Anne, some of her co-workers and women from other programs move to one of the classrooms for the 'bag lunch lecture series.' Anne notes that the series is quite popular and credits her primary worker and other staff for organizing these noon hour activities.

After the lecture, Anne attends a pre-release program. Anne is quite excited about her upcoming release. The instructor who runs this program, gives an animated session on job interviews – do's and don't's. In the second part of the program, budgeting and household management, he provides a good review, an exercise designed to build confidence. Anne feels her skills in these areas are quite good because of her house arrangements and her business courses/experience. At the end of the session, the instructor does a count.

On her way home, Anne stops at her mailbox. Nothing today but she runs into her case worker who tells Anne about an informal community network presentation scheduled for Saturday in the recreation area. Her worker also might have a lead on some employment opportunities. They agree to discuss these possibilities during Anne's regular counselling session the next day. She always looks forward to these sessions but it has been difficult to deal with some of her feelings about the abuse she experienced in her relationship with her common-law husband, from whom she is now separated.

Continuing home, Anne stops to visit a woman who lives in another house and has a daughter the same age as Katie, to make arrangements for a weekend 'play date.'

Anne's house mate has invited her primary worker to have dinner with them in the house. She gets the feeling that not everyone wants staff around at dinner time, but her worker is fairly well accepted so Anne isn't too worried. During the meal, everyone is pleased to learn that one of their house mates is progressing well in the enhanced unit where she has been temporarily transferred, and may be able to return to the house in the next few weeks. Anne helps with dinner and together the women do the dishes. Anne's friend has her survivor support group meeting this evening which she and her primary worker will attend. The weekly meeting is held in the municipal social services building.

After dinner, Anne makes a quick trip to the resource centre to check an accounting reference. The reference raises a few other questions. Anne resolves to look for the answers in the town's library collection during her bi-weekly visit. Anne heads towards the recreation centre for the evening's special events. Every month there is a movie night open to all women and their guests. Tonight, Anne's sister is coming. The movie is not great but the atmosphere is congenial. It is nice to see the mix of women, staff and visitors.

By 9:30 p.m., all women are supposed to be in their own houses. Anne and her house mates watch television and chat about plans for the upcoming weekend. Since Katie will be visiting all weekend, Anne has planned to do her weekly household chores and her laundry tomorrow after work. Although Anne's primary objective for weekends is to be with

Katie, she would like to attend the special presentation. A house mate offers to stay with Katie while Anne is at the presentation.

At 11:00 p.m. a correctional worker takes the last count of the day.

This description of a supportive, homelike environment in which women work co-operatively and live with prison staff was highly ambitious – and highly inconsistent with most visions of imprisonment. The plausibility of such lofty ideals is further discussed in chapter 6.

From Vision to Practice

Since the release of *Creating Choices,* four new women-centred regional facilities (prisons) have opened in Truro, Nova Scotia (1995), Joliette, Quebec (1997), Kitchener, Ontario (1997), and Edmonton, Alberta (1995), as well as Okimaw Ohci Healing Lodge – the aboriginal healing lodge in Maple Creek, Saskatchewan (1995). Architecturally, these prisons are innovative. The designs vary slightly, but each prison has residential-style houses for six to ten women, a central core building for programs[21] and administration, and an enhanced security unit. The Okimaw Ohci (which means Thunder Hills) Healing Lodge and Joliette Prison provide accommodations for mothers and their children.[22] The other facilities do not have operational mother/child programs.[23] P4W remained open until May 2000 for fewer than twenty maximum-security offenders. The Canadian government maintains that the segregated units for maximum security women in men's prisons will close in 2001 once new accommodations for these women have been built at each of the regional prisons (see chapter 6).

Site Selection

Local communities responded to the building of the new prisons in mixed and largely unanticipated ways. While many local people sympathized with the plight of federally sentenced women and acknowledged the limits of P4W, the public generally was resistant to the building of prisons that would include luxuries and accommodations that were better than those of non-offenders. For some of these new prisons, the site selection process was controversial. In both Edmonton and Kitchener, there was a great deal of vocal opposition to being chosen as a site.[24] As Druar, Carrington, and Goyder (1998:48) have observed, 'prisons, like power plants, airports, garbage incinerators, toxic waste disposal sites, freeways, half way houses, and shelters for the homeless represent locally unwanted land uses or LULU's.' In Kitchener, local residents armed with clear memories of the sensational case of Karla Homolka and an inflated 'fear of crime' feared that a prison in their community would compromise public safety and lower property values. Groups like People for the Protection of Homes and Children erected makeshift signs and distributed flyers to solicit support for keeping the prison out. The openness of CSC's public consultation processes varied considerably across the country.

Meanwhile, feminist reformers like CAEFS also expressed their concern that the new prisons were to be built in small and in some cases remote communities, where it would be more difficult and expensive for prisoners' families to visit and where there were fewer services. *Creating Choices* (TFFSW 1990: 80) had stated that it was critical for the of new facilities to be in 'proximity to large urban centres in order to facilitate visits by family members, attract professional, community and business resources, and to take advantage of existing educational health, cultural and recreational facilities.' The task force had added that two key variables to be considered in the placement of the new prisons must be proximity to the home communities of the incarcerated women and the availability of community resources. On this basis, Halifax, Montreal, Central Southwestern Ontario, Edmonton, a Prairies location suitable for the Healing Lodge, and the B.C. Lower Mainland had been suggested as sites for the new women's prisons (TTFSW 1990: 83). Yet three of the four regional facilities (Truro, Joliette, and Kitchener) were placed about 100 km outside major urban centres (Halifax, Montreal, and Toronto respectively). And rather than building a separate facility for federal female offenders in British Columbia,[25] Corrections Canada decided to accommodate these women at the provincial Burnaby Correctional Centre for Women. The continued incarceration of federally sentenced women in provincial facilities has resulted in inequitable practices; in the wake of this, two federally sentenced women have taken legal action against the Solicitor General and CSC (CAEFS 1999a). Considerable governmental resources have been devoted to building new prisons, yet few if any resources have been allocated to implementing community strategies. This amounts to a substantial departure from the implicit intent of *Creating Choices*, which was not to build more prisons but rather to decarcerate and provide better services for women, who present minimal risk to the community and who have few if any community resources to facilitate their timely and inevitable reintegration into the community.

Redefining Women-Centredness

CSC operational documents (1994a: 3) have stated that a women-centred approach means 'that programs must reflect the social realities of women and respond to the individual needs of each woman.' To implement the women-centred philosophy, the government has established five 'operational' principles:[26] 'contextual analysis,' 'cooperative,' 'challenging,' 'connection,' and 'agency.' These operating principles selectively incorporate the feminist analysis and ideals outlined in *Creating Choices*. The 1994 Operational Plan incorporates some of the main ideas of *Creating Choices*; however, it is different.

The principle of **contextual analysis** draws on the premise that the lives and actions of federally sentenced women must be placed in a wider social, political, and economic context and on the belief that programs must reflect the social realities of women while responding to their individual needs. The second principle, **cooperation**, argues in favour of a correctional model that is not based on hierarchical relations of power. Women are to be valued as experts on their own needs, and thus are to be afforded some decision-making autonomy. Regardless of this, women prisoners have limited input into the decision-making processes that shape their incarceration. It is virtually impossible to create a nonhierarchal model in a prison setting.

The third principle, **challenging,** is expected to promote 'the most effective interaction between women and the facilitator in a supportive, encouraging, empathic, accepting, *challenging*, and non-confrontational manner' (CSC 1994a: 10). The principle of 'challenging' is vague, but it seems to imply that penal regimes should encourage prisoners to question their life choices. Yet this concept undermines the ideal of cooperation. Presumably, it is the staff's role to question or 'challenge' the life choices of incarcerated women. Undoubtedly these 'challenges' are informed by middle-class (often white) standards of normalcy and morality, which for instance shun employment in the sex trade, the failure to have a bank account, unstable residence, and the frequent use of social services.

The fourth principle, **connection**, invites women to learn from one another through a process of dialogue and sharing that is designed to promote trust. However, developing 'positive' relationships with other offenders does not always mean that institutional officials will perceive these relationships as fostering rehabilitation and reintegration. Sometimes relationships between offenders (in particular same-sex prison romances) are used by authorities as evidence to support claims about a woman's continued involvement in, identification with, and commitment to a criminal subculture – especially if she is also reluctant to engage in a 'meaningful and trusting relationship with institutional staff.'

The final principle of women-centredness is **agency**, which envisions women as active agents rather than passive victims. While they are accountable for their actions, including there criminal activities, all their activities are understood in the context in which they occur. Many women have been victimized but have survived even when their options were very limited. The strength and creativity employed by women demonstrates their potential power to effect change. This strength can be used and refocused towards empowerment (CSC 1994a: 10).

The issue of agency with respect to incarcerated women is complex. On the one hand, feminist reformers support the attribution of agency to the female offender because it creates an active subject capable of making choices, putting up resistance, and changing her situation. When we identify the prisoner as a survivor and active agent rather than as a victim, we open the door for empowerment and for her acceptance of responsibility for her own destiny. On the other hand, for CSC the concept of agency is not rooted in a politicized understanding of women's oppression, but rather in the objective of making the offender accountable for her crimes, and ultimately for her rehabilitation.

Overall, the women-centred approach was meant to 'empower' federally sentenced women. These operating principles, like those in *Creating Choices*, are lofty ideals; women's corrections in Canada may aspire to them but it has not yet achieved them.[27] These principles, like those of *Creating Choices*, reflect a shift toward a strategy of responsibilization (O'Malley 1992). The governance of women prisoners is no longer conceptualized as the sole responsibility of the federal government; rather, it is seen as the collective responsibility of the community and even the individual responsibility of the offender. In this new correctional framework, the offender is responsible for her own self-governance and for minimizing and managing her needs and the risk she poses to herself and the public. (This issue is developed further in chapter 6.)

The Healing Lodge

An entire chapter of *Creating Choices* was devoted to aboriginal women. This chapter and a companion document by Sugar and Fox (1990) clearly and concisely outlined the needs of federally sentenced aboriginal women and the unique experiences of racism and discrimination experienced by them. The task force documented the absence of aboriginal programs, aboriginal women's limited means to practise their spirituality, and the unfamiliarity of many staff with aboriginal culture and spirituality. For example, for a long time CSC treated sweetgrass (which is central to the teachings in most aboriginal cultures) as a contraband substance. In terms of programming, it was observed that aboriginal women often refused to attend various treatment programs that were foreign to their culture; consequently, their parole applications were not supported and they were viewed 'as not addressing their treatment needs' (Sugar and Fox 1990; also see Morin 1993, 19; Nahanee 1995, and Weibe and Johnson 1998). Besides these forms of discrimination, aboriginal women felt that they were being treated prejudicially and labelled violent, uncontrollable, and unmanageable because they refused to cooperate with correctional staff. As one woman noted, '[maximum] security classifications were applied to us because, as native women, we were seen as a collective, war party, that posed a risk to the good order of the institution' (Sugar and Fox 1990, in Morin 1993: 20). Federally sentenced aboriginal women interviewed by Sugar and Fox (1990) outlined several other issues that affected their lives in P4W: archaic conditions (no hot water until 1987, and no heat in segregation units), poor medical treatment (which was believed to have contributed to the death of women who self-injured or slashed), arbitrary mass punishments, and sexism and racism barriers imposed by the administration (Morin 1993: 20).

Aboriginal women prisoners were and still are overrepresented in the Canadian prison population.[28] The task force was particularly concerned with reducing the number of federally sentenced aboriginal women and with providing culturally appropriate services and programs. Ideally, the Healing Lodge recommended by the task force was to be a 'new concept of incarceration' that would provide women with an opportunity 'to heal their wounds, to deal with their present circumstances and to prepare for their responsibilities for the future'(Morin 1993:35).

The Healing Lodge is different from the other regional women-centred prisons in that it is semi-autonomous and emphasizes Aboriginal traditions. According to Jane Miller-Ashton, a member of the Task Force, there was an absence of detail on the Healing Lodge in *Creating Choices* because it was deemed essential for native people themselves to develop a vision for the lodge (Palumbo and Palumbo 1992: 12). In the end, a Planning Circle developed the lodge independently, with a result that is significantly different from the other regional facilities in terms of both architecture and its operational plan.[29] The Planning Circle was established in March 1992 and included several elders as well as representatives from aboriginal women's organizations (the Aboriginal Women's Caucus and the Native Women's Association of Canada), the Nekaneet Reserve, the town of Maple Creek,[30] and CSC. That both government and nongovernment officials were represented on the Planning Circle was an acknowledgment of the importance of a 'more active and influential role for Aboriginal women and Elders in the planning process' (CSC 1992: 10). CSC (1994c: 6) notes that the operational plan for the Healing Lodge ensures that every facet of the lodge reflects native traditions and spirituality. When the Healing Lodge opened in November 1995, the Planning Circle was replaced by Kekunwem Konawuk, or 'keepers of the vision,' who were to ensure that the initiatives recommended by the task force were maintained (Sparling 1999: 119).

The concept of the Healing Lodge 'was derived from the teachings of the Four Directions in the Circle of Life with a holistic healing focus to develop the Spiritual (East), the Emotional (South), the Physical (West) and the Mental (North) aspects of the lives of federally sentenced aboriginal women' (Morin 1993: 29). The unique architectural features of the Healing Lodge include an elders' lodge, a cedar tipi, and a day care. The Healing Lodge is based on a circular design. It has several aboriginal staff members under the direction of a *kikawinàw* (Cree for 'mother,' equivalent to a warden), who depends on elders and medicine people for advice and for teaching the prisoners and staff. It was hoped that eventually at least 60 per cent of the staff will be aboriginal.

The Okimaw Ohci Healing Lodge focuses on promoting the following: 'a safe place for women; a caring attitude towards self, family and community; a belief in individualized client-specific planning; an understanding of the transitory aspects of Aboriginal Life; an appreciation of the healing role of children who are closer to the spirit world; and pride in surviving difficult backgrounds and personal experiences' (CSC 1997a: 11).

At the Healing Lodge, 'healing' is operationalized as 'self-knowledge – to acquire a thorough awareness of self and the issues that affected one's life in order to start the journey towards healing; equality – to acquire the knowledge and ability to empower oneself so that one can deal with the work from an equal position; and Aboriginal spirituality and tradition – to acquire and/or deepen knowledge and understanding of one's role as a woman, mother and community member through Aboriginal teachings, traditions and spirituality' (CSC 1997a: 12).

Clearly, the prison is constructed as a place of healing, notwithstanding aboriginal reformers' concerns that imprisonment is inherently incompatible with aboriginal culture and traditions. The concepts of healing, caring, and community are used to govern the conduct of prisoners, and to foster the development of self-governing aboriginal citizens who understand their responsibilities as a 'woman, mother, and community member.' A woman who resists this caring and well-intentioned intervention is subject to 'mediation and conflict resolution,' wherein she is 'held accountable for [her] actions, and the consequences to [her] actions focus on reparation to the community of the Healing Lodge and learning to handle conflict in a responsible manner' (CSC 1997a: 12).

The Healing Lodge depends heavily on community involvement and the notion of a shared responsibility between the community, women prisoners, and correctional officials. The community, reformers, advocates, and CSC see the Healing Lodge as a 'success.' It is perhaps the closest that the Canadian government has come to resolving the 'predicament of governing' aboriginal prisoners in a politically acceptable way. Although the Healing Lodge is not without it critics, its widespread acceptance as an alternative mode of governing suggests a potential reconfiguration of state and 'community' relations and a growing trend toward the 'privatization' and 'civilianization' of state punishment.[31] However, before embracing the Healing Lodge as an innovative model of correctional progress, we need to examine its impact on the lives of incarcerated aboriginal women, and the consequences of trying to blend a two distinct cultures (aboriginal and correctional).[32] While the Healing Lodge is unquestionably different from mainstream white prisons, it is still a federal prison. Some observers suggest that while the Healing Lodge has advanced aboriginal justice in theory, in practice its vision has been compromised by CSC's wider ideological and systemic constraints, and that many elements of aboriginal culture have been appropriated and redefined to fit the wider correctional agenda (Hayman 2000; Monture-Angus 1995, 2000).

Today, many observers feel that the once revered Healing Lodge is becoming more like a prison and that its 'aboriginal ideals' are slowing being lost or compromised. For example, the Healing Lodge was at first able to resist many static security measures; however, security is becoming increasingly intrusive. The original *kikawinàw* (warden) of the Healing Lodge came under a lot of pressure to comply with CSC's wishes in terms of standardizing operating practices with those of other prisons. Some authors have argued that the Healing Lodge has experienced a form of 'prisonization' (Monture-Angus 2000). As the vision of the Healing Lodge matures as it departs further and further from its original roots in aboriginal culture and tradition – and it gets closer to the traditional colonial legacy of imprisonment. While it was envisioned that the *kikawinàw* would be accountable to the Planning Circle, increasingly CSC is directing decision making, and marginalizing other members of the circle. Interestingly, in 1992 aboriginal women at P4W expressed some concern and anxiety about the Healing Lodge concept. They felt that 'as a correctional facility, it would not work, it would be another prison' (Morin 1993: 23).

According to Monture-Angus (2000), the bottom line is that the Healing Lodge is a *prison*, no matter how much it was inspired by aboriginal culture and traditions. She contends that while the Nekaneet people (whose land includes the lodge) and aboriginal women generally, understood that the lodge was to be part of the larger bureaucratic structure of CSC, they did not fully anticipate just how much the lodge would move away from emphasizing meaningful choices and opportunities to heal, towards a more punitive, punishment-centred mentality. As time passes, the local Aboriginal community, which was so central to the development of the lodge, and other concerned people, are increasingly being excluded from the Healing Lodge, its regime, and its vision.

The original vision of the Healing Lodge included community governance and the direct (i.e., not peripheral) involvement of the local aboriginal community. Unlike the CAEFS experience in the development of the other four prisons, aboriginal people were to remain part of the process to an unprecedented degree (Hayman 2000). Elders played a pivotal role in selecting the site for the lodge – a site chosen in part because of the good will and commitment of the Nekaneet Band, which resulted in their providing a sizable piece of land for the facility (Hayman

2000). That band also expressed an interest in helping shape the philosophy of the lodge through their elders . However, by the end of 1998 Nekaneet's elders were no longer as actively involved as when the lodge first opened, and increasingly, nonaboriginals are occupying senior management roles. Hayman (2000: 48) fears that 'there is a considerable risk of the expropriation of the Neekaneet's goodwill and their incorporation into a venture whose outcome they had not envisaged.' In terms of the Healing Lodge, one of the most disturbing departures from the vision of *Creating Choices* pertains to the fact that not all aboriginal women have access to it. If a woman has a maximum security classification, she cannot transfer to the Healing Lodge. Many aboriginal women remained at P4W, or in segregated maximum security units in men's penitentiaries such as Saskatchewan Penitentiary, or Regional Psychiatric Centre, or the newly opened maximum security units in regional facilities, where they have limited access to aboriginal programs and services. Sky Blue Morin's 1999 report, 'Whatever Happened to the Promises of *Creating Choices*: Federally Sentenced Maximum Security Women,' shows that the ethnic, cultural, and spiritual needs of aboriginal maximum security women continue to be neglected. She contends that CSC has not fully adhered to the recommendations of *Creating Choices* as it relates to federally sentenced aboriginal women, that these women have not been 'empowered' or provided with meaningful and responsible choices, and that they have not been incarcerated in supportive environments (1997: 23). Furthermore, 'although the *CSC Corporate Mission Objectives*, the *Corrections and Conditional Release Act*, *Creating Choices* recommendations and *Commissioner's Directives* have mandated intentions to implement programs that recognize Aboriginal culture and spiritual beliefs, *discrimination and racism against Federally Sentenced Aboriginal Women have been sited.* Against these odds, FSAW have not been able to reintegrate into their home communities and society successfully' (emphasis added; 1999: 24). Sadly, the women most in need of the Healing Lodge cannot access it.

Conclusions

The past twenty years of Canadian women's prison reform reveals that the concerns of women reformers about women's difference have been institutionalized, but they have also been recast. CSC claims to have developed a correctional model that satisfies the 'unique needs' of women prisoners, and with the opening of the new prisons, P4W was closed. The darker side of the institutionalization of women's concerns is the unanticipated redefining of women's issues to make them compatible with the existing institutional arrangements of incarceration. Various terms used in current correctional narratives such as 'empowerment' and 'healing' serve to make the activity of punishing less visible and less open to scrutiny. After all, few oppose or question the logic of 'empowering' oppressed groups or the 'healing' the 'sick.' Yet this language obscures the reality of who is doing what to whom. The next chapter explores this issue as it relates to notions of empowerment and shared responsibility. We could argue that in hindsight, feminists and other advocates for women prisoners should have pursued a more vigorous campaign for formal legal equality rights. This strategy might have won inmates more tangible benefits as opposed to the dubious benefits delivered through the CSC's cooption of the feminist politics of difference and empowerment. While many feminists and activists succeeded in having their philosophies reflected (at least in part) in the report of the task force, the outcome of their involvements was largely unanticipated.

Chapter Six

Empowering Prison: Neoliberal Governance

Penal governance has changed in the years following the tabling of *Creating Choices*, but not in the ways envisioned by the task force and reformers. As outlined in the previous chapter, many of the ideals reflected in *Creating Choices* were compromised while the most recent reforms were being operationalized. While Corrections Canada has adopted a more feminized penal discourse and improved the material conditions of some women prisoners, the more sinister and oppressive punitive elements of incarceration persist.[1] In this chapter, instead of continuing to document the widening gap between the ideals of *Creating Choices* and the vision of reformers,[2] I discuss in depth the complex dynamics of penal governance that are embedded in the recent changes. I will concern myself mainly with the recently tightened security in the new women's prisons, the ideal of empowerment, and the reintroduction of traditional forms of discipline (therapeutic and punitive).

Theorizing Changes

The recent literature on governmentality allows for a more complex analysis of the relations between state power and other modalities of governance, and of how power is exercised over individuals (Hudson 1998: 585). This provides an opportunity for those who are interested in the sociology of punishment to re-examine the dynamics of penality. Drawing on Foucault's claim (1991: 102) that 'we cannot see things in terms of the replacement of a society of sovereignty by a disciplinary society and the subsequent replacement of a society by government; in reality one has a triangle, sovereignty-discipline-government,' O'Malley (1996: 194) contends that the scholarly objective 'is not to map the unfolding of an evolution, but to understand the dynamics of such triangular relations, and the conditions that affect the roles taken by various elements in specific combinations.' Penal governing reflects various fragmented and flexible exercises of power that are inter-dependent (Hannah-Moffat 1997). Changes in contemporary penality cannot be viewed in isolation from past strategies of governing. We can combine past analyses of penal discipline with the more recent ac-counts of neoliberal strategies of governing to demonstrate changes in penality, and to enhance our understanding of the interrelatedness and interdependence of various strategies and logics of punishment.

Several analyses of juridical and welfare models of punishment have drawn on classic texts such as *Discipline and Punish* to emphasize the exercise of sovereignty and discipline. Without minimizing the impor-tance of these studies, it is important to note that they have focused mainly on repression, discipline, social control, and welfare interven-tions. More recent analyses of neoliberal strategies of government draw our attention to how 'public authorities seek to employ forms of exper-tise in order to govern society at a distance, without recourse to any direct forms of repression or intervention' (Barry, Osbourne, and Rose 1996: 14). Analyses of neoliberal forms of governing adopt a range of 'techniques of government that create a distance between decisions of formal political institutions and other social actors, conceive of these actors in new ways as subjects of responsibility, autonomy and choice, and seek to act upon them through shaping and utilizing their freedom' (Rose 1996a: 54; see also Rose 1993). In general, Rose contends that governing in advanced liberal societies includes three elements. *First*, a new relationship between politics and expertise, wherein the calculative regimes of positive knowledges of human conduct are replaced by the calculative actuarial regimes of accounting and financial management (1993: 295).[3] *Second*, a pluralization of new social technologies – a 'de-governmentalization of the state' – which according to Rose (1993: 296) involves ' a detaching of the centre from the various regulatory tech-nologies that it sought, over the twentieth century, to assemble into a single functioning network, and the adoption instead of a form of government through shaping the powers and wills of autonomous entities.' And *third*, a new specification of the subject of government, wherein 'the regulation of conduct becomes a matter of each individu-al's desire to govern their own conduct freely in the service of the maximization of their happiness and fulfilment that they take to be their own' (1996: 59). This neoliberal conception of the self-governing subject constructs the individual as a rational, free, responsible, and prudent consumer who is capable of minimizing and managing risk. Here, the exercise of authority is the outcome of free choice.[4]

Using this perspective, contemporary scholars have argued that techniques of crime control, prevention, and punishment are being transformed, and that new modes of governing crime and criminality are emerging (Feeley and Simon 1992, 1994; O'Malley 1992, 1994, 1996, 1998; Simon 1993; Garland 1996a, 1997; Pratt 1997; Hudson 1998; Rose and Valverde 1998). David Garland (1996a), in his analysis of neoliberal strategies of crime control, contends that the pervasiveness of high crime rates and the well-recognized limits of criminal justice agencies have created a new predicament for governments searching for new strategies[5] to cope with the social and political demands of crime control. He outlines some of the dynamic aspects of new neoliberal strategies of crime control, 'governing at a distance,' and related criminological knowledges.

In this chapter I build on these analyses by showing how these strategies and knowledges have affected recent reforms to Canada's federal system for imprisoning women, and how these new strategies function in a triangular relationship with sovereignty and discipline. I discuss the centrality of responsibilization strategies to the Correctional Service of Canada's new women-centred approach to the management, reform, and healing of incarcerated women. I analyse the government's new emphasis on 'empowerment' (as outlined in the 1990 Task Force on Federally Sentenced Women and related policy documents), and evaluate the logic and interpretive politics of empowerment strategies. I show how 'empowerment' – a term previously associated with radical activists and social movements – was used just as easily by CSC to justify the establishment of the regimes at the five new regional prisons for women. I examine reflexively how feminist and aboriginal knowledges contributed to the construction of empowerment as a legitimate and viable penal reform strategy; and show how feminist and aboriginal reformers' notions of empowerment came to be aligned with very different political rationalities and used by policymakers and correctional officials as a strategy of responsibilization and further linked to actuarial models of risk management.[6] In particular, I show how these knowledges become linked to penal power and come to be used to create new regimes of governing *and* to reinforce pre-existing relations of power. Finally, I consider some of the limitations of neoliberal responsibilization strategies. I discuss the reassertion of sovereign and disciplinary power, when it comes to governing those who fail to take responsibility for their own empowerment, to show how neoliberal strategies of government develop alongside, and operate in conjunction with, other forms of power.

Renegotiating Boundaries: Responsibilizing the Community and the Offender

Of particular interest is Garland's description (1996a: 452) of *responsibilization strategies*, which involve 'the central government seeking to act upon crime not in a direct fashion through state agencies (police, courts, prisons, social work, etc.) but instead acting indirectly, seeking to activate action on the part of non-state agencies and organizations.' Responsibilization strategies involve a series of new techniques and methods 'whereby the state seeks to bring about action on the part of private agencies and individuals – either by *simulating new forms of behaviour* or by *stopping established habits*' (emphasis in the original; Riley and Mayhew 1980; also cited in Garland 1996a: 452). As the previous chapters illustrated, the use of volunteers and private organizations in punishment is not new. However, the relations between the state and these agents have changed.

Through strategies such as responsibilization, the central government is 'seeking to renegotiate the question of what is properly a state function and what is not' (Garland 1996a: 453). According to Garland (1996a: 453), 'the reoccurring message of this approach is that the state is not and cannot effectively be responsible for preventing and controlling crime.' The new responsibilization strategies depend on the creation of partnerships between the state and 'private'[7] organizations and individuals. This devolution of the state's responsibility for crime prevention and offender reform is taking place at a number of levels in Canadian women's penality. For example, nongovernmental agencies and volunteer services are increasingly being expected to participate as 'partners' in crime prevention strategies and in the development and implementation of offender reform strategies. Thus, the report of the Task Force on Federally Sentenced Women, like other recent task forces, stresses the 'shared responsibility' of the offender, the community, and the state in the reform process.[8] In keeping with this 'message,' the preface to that report, *Creating Choices*, notes that community partnerships are central to the production and implementation of long-term solutions to the problems that Canadian federal female offenders have long faced. The task force's conceptualization of shared responsibility emphasizes the responsibilities of the prisoner, the government, and the community. Offenders are now seen as being responsible for their own reform; but more importantly, strategies such as empowerment, risk management, and shared responsibility are now being mobilized to responsibilize prisoners. These discursive shifts are examples of how penality in certain situations is being reconfigured through the responsibilization of the community and the offender.

The governance of women prisoners is no longer conceptualized as *solely* the responsibility of the federal government; rather, it is also perceived as the collective responsibility of the community and even the individual responsibility of the offender. Clearly, the government's responsibility for reforming and reintegrating offenders has in some ways shifted to community agencies and to the offender; yet at the same time, the government's new strategies of responsibilization do not entail the simple off-loading of state functions (cf. Garland 1996a: 454). Rather, a new form of government-at-a-distance has emerged. It consists of 'a new mode of governing [offenders] with its own forms of knowledge, its own objectives, its own techniques and apparatuses' (Rose and Miller 1992, cited in Garland 1996a: 454). The following analysis shows how Corrections Canada's reliance on empowerment clearly indicates both a new mode of government-at-a-distance *and* a continued reliance on past modes of disciplinary government, which persist alongside neoliberal forms of governing.

Creating an Empowerable Subject: Supporting Knowledges

Arguably, 'subjects are constituted in a whole variety of ways in different legal contexts and forums,' and 'each of these subjectifications has a history, each is differently suffused by the norms and values of positive knowledge' (Rose and Valverde 1998: 575). One of the preconditions for a new form of governing appears to be the ability to reconstruct subjectivity – in this case, the female criminal subject. In exploring this element of governance, Garland (1996a: 461) suggests that 'increasingly dualistic, polarized, and ambivalent' criminological knowledges play a critical role in this reconstruction. He suggests that 'there is a *criminology of the self,* that characterises offenders as rational consumers, just like us; and there is a *criminology of the other,* of the threatening outcast, the fearsome stranger, the excluded and embittered' (1996a: 461). The 'criminology of the self,' which offers a neoliberal image of the responsible and rational individual, is quite apparent in feminist, aboriginal, and reformers' portrayals of the woman prisoner. This image is simultaneously embraced and rejected by the state – in this case, the criminal justice system. The narratives of reformers shape and are integrated into certain institutional policies and practices.

Feminist criminology has expanded, as has our awareness and understanding of the issues and experiences of women in conflict with the law. Feminist research on female offenders, victims, and workers in the criminal justice system has revealed a number of disturbing patterns of discrimination and ignorance. Feminist/aboriginal advocates on the task force argued that correctional policies should reflect the specific and unique reality of the female offender. This reality is characterized by qualitative differences in the types of crimes committed by women and by women's social, economic, cultural, and political experiences, which are generally different from men's. Echoing the concerns of critical criminologists and political lobbyists, task force members contended that women in conflict with the law are different from their male counterparts on a number of levels. Examples: women tend to commit fewer and less violent offences than men; they have fewer vocational and educational skills; they have more extensive histories of physical, sexual, and emotional abuse; they are more likely to have substance abuse problems and to be single parents. It follows from all this that a penal system designed with men in mind cannot meet the specific needs of women prisoners. The research completed for the task force verified all of this and stressed that 'issues such as poverty, racism, wife battering, and sexual abuse are central to women's crime' (TFFSW 1990: 83). The task force also contended that each of these issues is more serious for aboriginal and visible minority women, who carry the additional burdens of racism and cultural alienation (TFFSW 1990; Sugar and Fox 1990). Thus, the task force recommended that culturally specific accommodations (i.e., a Healing Lodge) be made for aboriginal women, who are overrepresented in the Canadian federal prison population.[9]

When feminist criminologists discuss the issue of 'risk' in relation to the female offender, they tend either to use 'anti-risk' language or to locate the source of risk exclusively in male behaviour. In the first instance, feminists point out that women prisoners have generally been convicted of relatively minor, nonviolent offences, and that when women are perpetrators of violence the victim is often an abusive partner. Reformers and even state officials have lobbied for improved prison conditions and additional community programming on the basis that women in prison do *not* represent a substantial risk to public safety. In the second instance, feminist researchers argue that not only do women prisoners present little risk to society, but they are in fact *at risk* – of being victimized by men, or of harming themselves through self-mutilation and other self-abusive behaviours. Women in prison are in a situation similar to that of women in the community, in the sense that women in general often find themselves in 'risky situations' with few structural supports. Unlike the male prisoner, the female prisoner is rarely constructed as a risk to the community; but like women in the community, she is often portrayed as being at risk of being victimized by men.

These themes are outlined clearly in *Creating Choices* (TFFSW 1990), which uses a 'criminological discourse of the self' and resists pathologizing women's criminality. The task force's feminist articulation of a women-centred politics rests on the assumption that women as a group have a common set of experiences, and that as a group women are commonly disempowered.

The 'Will to Empower'[10]

Strategies such as empowerment are capable of assuming multiple meanings depending on how they are used and by whom. *Empowerment* is a common term, which was originally associated with the social movements of the 1960s and 1970s that sought radical political changes in social relations. More recently, the concept of empowering individuals (whether they be the poor, workers, patients, immigrants, students, citizens, or prisoners) has become popular in various political and policy circles.[11] The widespread use of this term everyday language has gradually depoliticized or deradicalized the language of empowerment, so that nowadays both advocates and policymakers easily resort to it. This malleability that is so characteristic of empowerment strategies is important when we come to consider how 'the will to empower has created a new series of relationships and conceptualisations of empowerment in academic disciplines, social services, neighbourhood agencies, social movements, and political groups' (Cruikshank 1994).

Thus, in Canadian women's penality, bureaucrats and feminist reformers alike uncritically champion empowerment. Part of the appeal of empowerment, for those who already have power, is that it enables them to informally and subtly govern marginalized populations in ways that encourage the latter to participate in their own reform; at the same time, it suggests that an alternative to past regimes is being offered. As Cruikshank (1994: 34–5) notes: 'The logic of empowerment targets the capacities of the powerless, measuring and seeking to maximize their actions, motivations and interests ... Here power works by soliciting the active participation of the poor in dozens of programs on the local level, programs that aim at the transformation of the poor into self sufficient, active, productive and participatory citizens.'

The feminist narrative of empowerment has contributed to a new and unique method of governing prisoners. Cruikshank (1994: 35) contends that the 'will to empower' marginalized groups often has these four characteristics: it is established by experts; it often entails a democratically unaccountable exercise of power, in that the relationship is typically initiated by one party that is seeking to empower another; it depends on knowledge of those to be empowered, which is often found in the social sciences and in the self-descriptions or self-disclosures of those being empowered; and it involves an exercise of power on the subjectivity of the empowered that is both voluntary and coercive.

The increased reliance on empowerment politics indicates a much wider systemic shift in governing; governments and corporations with little or no interest in politicizing disempowered groups are adopting discourses of empowerment to advance a neoconservative agenda of responsibilizing citizens. In coercive institutions such as prisons, governing is most commonly associated with the external policing and regulation of the behaviour of individuals. An emphasis on strategies such as empowerment suggests a greater reliance on self-governing. In this setting, empowerment discourses make links between the aspirations of individuals and those of government; and they contribute to the formation of prudent subjects who are prepared to take responsibility for their actions, and for whom the ethic of discipline is part of their mental fabric and not a product of external policing (cf. Rose 1993). Below I examine the instability of empowerment's meaning; I also illustrate on a material level some of the limitations and contradictions that arise when the language of empowerment is used to achieve organizational changes.

Empowerment: A Flexible Strategy of Government

Iris Young (1994: 49), in her article on the treatment and punishment of female drug addicts, notes that 'empowerment is like democracy: everyone is for it, but rarely do they mean the same thing by it.' Young's comments capture some of the difficulties associated with the current emphasis on empowerment in women's penal and treatment regimes. In this context, at least two interpretations of empowerment can be identified. Traditionally, feminists have embraced empowerment (ideological, political, and economic) as a means for transforming the lives of women; when power relations are restructured, women are able to make choices and regain control of their lives. Young notes that for feminists, service providers, and activists, empowerment can mean 'the development of individual autonomy, self-control, and confidence' and/ or 'the development of a sense of collective influence over social conditions in one's life' (1994: 49). Empowerment, as defined by Young and social advocates, is particularly difficult to accomplish in a prison setting because the flexibility to make choices and control one's surroundings does not exist. In general, feminists' interpretations of empowerment and their reliance on this strategy of reform fail to take into account a broader institutional context and history. Prisons are organized to limit individual expressions of autonomy, control, and choice. They are sites of repression; behind their walls we find an undeniable imbalance in the relations of power between the 'keepers' and the 'kept.' Rarely are the 'keepers' able or willing to relinquish their power to facilitate empowerment. While incarcerated, women prisoners have little influence, collective or otherwise, over the conditions of their lives. In the end, the techniques typically associated with empowerment are in the control of the prevailing organization.

A 'women-centred empowerment model' of punishment feminizes the discourse and practices of imprisonment without fundamentally challenging or restructuring the disciplinary relations of power in prisons. This is born out by CSC's approach to adopting an empowerment discourse in state narratives on women's penality. Ironically, CSC claims it is committed to empowering women prisoners; yet empowerment for CSC is not about fundamentally restructuring relations of disciplinary power in the prison, but rather about adding a new dimension to existing relations by using empowerment strategies to responsibilize prisoners.

In the description of the principle of *empowerment* in *Creating Choices* (TFFSW, 1990: 105–6), it is claimed that the structural inequities experienced by women prisoners are similar to broader gender inequalities. It is noted that the 'research and the words of federally sentenced women have repeatedly stressed the connections between women's involvement in the criminal justice system and the inequalities, hardships, and suffering experienced by women in our society.' Empowerment is connected to the perception that women prisoners, like women generally, lack self-esteem and as a result believe themselves to have little power to direct their lives: 'They feel disempowered, unable to create or make choices, unable to help create a more rewarding, productive future, even if realistic choices are presented to them' (1990: 105). The task force locates the disempowerment of women in two sites: in the structural arrangements of society, and in the woman herself, with an emphasis on the latter.[12]

The task force contends that 'the attitudes, barriers and suffering, which are consequences of sexism and racism erode the self esteem of women in general' (1990: 106). This incidence of 'general low self esteem' is particularized to the federal female offender. For example, the report notes that 'federally sentenced women typically are poorly educated, unemployed, and have survived physical and/or sexual abuse. Their life circumstances, along with feelings of guilt, fear, anxiety, alienation and confusion which are often elicited when they are apprehended and sentenced by the justice system, combine to produce a group of women with extraordinarily low self esteem' (1990: 106).

It is further argued that low self-esteem reduces women's ability to cope, and creates circumstances in which they are unable to accept responsibility for their actions and choices. Criminal and self-destructive behaviour are both attributed to women's low self-esteem and disempowerment. The task force suggests that empowerment and improved self-esteem will give women the 'ability to accept and express responsibility for actions taken and future choices' (1990: 107). In the report, all of this is used to reaffirm a commitment to women-centredness and to reinforce a construction of women's shared disempowerment and marginalization.

Feminist and aboriginal knowledges are used selectively to support an empowering/responsibilization strategy. Not surprisingly, however, feminist and aboriginal understandings of women's disempowerment and its remedy cannot be neatly incorporated into correctional narratives and practices. Quite independently, CSC has redefined and constructed empowerment and notions of shared responsibility so that these are compatible with its own independent strategy of penal government. Thus, a 'critical feminist criminology of the self' is being used to construct a rational, prudent, and reformable subject[13] who can be empowered so as to change her life circumstances and to take responsibility for her future and past criminal behaviour.

As noted, the difficulty is that strategies of empowerment tend to resonate with multiple and conflicting objectives. While the strategy of empowerment coincides with the feminist objectives of the reformers, it is also compatible with the longstanding objectives of correctional officials. Empowerment alternatively is defined by CSC as 'the process through which women gain insight into their situation, identify their strengths, and are supported and challenged to take positive action to gain control of their lives' (1994a: 9). Empowerment in this context has a different meaning from empowerment in feminist reform narratives. CSC further indicates that its empowering process 'acknowledges and holds FSW [federally sentenced women] accountable for their actions, but also recognizes their actions in a wider social context' (1994a: 9). Previous welfare penal strategies of rehabilitation viewed the state as responsible for reforming the offender; in contrast, this empowerment strategy makes the offender responsible for her own rehabilitation. Because new strategies of responsibilization seem less intrusive and less regulatory, few contest them.

In this new correctional framework, the offender is responsible for her own self-governance and for minimizing and managing her own needs and the risk she poses to both the public and herself. This is similar to what O'Malley (1992) calls *prudentialism*. Prudentialism refers to a construct of governance that removes the key conception of regulating individuals by collectivist risk management, and throws back upon the individual the responsibility for managing their own risk' (O'Malley 1992: 261). It is implicitly accepted that the prison does not rehabilitate the offender; instead, it is the woman who makes prudent choices that ensure a responsible, self-sufficient future. The responsibility of CSC is to provide women with opportunities and to facilitate this process.

A Meaningful and Responsible Choice?

This strategy of neoliberal penality is different from the welfarist models of the past. A neoliberal penality

> seeks through the calculus of punishment primarily to press upon the offender (and the potential offender) the model of individual responsibility. Accepting responsibility for one's actions does not imply accepting or obeying any specific set of morals. It implies accepting the *consequences* of one's actions. The individual may choose, are free to choose, in a way and

to a degree never envisaged by normative disciplinarity – but if those choices lead into criminal offending, they must take the burden of their choice (O'Malley 1994: 15).

A recent phenomenon of modern forms of government is a shift in emphasis away from 'choice and responsibility for choice' toward 'creating the conditions for responsible choice' (Simon 1994) whereby making choices is as much a process of government as a practice of freedom. Given Simon's understanding of choice as a process of government, the provision 'meaningful and responsible choices' in new, women-centred prisons takes on a new meaning.

In the prison context, empowerment becomes a technology of self-governance that requires the woman to take responsibility for her actions in order to satisfy not her own objectives but rather those of the authorities. The choices that women are empowered to make are censored and predetermined by the wider penal structure. Women in prison are allowed only those limited choices that the *administration* deems to be meaningful and responsible. Thus, programming choices to accept treatment, such as feminist therapy and Alcoholics Anonymous, are deemed meaningful and responsible, while to escape or join a riot is not meaningful or responsible, even though these latter choices may be truly empowering. It is judges, parole boards, correctional officers, and therapists, not the prisoner, who ultimately determine which actions are a meaningful and responsible or empowering. Under a new, self-governing regime of empowerment, the authorities can regulate women through the decisions the women themselves make, without resorting to overt expressions of power. The new technologies steer choices and prevent misbehaviour, instead of deterring through punishment.

For example, the new prisons have a written program strategy that is designed to 'ensure that women receive the most effective programs at appropriate points in their sentence' (CSC 1994a: 4). This document identifies four core programs: Abuse and Trauma, Substance Abuse, Parenting, and Education and Employment Skills. The government sees these programs as addressing of the primary needs of women in prison, and as providing women with the opportunity to make 'meaningful and responsible choices' within a 'supportive environment,' and thus to be empowered. For example, the policy literature supporting the substance abuse program suggests that programming should be based on the 'the premise that learning to make well-informed choices and accepting responsibility for those choices is key for women to take control of their lives' (CSC 1995b: 1). This program, like the others, is based on a 'model of self change' rather than traditional 'therapy,' which is constructed as a more in-depth form of treatment.

The 'self-change model' places responsibility for change and risk minimization squarely on the shoulders of the offender. Thus, if a known substance abuser chooses not to participate in these programs, she is constructed as being in denial or as defiant and uncooperative, and therefore as more risky. Women may well choose to participate in certain programs simply because they know that doing so will improve their chances for parole/release. Nonetheless, a woman can be encouraged to participate in her own empowerment or responsibilization without threats. She is expected to constantly monitor herself and to control her own risk-generating behaviour. When she fails, more coercive disciplinary techniques of government are mobilized. For example, a positive urine test for drugs or visible signs of drug or alcohol use can lead to institutional charges, segregation, revocation of privileges, cancelled visits, or (in the case of community supervision) a return to prison. However, it is also evident that 'these new techniques do not so much replace these traditional measures as embed them in a far more comprehensive web of monitoring and intervention' (Simon 1994: 33). In some respects, models of self-help and responsibility ultimately re-legitimate the prison and the continued reliance on discipline.[14]

It can be argued that the governance or regulation of women prisoners is transformed into a question of self-governance through strategies of empowerment and shared responsibility. Power is exercised through formation strategies designed to encourage subjects to take responsibility for their actions, with only limited involvement of external mechanisms of policing. In this sense, individuals become responsible for carrying out actions that were previously state functions. In this way, the new or renewed emphasis on responsibility merges with old correctional methods of disciplining and reforming the irresponsible deviant. The proposed new solution to governing or regulating inmates is located not in the capacity of the penal regime to alter the behaviour of prisoners, but rather in self-governance or regulation. While the offender is still targeted for punitive interventions, accountability for reformative results shifts from the state (as in a welfare-based model) to the offender.

The individual prisoner is now responsible for her own discipline, which is facilitated by social science professionals at the request or choice of the prisoner. When defined in terms of responsibility, empowerment has a self-disciplinary quality that allows the state to govern at a distance. In penal settings, empowerment can be used to justify a variety of disciplinary techniques through the language of responsibility. It implicitly erodes the notion that CSC alone is responsible for reforming women prisoners. An 'empowering-responsibilizing strategy' leaves the state more powerful than before, and extends its capacity for action and influence. Women are expected to conform to a series of normative standards by attending vocational classes and programs in parenting, life skills, anger management, and so on. Ironically, it can be argued that women are now being sent to prison, and being kept longer in prison, with the goal of empowering them!

For CSC, empowerment is clearly about responsibilization and accountability. As Cruikshank noted (1994: 35), power in these situations tends to work by soliciting the active participation of prisoners in institutional 'programs that aim at the transformation of the [prisoner] into self-sufficient, active, productive, and participatory citizens.' Empowerment is used to justify and rationalize a variety of disciplinary techniques through a parallel discourse of responsibility. Having the offender take responsibility or ownership for her actions is of paramount importance for correctional institutions. This emphasis on responsibility coincides with feminist demands that women's experiences be integrated, and for a feminist strategy of empowerment, which after all does not require that offender 'agency' be displaced. In fact, feminists have fully acknowledged that the negation of personal accountability often results in the 'disempowerment of women by rendering them harmless victims, thus stripping them of self-determination' (Allen 1987a; Shaw 1991a, 1991b, cited in Kendall 1993: 14). Feminists agree that women prisoners are not simply victims, but add that their life circumstances and the social context of their offences must be acknowledged. This aspect of feminist notions of empowerment corresponds with CSC's agenda, which clearly constructs the offender as accountable and responsible for her actions, irrespective of structural impediments and her 'level' of victimization. The difference is that CSC perceives empowerment as linked to *responsibility* rather than to relations of power.

CSC, which has a legal responsibility in the criminal justice process, seeks to make the offender accountable and responsible for her criminal behaviour, irrespective of structural or situational constraints. It is this process that CSC terms empowerment. This individualistic approach contradicts feminist perspectives, which place women's actions in a wider social, political, and economic context. Despite the rise of empowerment discourse, women-centred corrections is about responsibilizing the prisoner rather than 'empowerment' as defined by those who wrote *Creating Choices*. This strong emphasis on responsibility decontextualizes feminist/aboriginal constructions of women's oppression; it also disregards feminist/aboriginal analyses of the social, economic, and political barriers experienced by women, in particular by marginalized women. The new strategy of empowerment softens disciplinary power even while reinforcing it. It is clear from all this that empowerment strategies can be aligned with different political rationalities. The 'will to empower' involves both coercive and 'voluntary' exercises of power over the subjectivity of the empowered (Cruikshank 1994: 35). The following illustrates how punitive punishments and empowerment-based responsibilization strategies depend on each other.

The Unempowerable Prisoner: The Triangle of Sovereignty–Discipline–Government

According to Simon (1994: 17), 'a shift in the acceptance of particular political rationalities may undermine the stability of a government, requiring efforts at redefinition and reform.' This claim is relevant to the problem of 'empowering penal government' that CSC currently faces. This dilemma is mainly about prisoners' resistance and the general failure of the new correctional regimes to adequately responsibilize 'problem prisoners.' Given that the 'will to empower' is more often than not imposed on a captive audience of prisoners, by a sometimes well-intentioned state armed with a body of knowledge about what is best for the prisoners, resistance is not surprising. Recent events and recent changes in government policy show how neoliberal strategies such as empowerment develop alongside, and operate in conjunction with, sovereignty and discipline. For example, consider recent events at P4W and at two of the new regional prisons (in Truro and Edmonton). In these prisons there have been a number of escapes, suicide attempts, cases of self-injury, and assaults on staff. In addition, one prisoner has died. The government's reaction to these incidents shows how the contemporary rhetoric of empowerment can disguise and conceal ongoing repressive (and sometimes abusive) penal practices.

When government-at-a-distance fails, techniques of disciplinary governance are reasserted and legitimated through administrative discourses of risk and public safety.[15] In adapting to some recent failures, CSC has reformulated some of its administrative objectives and priorities. It has developed new managerial techniques and rationales for controlling the 'resistant prisoner,' who presents too great a risk to public safety and/or to the 'good order of the institution' to remain in one of the regional prisons. Here, the objective of responding to the unique needs and experiences of women prisoners is perceived as secondary to the objective of protecting the public from 'dangerous criminals.'

CSC's redefinition of some prisoners as 'difficult to manage' – in essence 'unempowerable' or 'high risk/high need' – requires the deployment of what Garland (1996: 46) calls *a criminology of the other*, which 'represents criminals as dangerous members of distinct racial and social groups that bear little resemblance to *us*.' Furthermore, 'it is a criminology that trades in images, archetypes, and anxieties, rather than in careful analysis and research findings' (Garland 1996a: 461). Until recently, feminist knowledges have not constructed women as violent or dangerous (Shaw 2000). Recent correctional policies and narratives of the 'unempowerable' (i.e., high-risk and high-need) offender demonize, pathologize, and medicalize women who resist well-intentioned, empowering correctional interventions. These women (who are mainly aboriginal or mentally ill) are ultimately portrayed as a danger – to the prison culture, to the public, and to themselves. They are constructed as needing more intensive and ultimately more punitive supervision to ensure public safety. The construction of this group of women as 'disruptive,' 'risky,' 'mentally ill,' and 'potential escapees' is used to justify the use of force, searches, involuntary transfers, and prolonged solitary confinement, as well as the transfer of some women to segregated units in men's maximum security penitentiaries.

Adjusting the Vision – Re-Forming Creating Choices

It is now held by many inside and outside corrections that *Creating Choices* promoted an unachievable ideal. Within CSC, *Creating Choices* is now simply referred to as a philosophy statement. While the benevolent rhetoric of empowerment and healing embodied in *Creating Choices* has permeated correctional discourses, the more sinister and punitive disciplinary reality of 'corrections' persists. In the wake of a number of serious incidents at the new regional prisons, significant changes have been made in the design of these penal regimes that amount to an abandonment of the approach urged in the task force report. These incidents have also fostered the construction of an 'unempowerable' and 'difficult to manage' woman prisoner.

Arbour Commission

In 1994 an incident occurred at P4W that led to the establishment of the Commission of Inquiry into Certain Events at the Prison for Women (hereafter the Arbour Commission), led by Madame Justice Louise Arbour. The initial incident and the resulting treatment of the prisoners while in segregation received national attention and revealed the 'dual personality' of women's corrections.[16] There remains a lack of consensus as to what exactly happened at P4W in April 1994. The report of the Arbour Commission (1996: 25) states that on the evening of 22 April 1994, at P4W, a brief but violent confrontation took place between correctional staff and six prisoners.[17] Afterwards, these women were placed in segregation and charged under the Criminal Code. Five of the six women pled guilty to these charges. The tensions in the segregation unit were high; the incident was seen by CSC as an unprecedented assault on staff, and generated tremendous hostility, resentment, and fear among those who worked in the prison (1996: 36). Also unprecedented was that the staff later ignored the warden's orders to unlock ranges, and demonstrated outside the prison demanding that the prisoners involved in the incident be transferred to a Special Handling Unit (which houses prisoners deemed to be particularly dangerous and as threats to institutional security).

In the days following the event, women prisoners were strip-searched by a male emergency response team, subjected to prolonged (and ultimately illegal) segregation, denied fundamental rights and freedoms (such as access to legal counsel), and involuntarily transferred to a makeshift Special Handling Unit in a men's penitentiary (Kingston Penitentiary). At several levels of the correctional bureaucracy, there was an overall disdain for the women and a blatant disregard for the law and correctional policy. The internal system of checks and balances devised to protect prisoners' rights, and to minimize abuses of power, failed. These violations of law and policy in the management of the women extended from the front lines all the way to the top of the administrative hierarchy, including the Commissioner of Corrections. Ultimately, Madame Justice Arbour found that 'in terms of general correctional issues, the facts of this inquiry have revealed a disturbing lack of commitment to the ideals of justice on the part of the Correctional Service ... the two areas in which the Service has been most delinquent are the management of Segregation and the administration of the grievance process.' Arbour's report paid particular attention to the absence of 'a culture or rights' and 'the rule of law' in P4W and in the prison environment more generally (1996: 179–89). She stated that while the rule of law is fundamental to penal governance and to the establishment of legal norms in penal institutions, and while there is an abundance of rules and laws governing penal relations, prisons can represent a complete negation of every principle of legality (Lemonde 1995; cited in Arbour 1996: 180–1). She then added that this 'dual characteristic' or contradiction was apparent throughout the inquiry. Although there were various rules, policies, and laws that govern every minute aspect of CSC and the conduct of its representatives at P4W, 'the applicable law or policy in a given situation appeared to be either unknown or easily forgotten and ignored' (1996: 181). Furthermore, 'despite this plethora of normative requirements, one sees little evidence of the will to yield pragmatic concerns to the dictates of legal order' (1996: 181).

In response to these violations, Justice Arbour reaffirmed the essential limits on the state's power to punish: 'One must resist the temptation to trivialize prisoners' rights as either an insignificant infringement of rights, or as an infringement of rights of people who do not deserve better. When law grants a right, it is no less important that such a right be respected because the person entitled to it is a prisoner' (1996: 183). She also noted that these rights provide protection to vulnerable populations, including prisoners: 'The right not to be subjected to non-consensual body cavity searches is not particularly valuable to those who are unlikely ever to be subjected to such an intrusive procedure. It is only valuable, and therefore should be enforced with the greatest vigour, in cases where such searches are likely to be undertaken. In the same way, the right for a woman not to be strip searched by a man is of little significance to someone who has never been and is realistically unlikely to ever be strip searched by anyone' (1996: 183).

These statements remind us of the due process claims of prisoners' rights advocates in the early 1970s. Madame Justice Arbour's findings and recommendations had a powerful impact on Canadian Corrections.[18] At the same time, the events that led to the inquiry were embedded in the correctional memory as an example of how dangerous and violent some women in prison can be in certain circumstances. These events have been used to legitimate differential and punitive treatment of 'difficult to manage women' who act out and resist institutional authority.

Increased Security

The April 1994 incident affected the plans for the new prisons – in particular, the plans for a newly defined population of 'difficult to manage' women. That being said, the intensification of static security at the new prisons prisons predated April 1994.

Creating Choices acknowledged that a small number of women 'have come to rely on violence in order to survive overwhelming abuse in their lives.' (TFFSW 1990: 90). However, the report also argued that 'these women will respond well to a more supportive environment' (1990: 90). In keeping with the wider academic literature, it contended that women present a risk to themselves, through self-injury, more often than to others; and that punitive environments exacerbate and possibly motivate such self-directed violence. The task force stated clearly that 'punishments such as segregation, whether in response to disciplinary offenses, the "good order of the institution," or whether in response to an individual being victimized by other prisoners, is *inappropriate when the aim is to empower women to accept responsibility and make good choices for themselves'* (TFFSW 1990: 9 – emphasis added). It consistently argued that every effort must be made to use dynamic (rather than static) security measures for women, and that in the event that women prisoners required separation, it should be for a limited amount of time and only as a last resort. However, when *Creating Choices* was operationalized, CSC imposed a different interpretation on the report's findings.

Briefing notes prepared by CSC on their 'strategy to manage federally sentenced women who behave violently' suggest that *Creating Choices* proposed that cottages at the new prisons be designated for women displaying signs of disturbance or who are unsettled, and that some cottages be designated for special use – for example, for high-risk or high-need women (CSC 1995c: 1). This interpretation is not literal: *Creating Choices* did not clearly specify how to deal with such women. Furthermore, the task force envisioned that all the cottages would be staffed, whereas this is not presently the case. During the operationalization phase it was decided that correctional staff would not be posted in living units, in order 'to minimize the possibility of administrative activities occurring in a residential setting' (CSC 1992: 37). Instead, a telephone was installed in each house so that women would have direct access to staff in an emergency.

The operational plan for the regional prisons, which was approved by CSC's Executive Committee in July 1992, contended that approximately 10 per cent of federally sentenced women required enhanced security measures because they were escape risks or because they had learned to rely on violence (CSC 1992: 38; see also CSC 1995c). The same plan proposed that enhanced units be built. This seems to be the first mention of the need for such units. To satisfy this requirement, each facility's design was altered to include an enhanced unit in the main administration and program building that would provide twenty-four-hour staffing. Women would be placed in the enhanced unit whose behaviour was 'deemed to constitute a security risk.' There, staff would provide them with opportunities for intensive one-on-one counselling and encourage them to modify their inappropriate behaviour, with the goal of returning them to, or facilitating their initial placement in, a regular house (1992: 38). Furthermore, it was anticipated that a classification system for women would be established specifically designed to estimate a woman's risk and ability to function in this environment (CSC 1995c: 1). To date, however, such a system has not been developed (Hannah-Moffat and Shaw 2000b). While a security management system has been drafted (Hannah-Moffat 1999), this gender-sensitive assessment tool is not presently being used in the regional prisons to make decisions about admitting or discharging women from enhanced units.

It is reported that during this developmental phase, concerns were raised about whether staff would be able to manage, in one small facility, women who presented a range of concerns (including acting out, self-injury, and risk of escape) along with new admissions whose behaviour was not yet known. These concerns were magnified by the April 1994 incident at P4W. However, it was acknowledged that because the regional prisons were too small to offer such specialization, the enhanced units would have to be designed to accommodate diverse groups of women. Various options were considered for separating newly admitted women from those who were 'acting out.' One option considered was separate accommodations for women who behaved violently in a separate regional or national facility or in a men's facility. This option was rejected at the time because it was deemed too costly in

terms of program delivery, because it might hamper the woman's return to her 'home' facility, and because it might result in further geo-
graphical dislocation for some women. A second option considered
was the enhancement of perimeter security. This approach was also
rejected, because of the costs involved and because it would penalize
the majority of women, who do not require this level of containment. A
third option, which *was* adopted, was to modify the enhanced units to
allow for the physical separation of the two populations, while maintaining the requirement that one permanent staff be present. To ensure
that a bed was always immediately available when a woman acted out
violently, the capacity of the units was increased. This expansion, which
was partly in response to the April 1994 incident, was justified as
follows: 'It is clear that the FSW [federally sentenced woman] may act
out on a group basis rather than individually and that effective intervention may require repeated separation over a period of time of a
woman from her colleagues' (CSC 1995b: 3).

CSC also advocated developing a regionally based protocol with
men's facilities to accommodate women prisoners on a short-term,
crisis basis until a longer-term strategy could be implemented. This
was in the event that a given enhanced unit was 'temporarily exhausted' (i.e., full).

Enhanced security cells were expanded in each of the new regional
prisons. This was in response to correctional and staff concerns about
security and discipline in the new regional prisons, which up until this
time had relied more heavily on dynamic (as opposed to static) security
measures. 'Enhanced security' cells in the new prisons have doubled in
number from the original designs; they have also been modified to
allow for double-bunking: 'The enhanced unit is contained within the
main building; it is a closed unit and has its own enclosed exercise yard.
The unit consists of four cells and program areas, with two levels of
supervision (Segregation – 23 hour restriction; or Maximum with access
to program participation). The unit has 24 hour supervision by staff. *It
provides housing for inmates who: exhibit violent behaviour and/or have special needs, and /or serve disciplinary sentences'* (emphasis added; Whitehall
1995: 22).

Going by this description, women who are considered 'high risk' are
not managed any differently from women who are 'high need' because
of 'mental health' problems. At present, CSC is developing separate
strategies for dealing with these two groups of women. Additional
concerns about the regional facilities surfaced in response to riots,
escapes, and suicides and to an alleged murder at the newly opened

regional prison in Edmonton.[19] Collectively, these events were used to justify increased levels of static security and the building of fences around all of the facilities except the Healing Lodge. These measures, which were previously rejected, ultimately intensified security in all prisons, and thus all federally sentenced women were affected. This was a significant departure from the philosophy put forward in *Creating Choices*. When static security was increased, the majority of prisoners, who do not require this level of security and who pose a minimal risk to public safety, found themselves in an environment that was much more restrictive than necessary. One of the often repeated criticisms of P4W that these new facilities had sought to rectify was that all women were subject to high security measures, regardless of their security classification. This situation has now been replicated in the regional prisons. Furthermore, minimum security women do not have access to living units outside the fence, as is the case in men's minimum-security prisons.

Some regional prisons were facing the prospect of overcrowding, with the demand for beds exceeding capacity. This, and the escapes and other incidents in Edmonton, reportedly prompted a decision by CSC to incarcerate all maximum security women and those with intensive mental health needs in small units in men's institutions and in P4W.[20] Thus, between September 1996 and May 1997, small, completely self-contained units for women classified as maximum security were opened in Saskatchewan Penitentiary, in Saint-Anne-des-Plaines Penitentiary, Quebec, and in Springhill Penitentiary, Nova Scotia. In 1997, CSC, in spite of its new commitment to women-centredness and the criticism received as a result of the Arbour Commission, attempted to transfer the maximum security women remaining in P4W to the Regional Treatment Centre, a men's treatment facility located inside the walls of Kingston Penitentiary. This transfer was thwarted by a court action brought forward by the women prisoners. As a result, they remained at P4W. This 'temporary' arrangement, which was in place until May 2000, has allowed the women to remain in their home region while security concerns are addressed. These transfers, and attempted transfers, of women into men's prisons – particularly Kingston Penitentiary – are highly ironic, given the history of federal women's imprisonment. Interestingly, the Board of Investigation report (CSC 1996b) that examined events at Edmonton was reportedly what led to the removal of maximum security women from the regional prisons; yet it had not recommended this course of action. Instead it highlighted a series of problems related to the inexperience of staff and poor security measures in a facility that was opened too quickly. Under the correct conditions, could maximum secuirity women have been managed in the regional prisons as they were first envisioned without additional static security measures? We will never know.

Just as the maximum security units were opening, CSC established an 'intensive healing program' (Canada 1999b) at the Regional Psychiatric Centre (Prairies). This program is designed to help women with 'borderline personality disorders' or 'who exhibit a combination of all or most of the following behaviours: persistent and severe self-destructive behaviour, identity disturbance, depression, difficulty controlling anger, severe disassociation, problems in intimate relationships, suicidality, severe anxiety, low self-esteem, and severe substance abuse' (Rivera 1996: 13). These are the women defined by CSC as 'traditionally most difficult to manage' and 'whose behaviours are an impediment to programming aimed at reducing recidivism.' This intensive healing program was also implemented at P4W for the women who remained there due to their maximum security status.[21] This program was based partly on Dr Rivera's 1996 assessment of the acute mental health needs of twenty-six women (Rivera 1996).

A national strategy for high-risk, high-need women is presently being developed.[22] The new Intensive Healing Strategy[23] developed by CSC proposes another expansion of the existing enhanced security units in the regional prisons to accommodate thirty women classified as maximum security. Also, a structured living environment or 'healing house' is to be built at each regional prison to accommodate thirty-five minimum or medium security women who have mental health needs that require more intensive support. Specialized staff will be hired for these units. These new facilities are expected to open between fall of 2000 and 2001 and to result in the closing of the women's units in men's penitentiaries and in P4W. Once again, this strategy (which is still in the planning phase) will involve upgrading security arrangements. However, it will not affect the Healing Lodge – it seems that aboriginal women classified as maximum security will continue to be denied access to the Healing Lodge. It is hoped that these new arrangements for the maximum security women and those with more acute mental health needs will present a more 'humane alternative.' However, critics are sceptical. According to CSC, all decisions on these populations will be based on individualized risk assessments. The belief is that the sharing of institutional space with the rest of the federally sentenced population will provide these women with incentives to improve.

CSC reports that 'as these women develop accountability and personal responsibility they will have their privileges increased and potentially be reintegrated into the general population.'[24] CSC feels that this new model will give them the 'capacity to contain' but also the 'capacity to reintegrate.' This model offers some women additional therapeutic interventions, but it also enhances the medicalization of women's deviance and relies heavily on punitive measures. The interventions planned for the maximum security population are highly restrictive and invasive.[25] This increased punitiveness, which is aimed at gaining the compliance of women who continue to resist institutional authority, has affected the governance of the entire population. All women are being punished for the actions of a few (Pate 2000).

Presently, not all women have access to the new prisons. Before they can be transferred to the Healing Lodge or to one of the new regional prisons, women prisoners must achieve medium security status. These facilities are not yet equipped to deal with women with acute mental health needs or who present other behavioural issues. This is a fundamental departure from the position articulated in *Creating Choices*, which saw all women being housed in the new prisons, and not returning to the deplorable conditions in men's penitentiaries, where they are 'too few to count.' Admittedly, one weakness of *Creating Choices*, and of feminist criminology and reform generally, lies in their failure to propose solutions for those women whom CSC labels 'difficult to manage' (Shaw 2000). Some women *do* present as challenges, but placing these women in men's penitentiaries is not by any stretch of the imagination a tolerable or 'women-centred' alternative.

Conclusions

On the surface, Canada appears to be at the cutting edge of women's corrections with its new, woman-centred regime, but many problems persist. While CSC maintains that 'most' women will benefit from the new regime at the regional facilities, it also acknowledges that it is 'on a learning curve' and that there are growing pains associated with any new regime. CSC now contends that many of the ideals embodied in *Creating Choices* are not easily operationalized and are sometimes too ambitious (Reynolds 1996; Drouin 1997; Stableforth 1997).

The implementation process has been characterized by exclusions and by redefinitions of the original meaning of women-centred corrections. Recent correctional practices suggest that more and more women are being classified by institutional staff as 'risky,' even though ten years ago many of these same women were believed to present more of a risk to themselves than to anyone else (TFFSW 1990: 41–2, 89–91). None of the new security developments I have discussed are perceived by CSC as contradicting its wider philosophy of empowerment, because it perceives *this* group of prisoners as resistant to, and thus not amenable to, the principles outlined by the task force. As a consequence, the 'difficult offenders' – those who are identified as resistant to kinder, gentler forms of punishment – are subject to a different type of punishment. The plans for the more 'disruptive' prisoners reveal, in its starkest form, the persistence of sovereign and disciplinary powers.

A high-risk, high-need prisoner's resistance to CSC's more 'benevolent' women-centred regime is constructed as a choice; this is especially true with respect to maximum security prisoners (those who are not low-functioning or mentally disordered). Risk management is constructed as the responsibility of the prisoners and the authorities. The prisoner is governed through the expectation that she will rationally choose to engage in self-governing strategies to minimize her risk 'to the good order of the institution,' and to avoid situations and behaviours that are 'risky.' The status of being 'maximum security,' of 'high risk,' which results in punitive treatment, can be altered if and when the prisoner chooses to comply with the carceral regime by engaging in risk-minimizing conducts such as participating in programs, refraining from self-injury and from injuring others, and complying with the institution's regulations. Such positive and empowering choices could result in a transfer out of maximum security into the general population at a regional prison. This illustrates how the 'success' of a neoliberal strategy of governing like empowerment is to a great extent contingent on the continued existence of more disciplinary strategies of governing.

The vulnerability and resistance of a newly marginalized group of 'unempowerable prisoners' illustrates the triangular interdependence of sovereignty, discipline, and government in penality. Prisons are governed by cultural sensibilities that limit the extent to which a regime's content can be changed. With respect to women-centred prisons, who is being empowered? Is it the prison or the prisoner? The answer is increasingly unclear. What *is* clear is that the state can now claim to be offering women programs and services that provide them with the opportunity to empower themselves. The punitive treatment of 'irresponsible' prisoners is not inconsistent with wider neoliberal strategies of responsibilizing. Thus, it becomes more difficult for advocates and reformers to show how the state is negligent in terms of recognizing the programming needs of women.

This chapter has only begun the task of unravelling some of the colonizations, resistances, and complexities of new strategies of penal governing, and the tenuous and complex ways in which these strategies relate to sovereignty and discipline. CSC has adopted new responsibilizing strategies of government that exist in a triangular relationship with discipline and sovereignty. Additional research is needed if we are to improve our understanding of the particularities of these relations.

This discussion of empowerment as a responsibilizing reform strategy demonstrates three points. *First,* that new forms of governing are flexible, and resonate with multiple and contradictory goals. *Second,* that new strategies of governing create and mobilize new series of knowledges to justify and legitimate their various interpretations and uses. And *third,* that in situations where forms of responsibilizing government-at-a-distance fail, the powers that be often resort to more sovereign or disciplinary exercises of power. This illustrates the interdependence of multiple forms of power: sovereign, disciplinary, and governmental.

Conclusion

Stumbling Blocks, Growing Pains, or More of the Same?

Historians have debates about its origins; sociologists have studied its internal structure and culture; policy analysts have tried to evaluate its effectiveness; social critics, reformers, and prisoners have exposed its inhumanity. The prison invariably emerges from this criticism as little more than a crude instrument for punishment and disposal: of dubious utility and near certain harm. Yet prison systems throughout the world not only remain intact, they are expanding. They are seemingly impervious to criticism and resistant to attempts to replace them by alternatives that are more humane, efficient and cheaper.   Blomberg and Cohen 1995: 27

This book has analysed how federal women prisoners have been governed and how various expert and nonexpert knowledges have shaped and given authority to various prison regimes. It has revealed that patterns of governing women's prisons in both the past and the present have relied on multiple and interrelated relations of productive *and* repressive power. At any given historical moment, multiple rationalities and technologies are available to reformers and state agents. Processes of governance incorporate a variety of possibly contradictory rationalities and mobilize various techniques for the purpose of governing a known object in a particular way. Strategies of reform can appear to satisfy reformers' demands for change, while simultaneously accommodating the often contradictory demands placed on correctional administrators to discipline and responsibilize prisoners. A consideration of these shifting processes of governing can help us understand how penality has evolved and how women's knowledges and reformers' involvement in these processes have contributed to present strategies of correctional management. Changes in contemporary penality cannot be viewed in isolation, or as independent of past strategies of governing.

Paradoxes of Women-Centred Corrections

The seeds of change were planted with *Creating Choices*, but wider organizational barriers are preventing this vision from germinating. Of central concern is the extent to which regimes of imprisonment can be modified for women. The history of women's imprisonment in Canada reveals that building an institution based on the perceived needs and experiences of women prisoners, employing only female staff and administrators, and integrating feminist, maternal, and therapeutic discourses with a penal regime, is not an original or radical concept. Strange's (1983) discussion of the Andrew Mercer Reformatory, the first separate institution for women in Canada, illustrates that past women's penal regimes were based on variations of the women-centred philosophy. Strange illustrates clearly that although maternal regimes ameliorated some of the pains of imprisonment, they also inflicted their own type of pain. I do not mean to suggest that past and current regimes are the same; they are not. But it does illustrate that various institutional dynamics have always undermined women-centred reforms.

Discussions about which women are amenable to 'kinder,' 'gentler,' women-specific techniques, and which women are 'risky' and even beyond the pale of womanhood, have always been part of Canadian debate on prison practices. The present practice of housing 'risky' women in federal penitentiaries for men, or in specially designed maximum security units in women's prisons, has fanned the debate about which prisoners are 'reformable' and which are not. The criteria now being used to evaluate a prisoner's potential for reform are different (Hannah-Moffat, forthcoming) from those that were applied by correctional personnel at the Mercer in the late 1800s (see chapter 2); yet the concerns about prisoners' resistance and about their unwillingness to comply with regimes that are supposed to be in their 'best interests' are surprisingly similar.

At the centre of both of these 'women-centred' correctional developments – the Mercer and today's women-centred facilities – we find an effort to develop programs for meeting the gender-specific needs of women. Both regimes relied on notions of difference and an ethic of care to create a feminized technology of penal governance; and this technology was ultimately undermined by problems associated with governing an involuntary population of prisoners. We are still trying to develop a model of punishment for women.

The emphasis in contemporary women's penality on gender and

cultural differences has reconfigured penal governance; but it has also failed to shatter the prison/punishment nexus. Contemporary strategies have provided some benefits, but they have failed to alter women's imprisonment in any fundamental way. Penal reforms such as the new emphasis on women-centredness do not question the centrality of imprisonment: the sanctioning of prisoners continues to rely heavily on techniques of imprisonment. It is ironic that prisons, which have never succeeded in providing a suitable therapeutic milieu for rehabilitation, are now being used to *empower* women. It should not surprise us when this new women-centred and culturally sensitive regime eventually fails. Prisons are resilient, flexible, and enabling institutions that can resist, incorporate, redefine, and absorb critical discourses.

The ways in which the ideals of empowerment, shared responsibility, and healing embodied in *Creating Choices* were operationalized suggest how the correctional bureaucracy is able to redefine, reinterpret, and in some cases appropriate women's needs and feminist visions of change. A comparable pattern of governing and process of redefinition is also visible in maternal reformers' efforts to create homelike prisons based on the 'women-centred' principle of maternal guidance, and in attempts to implement the therapeutic ideal of rehabilitation in prison settings. The discussions of the Mercer and of earlier initiatives at P4W illustrate this point. Such 'benevolent' regimes can make tangible improvements; however, they also obscure wider power imbalances and mark the punitive context of imprisonment. The moralistic aspects of these regimes persist, albeit suitably disguised by benevolent presumptions about helping and improving the lives of wayward and disempowered women. As was the case at the Mercer, resistance to such a well-intentioned regime is deemed unconscionable. Women who assert their power and resist are subjected to repressive, intrusive, and punitive regimes until they are willing to participate in their empowerment.

The language of women-centred corrections incorporates tenuous assumptions and overlooks certain material experiences of incarcerated individuals. Interestingly, the language that defines the new women-centred regime is not being contested, even though it is increasingly apparent that feminists and correctional officials have conflicting interpretations of terms such as *empowerment* and *healing*. This history of women's penal reform raises a number of important considerations. Below, I outline some of the difficulties that underlie many well-meaning efforts at penal reform. I address three problems: the category 'woman,' the false dichotomy of female- and male-centred prisons, and the legal/material 'reality' of women's imprisonment.

Fracturing the Category 'Woman'

Recent government reports have adopted the same assumption as many feminist criminologists: that women in prison have more in common with other women than they do with male inmates. They stress the commonalities shared by women as a disempowered and marginalized group. This assumption of common disempowerment reflects some of the undeniable experiential and demographic similarities between women prisoners and 'free' women, but it also ignores the heterogeneity that exists among women. In particular, differences of race, class, sexual orientation, and – more importantly – power are minimized. The most fundamental difference between women prisoners and other women is that they are not free! Saying that all women are the same obscures wider relations of power. The concept of women-centred corrections gives priority to gender over all other factors. The experiences of women in prison are much more than a microcosm of the experience of all women. Prisoners experience the dehumanizing pains of imprisonment – a unique experience shared by a small portion of Canadian women (and men). The construction of women prisoners, in *Creating Choices* and other narratives, as 'no different from other women,' or as 'having more in common with other women than with male prisoners,' denies the involuntary and unique aspects of the experience of incarceration. An emphasis on the commonalities of women results in an insensitivity to the differences among women; as a result, the experiences of women as prisoners are trivialized. This lack of attention to difference leads to many flawed assumptions, such as a belief that if women are employed as guards, run programs, and administer prisons, women in prison will be better cared for.[1] Another common false assumption is that women in prison often identify with middle-class reformers and are willing participants even though they are being involuntarily confined in prison. Further fractured is the category 'woman prisoner.' Women in prison present a wide range of needs.[2]

A related point is that the language of women-centredness has the capacity to deny other forms of oppression, such as those based on race and class. In feminist criminology and critical legal studies, there has been extensive discussion of how the experiences of black and minority women have been neglected because of the hegemony of analytical categories such as 'woman' (Rice 1992). There are several excellent analyses of how multiple forms of oppression coexist, and how feminists, antipoverty activists, and antiracism activists share certain concerns but conflict over others (Crenshaw 1992; Martin 1993; Razack 1993, 1994; Bannerji 1995). These authors contend that women of different backgrounds are regulated and governed differently and have different experiences and understandings of those experiences.

The women-centred prison and the expectations placed on women prisoners are informed by white, middle-class sensibilities.[3] *Creating Choices* discusses at length the importance of cultural sensitivity; however, these sensitivities are limited to the context of aboriginal women's experiences.[4] Such an awareness is crucial because aboriginal women are overrepresented in Canadian prisons (Adelberg and the Native Women's Association of Canada 1993; Boritch 1997). Even so, it overlooks the needs of other minority women. This oversight has left black women inmates 'feeling slighted because they have not been asked for their opinions on any of the proposed facilities or programs' (Stewart and MacKay 1994: 34). Issues of systemic racism[5] are limited to a discussion of aboriginal culture. There has been a failure to consider the complexity and diversity of women's ethnic and cultural experiences.

When CSC bureaucrats (and many researchers) discuss aboriginal issues, they tend to use the term 'aboriginal,' as if it were a homogenous category. In fact, there is a great deal of diversity among aboriginal people, and among Aboriginal women prisoners (just as there is among women, and among women prisoners). This is significant when it comes to considering issues such as aboriginal women's access to elders. Within aboriginal culture, elders provide various functions: some conduct ceremonies, and others perform nonceremonial duties. Also, elders are associated with different Nations and have different traditions and customary practices. Thus, a woman of Cree descent may not be comfortable with a non-Cree elder. In the same vein, the hiring of aboriginal or nonwhite staff at the Healing Lodge and in the regional facilities may improve awareness of certain cultural issues, but profound differences will still exist between staff and prisoners that override any cultural similarities. Unequal and disciplinary relations of power between guards and prisoners can and likely will override any cultural identification. When we speak of 'aboriginal culture' as if it was homogenous, and when we speak of 'aboriginal programs' or 'culturally sensitive programs' as if they were sufficient, we are not serving the needs of incarcerated women, and in fact are probably creating a number of practical misunderstandings. CSC can indeed claim that it is sensitive to the needs of aboriginal women in prison, but it cannot claim that it is sufficiently meeting the needs of nonwhite women.

Cultural sensitivity is limited to the content and not the structure of the regime. Some of the frustrations expressed by the aboriginal women involved in the wider *Creating Choices* process articulate a similar concern. For example, aboriginal women reformers were not fully empowered to explore carceral alternatives consistent with their abolitionist philosophies. Adelberg and the Native Women's Association of Canada's discussion (1993: 77) of the *Creating Choices* process describes some of the frustrations aboriginal women experience in engaging with 'federal correctional officials and other organizations said to represent women in cages which had already conducted study upon study.' For many women, the bureaucratic discourse had little relevance and connection to the 'reality' they had experienced:

> No amount of tinkering with prisons can heal the before-prison lives of the aboriginal women who live or have lived within their walls. Prison cannot remedy the problem of poverty on reserves. It cannot deal with immediate or historical memories of genocide that Europeans worked upon our people. It cannot remedy violence, alcohol abuse, and sexual assault during childhood, rape and other violence aboriginal women experience at the hands of men. Prison cannot heal the past abuse of foster homes, or the indifference and racism of Canada's justice system in its dealings with aboriginal people. However, the treatment of aboriginal women within prisons can begin to recognize that these things are realities of the lives that aboriginal women have led. By understanding this, we can begin to make changes that will promote healing instead of rate. (Adelberg and the Native Women's Association of Canada 1993: 79)

However, the same authors also maintain that although prisons have been a site of problems in the past, they still have the capacity to 'promote healing instead of rage.' That being said, prison regimes are not safe places for healing, even if they are named 'healing lodges.'

The point here is not to discourage gender and culturally specific initiatives on a practical or political level. Rather, it is to argue for a fuller understanding of gender and racial oppressions, and to highlight differential relations of power among women in different situations. Most correctional reform narratives (both maternal and feminist) imply that the category of 'woman' is homogenous and unitary. Women-centred techniques of penal governance administered by female staff and advocated by female reformers, may alter the material experience of imprisonment, but they remain problematic because they obscure relations of power among women and assume that the oppression of women prisoners is narrowly linked to gender discrimination and harassment. The repression and oppression of women in prison is only partly linked to their status as women. The concepts of 'woman' prisoner and 'woman' reformer are poor ones to embrace. Relations of power exist among women of different socio-economic, ethnic, and racial backgrounds. Experiences of gender oppression in prisons, as elsewhere, are related to and intersect with other forms of oppression (Crenshaw 1992; Razack 1994; Bannerji 1995). As noted by Bannerji (1995: 121), 'we are still in the process of working out how to think of gender, "race" and class in terms of what is called "intersectionality," that is, in terms of their interactiveness, their ways of mutually constructing and reinforcing each other.' In this book I have attempted to begin unravelling these elusive relationships by showing how the governance of women in prison is linked to various historically specific gender, class, and racial or ethnic rationalities.

Besides legitimate concerns about the abuse and protection of prisoners' rights, there are also concerns about the degree to which relations between guards and prisoners can be fundamentally altered. According to CSC's new, women-centred correctional philosophy, the institutional staff, including the guards, are expected to engage in meaningful, respectful, and supportive relations with the prisoners in their charge. Yet as one incarcerated woman notes, even though guards are now *program deliverers* and newly classified under case management, 'they still wear the uniform of guards' (Horii 1994: 14). It is difficult to imagine how meaningful, respectful, and supportive relationships can develop when guards continue to perform strip searches, open women's mail, monitor their relations with others within and outside the institution, and at times punish prisoners for infractions against institutional order.

Although the women-centred model may downplay the coercive and oppressive powers of the keepers, unequal relations of power and the legal responsibilities of the prison will continue to shape institutional responses to women in prison. The inevitable tension between guards and prisoners is reduced by the presence of female staff, but it is not eliminated. Many of the allegations of abuse of prisoners' rights investigated by the Arbour Commission involved female staff. The point here is not that women can be cruel, but rather that governing is shaped by institutional structures.

False Dichotomy of Women- and Male-Centred Prisons

The construction of two separate and distinct models of corrections – women-centred and male-centred – sets up a false dichotomy. Some feminist critics argue that women's penal regimes have epitomized male-centred corrections in that they have emphasized security, discipline, and control. Conversely, the women-centred approach has been characterized by some as caring, empowering, supportive, respectful, and meaningful. In the correctional discourse, this split has reproduced and reinforced normative standards of femininity. Yet this dualism does not adequately reflect the diversity or complexity of either women's or men's prisons.

The women-centred trope reproduces male-centred views about what women need and want. The image of a women-centred prison as benevolent, caring, therapeutic, and supportive denies that similar relations exist in men's prisons. Conversely, the dominant conceptualizations that women-centred prisons are therapeutic in nature tend to minimize and obscure the oppressive aspects of involuntary treatment and disciplinary regimes. It is assumed that women prisoners will experience women-centred punishment as less oppressive than earlier, male-centred approaches, and that the ideals of women-centred regimes are applicable to all women. These assumptions are false: the coercive and sometimes inhumane nature of therapeutic regimes have been well documented in many correctional histories (Mitford 1973; Foucault 1977; Strange 1983; Dobash, Dobash, and Gutteridge 1986; Hornblum 1998).

It is generally assumed that the ideals of the women-centred approach can be achieved in a prison setting. To date, reformers have taken for granted that therapeutic, healing, and empowering programs can be implemented in prisons; the limits of this approach have never been clearly acknowledged and articulated. The feminization of penal regimes does not forgive their punitive and oppressive tendencies, especially when we consider that the subjects of the regimes are involuntary:

[Whereas] feminist therapy is premised on helping the woman see their own power so they can resist harm and take self-determined action,

> prisons generally remove whatever autonomy women have in their lives by enforcing rigid control over inmates, restrictions on movement, scheduling of activities and communication. Such control, coupled with arbitrary enforcement and application of rules, merely reproduces a sense of powerlessness and unpredictability present in the lives of women prior to their imprisonment. (Kendall 1994: 21)

Kendall (1993a, 1993b) further notes that it is this *control* that women prisoners identify as most damaging. She suggests that therapy *in* prison is 'a contradiction in terms.' Nonexistent opportunities and institutionally structured choices make it almost impossible for women prisoners to make what they regard as 'meaningful choices.' Women in prison lack the power and autonomy to make even the most mundane decisions, such as when to get up and go to sleep, when and what to eat, and when and whom to visit. This paradox frames women's experiences as prisoners, as well as the experiences and frustrations of many well-intentioned therapists and correctional staff.

Arguably, therapeutic ideals are compromised by the pre-existing structure under which correctional authorities are legally accountable for those in their charge. Remember here that CSC's main priority is to protect the public, not heal the offender. Frequently, therapy is aligned with control and security. Women prisoners who are believed to be dangerous or violent are often defined as needing 'more structure and more intensive therapeutic programming' (CSC 1995c: 42). If we have learned anything from correctional histories, we will be cautious when embracing ideological shifts away from punishment and toward healing and treatment in prison settings. Women-centred ideals have embraced therapeutic notions of healing and holistic regimes without questioning them. We must not forget the tragedies and abuses that led to the demise of the rehabilitative ideal in Canada and elsewhere (Mitford 1973; McNeil and Vance 1978; Culhane 1979; Gosselin 1982; Ekstedt and Griffiths 1988; Hornblum 1998). Academics and reformers have recently raised many concerns about the new mental health strategies that CSC has adopted for federally sentenced women (Laishes and Lyth 1996; Laishes 1997; CAEFS 1998).

The key point here is that advocates for women-centred prisons have failed to challenge the *use* of prisons. Most feminists discuss penal policy in ways that accept the current institutional framework. The women-centred approach implicitly assumes that while 'male models of corrections' are not suitable for women, prisons are suitable as long as they are based on a feminist vision of justice, punishment, and care. The restructuring of women's imprisonment based on such a vision is problematic because there is no uniform or essential 'female approach.'

The prison is tied into wider networks of social action and meaning (Garland 1990). Simply changing the content of a penal regime to reflect a women-centred approach leaves this wider institutional framework unchallenged. The way we currently think about and define punishment is derived from the wider context of criminal justice. To some extent, the feminizing of women's penal regimes *legitimates* the incarceration of women. Feminist discourses, instead of presenting a viable alternative to the problems faced by incarcerated women, are selectively mobilized. This selective integration of some feminist ideas and not others contributes to the production of a feminized social control dressed up in therapeutic and feminist language.

The Context of Imprisonment

Another major barrier to the realization of the women-centred ideal (whether based on maternalist or feminist principles) is that it denies the material and legal reality of carceral relations. The criminal justice system is perhaps the quintessential arena in which the state applies coercive measures against its citizens (Hannah-Moffat and Singh 1996: 6). In a liberal state, the explicit intention of imprisonment is to punish and to limit the freedom and autonomy of individuals subject to this sanction. When we reform the content of a regime, we tend to obscure the oppressive aspects of prisons and the unequal relations of power that characterize this sanction. Prisons are governed by material structures, cultural sensibilities, and mentalities that limit the extent to which the content of a regime can be changed. Regardless of the form and content of a women-centred regime, it is still in many respects about punishment, security, and discipline.

The limits of current women-centred reforms are perhaps most clearly reflected in the findings of the 1996 Arbour Commission. This report documented vividly the violations of prisoners' rights and abuses of power that took place in April 1994 (see chapter 5). Post-liberal reform strategies such as 'empowerment' and 'healing' require and assume that women in prison already enjoy certain rights. Madame Justice Arbour's (1996: 198) inquiry raised serious questions about a repressive state's capacity to 'empower' individuals who are not even deemed by that state to be legitimate recipients of the most basic of human rights. Five years after the release of this report, few of its recommendations have been implemented in the spirit in which they were intended.[6]

The legacy of women's penal reform raises questions about the ability of well-intentioned reformers to fundamentally alter the uneven relations of power that shape the governance of an involuntary population such as prisoners. Relations of power are complex and fractured, and feminists and others need to explore institutional power relations more fully. In spite of feminist efforts to redefine women's corrections, patterns of governing similar to those which prompted the 1990 Task Force on Federally Sentenced Women have resurfaced.

There remain a number of serious concerns: about women's access to meaningful programs in the community and in institutions; about neglect and abuses of power; about the sexual harassment and assault of prisoners about the medicalization, psychiatrization, and infantilization of women in prison; and about the continued housing of women in men's penitentiaries and in provincial facilities (namely in Burnaby Correctional Centre in British Columbia), which are not well equipped to deal with federally sentenced women. There are also ongoing debates about whether men should be employed in women's prisons,[7] and about how women should be classified in terms of minimum, medium, and maximum security. While some positive attempts have been made to house women closer to their homes, many remain dislocated, and few have benefitted from the mother/child program that was established to lessen the pain of separation from children. With the opening of five new prisons, capacity has been greatly expanded. Yet CSC is facing concerns about prison crowding. In the past, judges rejected the option of sending women to P4W because of its many failings; many now view regional prisons as places that can provide women with greatly needed programs and services.

Critics of the new prisons are concerned about how this innovative program of reform has been co-opted and used to justify more of the same. The failure to implement the radical ideal of *Creating Choices* and to fundamentally restructure women's prisons is a systemic problem, not an individual one. There are, without question, many hard-working and dedicated staff in CSC who are committed to the ideals of *Creating Choices* and who face the difficult task of operationalizing a different concept of punishment for women. While these individuals offer some hope, they are working in a wider correctional bureaucracy whose focus is mainly on managing the much too large male prison population.

Although correctional practices and logics may *appear* to incorporate feminist logics, pre-existing relations of power have not been displaced by them. The feminist logic of women-centred prisons coexists with other, often contradictory, modes of disciplinary governance. This is why the feminist and aboriginal vision of *Creating Choices* cannot on its own bring about a radical restructuring of women's penality. In this book I have shown how gender-based (more recently culturally based) concerns were institutionalized and how demands for change were neutralized to present the *appearance* of change without addressing many underlying problems.

Reformers have long been critical of the prison system's failure to represent or address women's interest; yet that same system is expected to play a central role in the empowerment and healing of women. The centrality of the prison is a common and unquestioned theme in reform narratives. We need to think more deeply about how and why we punish, and question our deeply ingrained assumptions about prisons and their potential for reform. Future reform initiatives should reflect more deeply on the history of well-intentioned penal reforms. Rather than engaging in projects that 're-form' the prison, we need to decentre the prison. While prisons cannot be ignored, they are not the solution. Had the money spent on the new regional prisons been used to implement other elements of *Creating Choices* – specifically, the community strategy involving the decarceration many federally sentenced women – this book might have ended quite differently.

Notes

Introduction

1 The five regional prisons are located in Edmonton, Alberta; Maple Creek, Saskatchewan; Kitchener, Ontario; Joliette, Quebec; and Truro, Nova Scotia.
2 For an excellent analysis of how expert and 'nonexpert' knowledge relates to the governance of alcohol, see Valverde (1998).
3 This is one of few reports that documents the experiences and needs of women offenders in the Northwest Territories. The terms of reference were to make recommendations on programming, custodial supervision, and rehabilitation services for the NWT female offender, and to determine whether the NWT female offender was a NWT or a federal responsibility.

1: Mothering the Flock: Maternal Discipline and Pastoral Power

1 One exception is Shaw (1992a; 1993), who examines the role of women's organizations in contemporary Canadian penal reform initiatives.
2 Freedman (1979: 521) notes that supporters of suffrage often argued that women needed the vote to perform their traditional tasks, to protect themselves as mothers, and to assert their moral force on society.
3 See Strange (1990). Her article offers some excellent examples of how feminists and maternalists mobilized maternal images in their protests, while having fundamental political differences.
4 For a more detailed discussion of the rise of a maternal ideal, see Bloch (1993). She notes that in the seventeenth and early eighteenth century, in America and Britain, 'motherhood was singularly unidealized, usually disregarded as a subject, and even at times denigrated' (101). She argues

that prior to the nineteenth century, literature did not emphasize mother-hood; instead, it tended to reflect dual images of women as 'help-mates' and 'ornamental refinement.' The 'help-mate' ideal downplayed the sexual differences between men and woman and stressed the utility of good housewives. As good wives, women were portrayed 'as pious, frugal, and hardworking' and were valued for the 'help they could be to men in furthering both spiritual and worldly concerns' (102). The more upper-class ideal of 'ornamental refinement,' however, 'concentrated on feminine graces and dwelt on the charms of female social companionship and in polite company' (103).

5 For additional examples, see Bloch 1993; Koven and Michel 1993; Koven 1993; Arnup 1994.

6 For a more detailed analysis of the role of nuns in penal discipline see Maurutto (1998) 'Philanthropic Governance: Church and State in Toronto's Catholic Archdiocese (1850–1950)' (PhD thesis, York University, Sociology). This imagery was also used by Fry. Fry's work, however, stressed the evangelical goal of salvation and thus, she is often portrayed as a savior in narratives, drawings, and lithographs.

7 The efforts of Elizabeth Fry were somewhat specific to large prisons in urban settings. The extent to which her ideas were adopted by women reformers and prison administrators in smaller local jails or in larger penitentiaries is unclear.

8 For a more comprehensive discussion of the life and activities of Elizabeth Fry, consult the following biographies: Fry and Cresswell (1848); Lewis (1909); Barne (1962); Kent (1962); Pitman (1969); and Smillie (1980).

9 Children were commonly incarcerated with their mothers if alternative caregivers were not available. Children who committed crimes were often incarcerated with adult prison populations until the early to mid-nine-teenth century, when classification measures designed to separate different types of offenders were instituted. In Canada, adult women and men were incarcerated with children. These populations were not separated until the mid-nineteenth century. For more information on delinquent children during this time, see Splane (1965), who discusses Canada's Prison Inspection Act of 1857, which resulted in the removal of one of the first groups of juvenile offenders from the adult penal system.

10 Fry's initial focus on children parallels her earlier work with impoverished children in her community. Before beginning prison reform, Fry was engaged in other social and moral reform efforts with the poor. One of her early achievements was the establishment of a girls' school in a poor neighbourhood. With the help of a cleric and the some of the ladies in the

area, she provided instruction for seventy girls. The school was regularly visited by the poor. A depot was filled with clothing, drugs, and soup. 'Madame Fry,' as she was known, attempted to persuade poor people to be more thrifty.

11 For more detailed information about the life and activities of Mary Carpenter see Koven (1993) and Young and Ashton (1956).

12 This association was initially started by the wife of a clergyman and eleven members of the Society of Friends. For additional information on the association, see Fry and Cresswell (1848).

13 Fry's ideal of separate institutions for women was not realized in her lifetime. Given that separate prisons were not immediately achievable, she argued for the classification of women prisoners. Early notions of classification were based on the belief that criminality was contagious and that criminal habits could be transferred through association. Thus the separation of experienced and inexperienced offenders was essential, as was the identification of reformable and nonreformable women. The concern about identifying women resistant to reform did not arise until Fry had been working with prisoners for several years. Initially Fry, like many novice reformers, believed that with proper training and supervision all women were reformable. A pioneering aspect of Fry's philosophy was her notion of classification, which in many ways foreshadowed the penal strategy advocated by Walter Crofton in Ireland several decades later. Fry encouraged the separation of convicts by age, gender, offence, and reformability. She felt that classifying convicts would make it easier to reform them. Her reform program included occupational, educational, and religious training (Fry and Cresswell 1848; Dobash, Dobash, and Gutteridge 1986; Zedner 1991b).

2: Mother Knows Best: The Development of Separate Institutions for Women

1 In Canada, a similar phenomenon occurred with the development of several rescue homes and homes for fallen or pregnant women. The Salvation Army and other Christian organizations played an active role in the development and operation of these homes.

2 For a comparison of the Mercer and other reform-oriented men's prisons, see Oliver (1994) and Wetherell (1979).

3 The hiring of matrons in women's prisons paralleled and was influenced by wider struggles to integrate women into the workforce. One movement that was particularly relevant in Canada and in the United States was the

'police matrons' movement. This was spearheaded by a variety of reform organizations, such as the Prison Association of New York (PANY), the Women's Christian Temperance Union (WCTU) and the National Council of Women of Canada (NCWC). This struggle was premised on the belief that women had a legitimate and valuable role to play in regulating and policing women – specifically criminal women.

4 One example of such a list is found in PANY's report, written by E.C. Wines and Theodore W. Dwight, titled Report on the Prisons and Reformatories of Canada and the United States. Some elements of this report's discussion of the selection of institutional staff, including matrons, are discussed in chapter 2. During the 1840s, middle-class women in New York City formed a women's branch of PANY.

5 Like matrons, male keepers were morally regulated. The qualifications for male officers, as stipulated in the Prison Association of New York's 1867 report, indicated that male officers had to be men who were honest, sober, mild-tempered, quiet-mannered, 'pure in their conversations,' decisive, energetic, humane, benevolent, sincere, discrete, efficient, impartial, vigilant, religious, moral, distinguished in habits of industry, order, and cleanliness, and knowledgeable of human nature in its various aspects and relations (PANY, 1867: 120–2). A detailed rationale for each of these qualifications can be located in PANY (1867: 120–1).

6 For a more comprehensive discussion of the development of women's prison reform associations and the motivations of their founders, see Freedman (1981), Rafter (1992), and Stewart (1993).

7 It is unclear why correctional responsibilities were divided the way they were in the 1867 Constitution Act. Shortly after Confederation, federal legislation declared that offenders sentenced to greater than two years of incarceration would go to a federal penitentiary managed by the federal government. Offenders sentenced to less than two years are sent to reformatories (now provincial correctional institutions), which are managed by provincial and territorial governments. There is, however, nothing in this legislation that prevents the housing of federally sentenced women (with a sentence of greater than two years) in provincial reformatories or the housing of short-term women in federal penitentiaries. The actual housing practices adopted at the turn of the century after the passage of the 1867 Constitution Act is difficult to ascertain. Nonetheless, it appears that most federally sentenced women were held in female units in men's penitentiaries (mainly Kingston Penitentiary) until P4W was opened in 1934. From 1934 onwards, most federally sentenced women were warehoused at this facility. In the mid-1970s, an Exchange of Services Agree-

ment was enacted between some provinces and the federal government to allow some federally sentenced women to reside closer to their home communities in provincial correctional facilities. For additional information, see Needham (1980), Friedland (1988), and Canada (1990).

8 According to Pollock-Byrne (1990: 44), the American women's reformatory movement was linked to four wider developments: the perceived increase in female criminality; women's Civil War experience; the development of charities and a prison reform movement; and the emergence of an 'embryonic feminist analysis' of women's place in American society. Pollock-Byrne suggests that the perceived increase in female crime was linked to an increase in prostitution and abortions during the American Civil War. After the Civil War, women reformers began to demand greater autonomy and authority over the public institutions that housed women prisoners (Freedman 1981: 22). This suggests that many citizens and antebellum reformers believed that the moral fibre of the American state was at risk and that a closer regulation of women's sexual and moral conduct was necessary.

9 Records on Canadian women's prison reform initiatives at the turn of the century are sparse and incomplete. Information obtained from research on this issue is discussed in greater detail later on. However, some of the earliest visitors to female units were Salvation Army officers and representatives of prisoners' aid associations.

10 Both Strange (1983) and Oliver (1994) provide evidence that confirms the cross-fertilization of ideas about women's punishment and its administration between Canada and various American states. Similarly, various Canadian historians and reports, such as Report on the Prisons and Reformatories of the United States and Canada (PANY 1867) and the Proceedings of the Canadian Penal Congress (Canadian Penal Congress 1949) illustrate that American reformers and penal administrators regularly visited Canada and shared their views on prison management with their Canadian counterparts.

11 The conditions that made the adequate classification of offenders in Ontario jails difficult are documented in Wetherell (1979).

12 For a more detailed history of the Andrew Mercer Reformatory for Women in Ontario, see Strange (1983), Oliver (1994), Ruemper (1994), and Berkovits (1995). These accounts focus on the reformatory as an institution, not on the wider social and political processes around it.

13 Specific examples of the activities of women associated with the Ottawa Elizabeth Fry Society (OEFS) can be located in Stewart (1993).

14 Both the Salvation Army and the Prisoners' Aid Association operated

homes for released women. For additional details on the activities of some of these reformers, see Wetherell (1979), Ruemper (1994), and Hannah-Moffat and Valverde (1996). Reformers such as the Prisoners' Aid Association (PAA) and the Salvation Army were involved in similar activities in men's facilities.

15 See note 7. The Mercer seems to have had little control over the type of women they received. According to sentencing legislation, all provincially sentenced women were potential candidates for the Mercer. However, not all of these women were considered 'reformable' by the Mercer's administration. Women not sent to the Mercer likely remained in local jails. It is difficult to determine how much power the Mercer officials had in screening the offenders they received (for reformability), or whether they were able to reject or transfer out unreformable candidates. The secondary literature suggests that Mercer officials had very little power in this regard and that the inability to screen offenders compromised the maternal reform project.

16 See previous note.

17 For a more complete discussion of the disciplinary regime at the Mercer, techniques of punishment, and concerns about the inculcation of unreformable women, see Strange (1983).

18 The surgeon, Dr John S. King, supervised and advocated the use of this technique during the reign of superintendents O'Reilly and O'Sullivan. This particular incident is cited in Berkovits (1995: 7).

19 Difficulties associated with the management of 'incorrigible women' were not specific to the Mercer. Several histories of women's reformatories have documented comparable problems and the use of punitive measures in the interest of maintaining order. For additional examples, see Freedman (1981), Zedner (1991b), and Rafter (1992).

20 This statement is not meant to suggest that the experiences of men in reformatories were not harsh and that they were not expected to conform to certain stereotypes of masculinity. However, the scope of this discussion does not permit an adequate analysis of the masculine components of men's regimes.

3: Finding a New Home: From Kingston Penitentiary to the Prison for Women

1 Upper Canada, Journals of the House of Assembly, App. 10, 1836–37: 4; cited in Beattie (1977: 106).

2 Female Convicts Punishment Book, 1850–1856, Penitentiary Museum Archives (PMA).

3 Untitled inventory of acceptable punishments for violations of prison rules (no. 73, volume 134), National Archives of Canada. There is also evidence of international consultations between wardens with respect to appropriate methods of punishment for incorrigible prisoners.

4 Records on the number of men and women received at Kingston Penitentiary are not available for the following years: 1854, 1917, 1918, 1920, 1921, and 1932. Calculations in table 3.1 are based on the average number of men and women received in the years for which there are data. Due to changes in the annual reporting dates for each fiscal year, there are some overlaps in reporting periods. Statistics published in the Annual Reports reflect developments during the respective fiscal years, except for the period 1852 to 1877, for which calendar years are covered. Therefore, it is difficult to determine the actual populations of various institutions during the calendar year. The numbers presented in this table represent the numbers of men and women received, which were reported for each fiscal year. These numbers were originally collected and compiled in a different format by Dave St Onge of the Penitentiary Museum Archives (PMA) in Kingston, Ontario.

5 In general, until the female unit at Kingston Penitentiary was established, women inmates serving sentences of greater than two years were the administrative responsibility of the federal government, and thus were sent to the closest federal facility that would accept them. This practice changed with the opening of P4W in 1934. After 1934, with few exceptions, all federally sentenced women were sent to P4W.

6 PMA.

7 PMA.

8 Annual Report of the Inspector of Penitentiaries, 1893–1894. Canada (1894).

9 PMA.

10 Annual Report of the Directors of Penitentiaries, 1868: 22. Canada (1868)

11 Warden Henry Smith to the inspectors of the Provincial Penitentiary, Annual Report 1836: 4. PMA.

12 She was succeeded by several other matrons and deputy matrons, including Mrs Parsons (1840–45); Mrs P. Martin (assistant, 1844); Catherine Coulter (1845–47); Mary Pollard (1847–49); Eliza Chase (assistant, 1847); Mrs Julia Cox (1849–56); Mrs Martha Walker (1856–65); Mrs Belinda Plees (deputy, then matron, 1864–70); Mrs Mary Leahy (deputy, then matron, 1861–71); Mary Bostridge (deputy matron, 1870); Margaret O'Loane (assistant deputy matron, 1880); Rose Anne Fuhey (1886–1920); M.G. Draper (1920–21); and E.A. Robinson (1921, transferred to P4W). The information about these women and their careers was originally compiled

from prison records by Dave St Onge at the Penitentiary Museum Archives.

13 This report was submitted by Mrs Julia Cox. PMA.

14 PMA.

15 Protestant Chaplain R.J. Rodgers, Annual Report, 1845, Appendix G. PMA.

16 Rev. Angus MacDonell, V.G., Roman Catholic Chaplain's Annual Report, 1851. PMA.

17 This comment was made by a Catholic chaplain at Kingston in 1851. Similar views were held by the Protestant chaplain and other administrators. Cited in Oliver (1994: 251). For additional examples, see Oliver (1994) and Cooper (1993).

18 Belinda Plees, *Remarks on the State of the Female Prison*. Annual Report to the Directors of the Kingston Penitentiary, 1869: 22.

19 *Remarks on the State of the Female Prison*. Annual Report to the Directors of the Kingston Penitentiary, 1869: 22.

20 Canada, Legislative Assembly Journals, App. 2G-AA, 1846 (cited in Cooper 1993: 37).

21 Report of the Inspector of Penitentiaries, 1889. PMA.

22 The original 1883 blueprints are in a service file at PMA.

23 This area of Kingston Penitentiary was later known as the Northwest Cell Block and is currently the location of the inmate training administrative offices, the office of the Deputy Warden, Reception and Classification. PMA.

24 Annual Report of the Commissioner of Penitentiaries, 1927–28.

25 While many federal commissions and independent reports recommended that federal women's prisons be transferred to provincial institutions because of the inequitable geographic dislocation of women prisoners from their families and home communities, this practice was not followed on a regular basis until the 1970s. After the Ouimet Report in 1969, federal exchange-of-services agreements were negotiated, which allowed some women to serve their sentences in their home provinces, and allowed the provinces to send 'high risk' women to P4W.

26 PMA.

27 Annual Report of the Commissioner of Penitentiaries, 1927–28.

28 For a more detailed discussion on the rise of positive sciences and their effect on the penitentiary, see Cullen and Gilbert (1982) and Garland (1985).

29 PMA.

30 Information about the administrative regulation of P4W is located in the PMA in documents that have not been filed and given numbers.

31 The Prisoners' Aid Association (PAA) provided religious services for Protestant inmates.

32 In keeping with wider maternal and evangelical obligations to care for the less fortunate, women from the Kingston area continued to visit the women in their new homes to provide them with Bible instruction and some limited training programs. Unfortunately, there is little information about the women who originally visited the prison and the role they played in Kingston Penitentiary and later in P4W. However, it is likely that these women were affiliated with the local religious and secular organizations mentioned earlier, such as the Salvation Army, the Prisoners' Aid Associations, and the Ladies' Auxiliaries.

33 During this time, inmate labour was often used in the construction of new prisons and institutions. Inmates at Kingston Penitentiary were also used during the construction of another local penitentiary, Collins Bay. The use of inmate labour in these particular circumstances can be linked to a more general concern expressed by penal administrators and politicians of the early twentieth century about the absence of useful and productive labour in penitentiaries. Historically, there has been a concern about idleness and a somewhat blind faith in the merits of 'hard labour,' regardless of the utility of that labour.

34 Notes from the Archambault Report (1938), Report of the Royal Commission to Investigate the Penal System in Canada, indicate that the cost of P4W, including material, labour, and departmental charges, amounted to $373,781.15. The accountant of the Penitentiary Branch informed the commissioners that it was impossible to figure out the extra cost to the state occasioned by alterations after the original plans were completed.

35 PMA.

36 In June 1923, the female department at Dorchester was permanently closed, in part due to the recommendations of the Nickle Commission (1921). The remaining three convicts were transferred to Kingston Penitentiary, along with the matron, Miss Edith Robertson, and her bilingual assistant matron, Mrs Allain. 'Historical Sketch.' PMA.

37 Annual Report of the Commissioner of Penitentiaries, 1932–33.

38 When Dorchester's West Wing was remodelled in the 1930s, all vestiges of the female ward were removed. Only a pair of small rooms on the third floor remained for accommodating a few transient female prisoners and a temporary matron, pending their transfer to Kingston's new P4W. PMA.

39 Most early P4W records are either missing or inaccessible. Hence, this discussion of the institution's first twenty years must be somewhat speculative.

40 Interview transcripts, 1994.
41 Interview transcripts, 1994.
42 Interview transcripts, 1994.
43 For a more detailed discussion of the persecution of the Doukhobors, see Hawthorn 1955, Maloff 1957, Johnson 1963, Woodcock and Avakumovic 1977, Yerbury 1984, Yerbury and Griffiths 1991, and Jackson and Griffiths 1991. Much of the conflict between the Doukhobors and the Canadian state involved issues related to the control of land (registration and ownership); Canadian citizenship, its obligations and privileges; taxation; and the registration of census information (Yerbury and Griffiths 1991: 335). One group of Doukhobors called the Svoibodniki, or Freedomites (more commonly known as Sons of Freedom), were engaged in nude protests and demonstrations (such as refusing en masse to comply with registration laws regarding births, deaths, and marriages and with compulsory secular education, which they regarded as immoral), and burning their own homes and cars. This led to legal conflicts and in some instances fines and imprisonment. Some more radical members of the Sons of Freedom allegedly participated in arsons and 'bombings.' These actions resulted in an amendment to the 1931 Criminal Code. This amendment provided for a mandatory penalty of three years' imprisonment for nudity in a public place. Yerbury and Griffiths (1991: 338) note that 'by May of 1932, 745 men, women and children were confined in an improvised detention camp at Nelson for nudity. More than 600 adults were sentenced to Piers Island in Haro Strait, and 365 children were placed either in orphanages or in industrial schools for delinquent children.' Difficulties with Doukhobor prisoners reportedly led to the opening of the Piers Island Penitentiary in British Columbia.
44 National Archives. file 23-21-23.
45 Annual Report of the Commissioner of Penitentiaries, 1950–51.
46 Annual Report of the Commissioner of Penitentiaries, 1952–53.
47 Annual Report of the Commissioner of Penitentiaries, 1939–40; 1940–41.
48 Annual Report of the Commissioner of Penitentiaries, 1937–38.
49 Annual Report of the Commissioner of Penitentiaries, 1947–48.

4: Laywomen's Expertise: Women's Prison Reform, 1945–70

1 Despite the prevalence of these changes in penality, it is critical to note that not all institutional regimes changed at the same rate. Some custodial institutions were only marginally affected by this wider transformation in governance. For example, Ruemper (1994) clearly indicates that while the

regime at the Mercer Reformatory reflected scientific ideals, these ideals did not exist to the same extent in other Ontario prisons. For a more detailed discussion of the development of specific rehabilitative programs in Canadian penal institutions, see Ekstedt and Griffiths (1988).

2 Annual Report of the Commissioner of Penitentiaries, 1957–58.

3 *Dorothy Mills Proctor and Her Majesty The Queen In Right of Canada, The Attorney General of Canada, George Scott, Institute of Psychotherapy Limited, Mark Eveson and Gerald Wilson.* Statement of claim – Ontario Court General Division. Court File Number: 98-cv-6618.

4 Isabel Macneill became the warden of P4W in 1960, when it was administratively separated from Collins Bay Penitentiary and Kingston Penitentiary.

5 For a more detailed description of the domestic science program at P4W, see Webb (1965). PMA.

6 However, the warden of Kingston Penitentiary, and later the warden of Collins Bay Penitentiary, retained responsibility for certain fiscal and administrative duties, which were transferred to the regional headquarters of the Correctional Service several years later, in 1963. As of 1 July 1962, the responsibility for certain administrative services at P4W was transferred, by order of the commissioner, from Kingston Penitentiary to Collins Bay Penitentiary. Surviving records do not explain clearly why these duties were transferred. Responsibilities withheld from the matrons and the first superintendent of P4W included the following: final compilation of annual estimates; accounting for money appropriated for the operation of P4W; administration of personnel; provision of rations; maintenance of buildings and services; and provision of tasks and overall supervision of industrial work. Superintendent Macneill repeatedly lobbied for financial autonomy for P4W. She insisted that the institution could not operate successfully unless it was financially separated from the larger men's penitentiaries. Regional headquarters (RHQ) Ontario, which came into operation on 1 April 1963, then assumed certain responsibilities vis-à-vis P4W and other institutions within its regional jurisdiction. In October 1963, those responsibilities were extended to include the recruitment of staff for all institutions in the Ontario region. PMA.

7 Interview cited in McNeil and Vance (1978: 81–2).

8 The 'little house' at P4W is no longer used for this purpose. Prior to P4W's closing, it was a private family visiting trailer used to accommodate occasional overnight visits from partners and families of federally sentenced women.

9 Mrs Hof was educated in Germany, where she studied household science.

10 PMA.

11 PMA and interview data.

12 See note 3.

13 See note 3. There is some issue here as to whether an incarcerated prisoner can ever provide informed consent. In this particular case, the defendant, Ms Proctor, was not informed of the potential long-term consequences of this drug, and as a minor and a prisoner she did not feel that she was in a position to decline treatment. There are outstanding allegations of assault and battery, breach of fiduciary duty, intentional infliction of mental suffering, and negligence. Punitive and exemplary damages are being sought. Also see the CSC 1998a, Board of Investigation Report.

14 Their interest in this population seems to have been prompted by inquiries from other clubs (specifically Halifax and Windsor) asking for guest speakers and for current literature on offenders. For instance, the 30 November 1948 minutes of the Group for the Study of Penal Reform indicate that all members of the group read and discussed John Kidman's book *The Canadian Prison*, and that they had a guest speaker attend their meeting to discuss Ontario training schools. The speaker, Mrs Sanderson, was the only female member of the Training School Advisory Committee, and she was a liaison member of the Ontario Board of Parole. After to this presentation, the group arranged visits to the Cobourg and St Mary's training schools for girls. Toronto University Women's Club Archives (TUCWA).

15 Address delivered by Major R. Gibson, Commissioner of Penitentiaries, on 16 February 1948, at a meeting under the auspices of the School of Social Work, University of Toronto, p. 1. TUWCA.

16 Report of the Group for the Study of Penal Reform, 20 November 1951. TUWCA.

17 The Department of Reform Institutions was established in Ontario in 1946. This department had jurisdiction over the Andrew Mercer Reformatory for Women, the Ontario Training School for Girls (formerly Cobourg), the St Mary's Training School for Girls, and all district, city, and county jails. It administered the sentences of women who received a custodial term of less than two years. Women offenders receiving sentences of greater than two years were sent to P4W in Kingston, a federal prison.

18 Noted in a report sent to Miss Elsie McGill by the University Women's Club's Group for the Study of Penal Reform to inform the Business and Professional Women's Club's Study Group. The report, written by L.E. Cruikshank, is dated 28 March 1953. TUWCA.

19 Part of the initial training of correctional officers was offered at the RCMP barracks under the supervision of Deputy Commissioner McCulley. This

program was six weeks long and covered a wide range of issues. The objective of the Penitentiaries Branch was to train professionally all of the officers working in penitentiaries. Address delivered by Major R. Gibson, Commissioner of Penitentiaries, on 16 February 1948, at a meeting under the auspices of the School of Social Work, University of Toronto, p. 6. TUWCA.

20 Address delivered by Major R. Gibson, Commissioner of Penitentiaries, on 16 February 1948, at a meeting under the auspices of the School of Social Work, University of Toronto, p. 6. TUWCA.

21 These concerns were also prepared as resolutions and presented to Major Foote, the Minister of Reform Institutions. Most of the University Women's Clubs in Ontario endorsed and submitted similar resolutions. TUWCA.

22 Report of the Group for the Study of Penal Reform, 18 November 1954. TUWCA.

23 For additional information on activities of local councils of women and the National Council of Women of Canada, and their involvement in penal reform, see Griffiths (1893), Shaw (1957), and Strong-Boag (1976).

24 Canadian Association of Elizabeth Fry Societies 1995–96 Annual Report.

25 For some additional information on the early activities of the Elizabeth Fry Societies, see Dorothy Hart (1959) and Lee Stewart (1993).

26 Initially, Macphail was not particularly interested in the plight of women convicts. Her interest in prison reform for women evolved out of her experiences with male convicts. Throughout the 1930s, Macphail lobbied for an 'impartial' investigation into the Canadian penitentiary system. She had many concerns about conditions in Canadian penitentiaries: the failure to reform convicts, the lack of proper classification of convicts, the absence of useful and constructive penal labour, the lack of adequate health care, the use of corporal punishment, and the blatant disregard for human rights (Pennington 1986). Conditions in the women's penitentiary were not much different from those in men's institutions. After the war, Macphail began to fight for improved prisons for women, and in the early 1950s she was instrumental in the founding of the Toronto Elizabeth Fry Society. For a more detailed discussion of the challenges Macphail faced, see Doris Pennington (1986).

27 Muriel McQueen Fergusson was the first woman to become the Speaker of the Senate. The Ottawa Elizabeth Fry Society's Fergusson House is named after her, in appreciation of her struggle for legal reforms for women and for the development of rehabilitative programs for women in penitentiaries. OEFS.

28 Meetings and social events were also used to raise funds for the philanthropic work of Elizabeth Fry Societies.

29 Cited in an unpublished essay by Brenda Cowley (1978: 8), 'The Political Effectiveness of Phyllis Haslam.' TEFS Archives – Haslam File.
30 'The First Forty Years of the Elizabeth Fry Society of Ottawa.' OEFS.
31 'The First Forty Years of the Elizabeth Fry Society of Ottawa.' OEFS.
32 Annual Report of the Commissioner of Penitentiaries, 1956–57.
33 Interview transcripts.
34 Letter dated 10 March 1964 from Rowan M. Paterson, Rehabilitation Officer, to Mr Guy Favreau, Minister of Justice. Kingston Elizabeth Fry Society (KEFS).
35 Letter dated 10 March 1964. KEFS.
36 Annual Report of the Commissioner of Penitentiaries, 1948–60.
37 Letter dated 10 March 1964. KEFS.
38 Annual Report of the Elizabeth Fry Society – Toronto Branch, 18 May 1955. Toronto Elizabeth Fry Society (TEFS).
39 The Annual Report of the Elizabeth Fry Society – Toronto Branch, 18 May 1955. TEFS.
40 The Annual Report of the Elizabeth Fry Society – Toronto Branch May 18, 1955. TEFS.
41 Initially only the Catholic Family Bureau responded and agreed to do referrals. 'The First Forty Years of the Elizabeth Fry Society of Ottawa' (Ottawa Elizabeth Fry – Historical Records).
42 Telegram (1952) media clipping. TEFS Archives.
43 'Recommendations for the Reorganization and Revitalization of the Prison for Women at Kingston,' February 1960. National Archives, Ottawa.
44 'Recommendations for the Reorganization and Revitalization of the Prison for Women at Kingston' February 1960: 1. National Archives.
45 'Recommendations for the Reorganization and Revitalization of the Prison for Women at Kingston' February 1960: 4 (Appendix C). National Archives, 73-56, file 1-6-40; vol. 2.
46 'Recommendations for the Reorganization and Revitalization of the Prison for Women at Kingston' February 1960: 4 (Appendix C). National Archives, 73-56, file 1-6-40; vol. 2.
47 See 'The First Forty Years of the Elizabeth Fry Society of Ottawa' (Ottawa Elizabeth Fry Society – Historical Records); and the Annual Report of the Elizabeth Fry Society – Toronto Branch, 18 May 1955. TEFS.
48 For an interesting discussion of the governance of alcohol and addiction, see Valverde (1998).
49 In 1968 the society urged that the detoxification unit set up by the foundation for men be extended to include women. For more information, see 'History of the Elizabeth Fry Society of Toronto.' TEFS.

50 Several copies of these briefs are located in the archives and libraries at the Toronto Elizabeth Fry Society and at the Canadian Association of Elizabeth Fry Societies.

51 These briefs are located in the archives at the Toronto Elizabeth Fry Society.

52 Comments by Mrs Helen Tracy. Newsletter of the Elizabeth Fry Society of Toronto (1978) – special issue in honour of Phyllis Haslam. TEFS.

53 Interview transcripts, October 1996.

54 Interview transcripts, October, 1996.

55 Haslam came from a prominent and accomplished middle-class family. Her mother, Dr Jean Jones, was one of the first women graduates in medicine from the University of Toronto in 1903. Her father, Dr Albert Haslam, was an Anglican minister and missionary to India, and later became the head of the theological college in Saskatoon. While in India, Dr Jones founded a hospital and remained one of its chief directors until succeeded by her daughter, and Phyllis's sister, Dr Florence Haslam. Phyllis Haslam's two other sisters became teachers, and her brother became a nuclear physicist (Cowley 1978). Phyllis Haslam and her sisters were educated at Havergal School in Toronto. Despite their privileged background, the Haslam children were taught the value of philanthropy and political consciousness. After Havergal, Haslam continued her education at the University of Saskatchewan, where she received a BSc, majoring in math and physics. In 1936 she acquired a degree in social work from the University of Toronto. She spent some time working at the Galt Training School 'developing records' and 'helping with recreation' to fulfil the requirements of her degree (Cowley 1978: 4). Shortly after returning from the Commonwealth Games (where she won a medal for swimming), she went to work for the YWCA in Montreal. In 1941 she became the Executive Director of the Cornwall YWCA, where she participated in the establishment of the Trinidad YWCA. After several years with the YWCA in several capacities, she decided to return to work in the field of corrections. This desire for a change corresponded with the emergence of the Elizabeth Fry Society of Toronto. According to Mrs Helen Tracy, founding president of the Elizabeth Fry Society of Toronto and volunteer co-ordinator between 1971 and 1976, in May 1953 Haslam 'took a substantial cut in salary' to begin working as the executive director of the newly formed Elizabeth Fry Society of Toronto.

56 At first, Haslam's salary was paid by the provincial Department of Reform Institutions.

57 Interview transcripts, October 1996.

58 Interview transcripts, October 1996.
59 Interview transcripts, October 1996.
60 Interview transcripts, October 1996.
61 Newsletter of the Elizabeth Fry Society of Toronto (1978), special issue in honour of Phyllis Haslam. TEFS.
62 The phrase 'women in conflict with the law' is the terminology that Elizabeth Fry Societies have chosen to use when referring to their clients. These agencies provide services for a wide range of women. This language was adopted in the late 1960s, presumably to avoid stigmatizing labels such as prisoner, convict, and offender.
63 In November 1953, the Toronto Elizabeth Fry Society joined with the Kingston and Ottawa Societies to form a Provincial Council of Elizabeth Fry Societies.
64 For a detailed description of the debate and ideas informing feminist therapies, see Kendall (1993b).
65 CAEFS, originally conceived in 1969, was incorporated as a voluntary nonprofit organization in 1978. In 1969, delegates from the Elizabeth Fry Societies of Vancouver, Kingston, Ottawa, and Toronto attending a Corrections Congress in Vancouver met to discuss a national association of Elizabeth Fry Societies (Stewart 1993: 11).

5: Breaking with Tradition: Feminist Reforms and the Empowerment of Women? 1970–96

1 For a detailed description of Claire Culhane's life and work, see Culhane (1979, 1985, 1986, 1991) and Lowe (1992).
2 For a detailed discussion of the violations of prisoners' rights in other countries, see Mitford (1973) and Hornblum (1998).
3 For a more detailed discussion of the experiences of female correctional officers, see McMahon (1999).
4 A more detailed description of female crime and of the characteristics of female offenders during this time can be located in Adams (1977).
5 Many of these nongovernment reports were produced by the Canadian Association of Elizabeth Fry Societies and by various local Elizabeth Fry Societies.
6 Interview transcripts, October 1996.
7 Interview transcripts, October 1996.
8 See *Women's Voices, Women's Choices* (Report of the Women's Issues Task Force), Ontario Ministry of the Solicitor General (1995), and Blueprint for

Change, Nova Scotia Correctional Services, Solicitor General's Special
Committee on Provincially Incarcerated Women (1992).

9 For a more detailed description of the events that led to the development
of the Task Force on Federally Sentenced Women, see Shaw (1993) and
Moffat (1991).

10 Research suggests that aboriginal offenders are more likely to be in
multilevel or maximum security than nonaboriginal prisoners; that they
are less likely to be released on full parole instead of mandatory supervision; that they are geographically dislocated from their home communities; and that they are more likely to have their conditional release revoked
(LeClair 1998).

11 In the few years before the task force was established, and while the task
force was sitting, there were several suicides and attempted suicides at
P4W. Many of the inmates who committed or attempted suicide during
this time were aboriginal women. This, and the inadequate living conditions at the prison, led to an increased public awareness of federally
sentenced women (Kershaw and Lasovich 1991).

12 There were thirty-one government and nongovernment officials on the
task force's Steering Committee and ten on the smaller Working Group.
See *Creating Choices* (TFFSW 1990: 1–4) for a detailed list of the membership on these committees.

13 Two native inmates at P4W – Fran Sugar and Lana Fox – completed some
research for the Task Force. Their report provides anecdotal information
on the lives and experiences of thirty-nine aboriginal women who have
been incarcerated at P4W. In the same vein, a survey of federally sentenced women completed by Margaret Shaw (1991a) outlines the views
and experiences of federally sentenced women in Canada.

14 A more detailed description of these concepts is available in *Creating
Choices* (TFFSW 1990).

15 A more comprehensive discussion of the recommendations proposed by
the Task Force on Federally Sentenced Women is found in *Creating Choices*
(TFFSW 1990). For this chapter, I have only summarized what I believe are
the most significant recommendations.

16 All staff working in the regional facilities are supposed to take special,
women-centred training in addition to the core training provided to all
newly hired correctional staff. Under the original staffing model at the
new regional facilities, the intention was to hire only those staff who were
appropriate for a women's facility; in other words, the candidates for the
new facilities would have to appreciate the needs and concerns of feder-

ally sentenced women, and of aboriginal women. At first, staff were
carefully screened and selected, and many of the new staff hired did not
have prior experience working in prisons. Many worked in women's
organizations and in the community, and several were women returning
to paid work outside the home after raising families. Currently there is
considerable debate as to the appropriateness of having men work in the
regional facilities on the front line. At present, men are working in these
positions. CAEFS has serious concerns about the safety and privacy of
women prisoners due to this practice. The Correctional Service of Canada
insists that men have a legal right to these positions and that appropriate
security precautions are being taken to ensure women prisoners' safety
and privacy. As the result of a recommendation made by the 1996 Arbour
Commission (Canada 1996), an independent investigation is presently
being conducted by Thérèse Lajeunesse and Christie Jefferson, who are
evaluating the issue of cross-gender staffing. See Lajeunesse and Jefferson
(1998, 1999) for a more detailed discussion of their preliminary findings.
17 Each of the four regional facilities is supposed to offer four core programs
– Abuse and Trauma, Substance Abuse, Living Skills (which includes
parenting), and Vocational and Educational Programs – as well as other
relevant woman-centred programs. For more information on these programs, see CSC (1994a), *Correctional Program Strategy for Federally Sentenced
Women*.
18 The policies for the new institutions, like all institutional policies, were
derived from prevailing legislation (the Corrections and Conditional
Release Act) and existing commissioners' directives. In the case of the new
facilities and their mandate, specific commissioner's directives had to be
written (i.e., The directive on the mother–child program). Prior to this
exercise, existing commissioners' directives were written to accommodate
the security and programming needs of the larger male population. Many
of these directives were not applicable to women.
19 Press release, Canadian Association of Elizabeth Fry Societies, 20 January
1997.
20 More detailed descriptions of these terms can be found in *Creating Choices*
(TFFSW 1990) and in the *Draft Correctional Program Strategy for Federally
Sentenced Women* – abridged version (CSC 1994a). Shaw (1993: 55–6)
provides a more detailed summary of these principles.
21 For additional details on the core programs at the federally sentenced
women's prisons, see CSC (1994a, 1995b, 1996a, 1998b).
22 For additional details on the Mother–Child Program, see Labrecque (1995).
23 When possible, the other regional facilities have tried to accommodate

federally sentenced women with children; however, they do not have functioning mother–child programs.

24 For additional information, see Druar, Carrington, and Goyder (1998), Van Nijnatten and Gregoire (1993), Conner and Fischer (1994), Keip (1994), and the transcripts of the public debate that took place at Conestoga College in Kitchener, Ontario, on 17 March 1994 (CSC file).

25 British Columbia is one of three provinces (the others being Manitoba and Newfoundland) with active exchange-of-service agreements (ESA) that permit the housing of federally sentenced women in provincial jails.

26 The operational principles do not appear to replace the original guiding principles outlined in Creating Choices (TFFSW 1990: 104–12). Instead, these operational principles are further elaborations and modifications of the guiding principles. In some correctional documents, both sets of principles are referenced.

27 For a more detailed discussion of the limitations of *Creating Choices* by a series of different authors, see Hannah-Moffat and Shaw (2000a).

28 Aboriginal people are presently overrepresented in the Canadian federal and provincial incarcerated populations, and the problem seems to be getting worse. Aboriginal people accounted for 11 per cent of admissions to federal custody in 1991–92, 15 per cent in 1996–97, and 17 per cent in 1997–98. Yet they represent only 2 per cent of the adult population (Canadian Centre for Justice Statistics 1999: 45). A fuller analysis of the direct and systemic racism experienced by incarcerated aboriginal people, and of Corrections Canada's responses, can be found in Waldram (1997). A recent article by Sangster (1999) attempts to trace the roots of the overincarceration of aboriginal women in twentieth-century Ontario. Also see Laprairie (1996).

29 For additional information on the Operational Plan for the Healing Lodge, see CSC (1993).

30 Members of the Nekaneet Reserve and citizens of the town of Maple Creek were included on the planning circle because the healing lodge is located on Nekaneet land just outside the town of Maple Creek.

31 The term 'privatization' in this context refers not only to the use of private corporations, but also to the government's increasing reliance on volunteers and nonprofit agencies or community groups. The term 'civilianization' is used by Garland (1996a: 456) to refer to the state's transfer of tasks that were performed by trained state agents, to volunteer citizens.

32 For a detailed discussion of the Hobbema Healing Lodge for federally sentenced men, see Braun 1998.

6: Empowering Prison: Neoliberal Governance

1 For a more detailed account of the continuance of an oppressive regime, see Arbour (1996), CAEFS (1996, 1997, 1998, 1999a), CSC (1995a, 1996b, 1996c), Pate (1999), Faith and Pate (2000), and Martel (2000).

2 For a discussion, see Hannah-Moffat and Shaw (2000a).

3 For further information on the adoption of actuarial techniques of governing in relation to crime and punishment, see Castel (1991), Feeley and Simon (1992), O'Malley (1992, 1996, 1998), and Hannah-Moffat (1999).

4 This is a brief outline of some of the key elements of neoliberalism. A more comprehensive discussion can be found in Rose (1993, 1996a, 1996b), Barry, Osbourne, and Rose (1996), O'Malley (1996).

5 For a more detailed description of these adaptive strategies, see Garland (1996a).

6 For a detailed discussion of the actuarial governance of federally sentenced women, see Hannah-Moffat (1999) and Hannah-Moffat and Shaw (2000b).

7 The term 'private' is meant to refer to all nonstate organizations, associations, and companies; this includes (but is not limited to) volunteers, churches, community groups, charitable and philanthropic organizations, and private businesses and corporations.

8 Some of these reports include J. Sauve (1977), Daubney (1988), Task Force on Federally Sentenced Women (1990), and *Creating Choices. Report of the Task Force on Federally Sentenced Women.*

9 Aboriginal women represent only 3 per cent of Canada's female population; however, they make up 15 per cent of Canada's federal female prison population. There is evidence that the problems of physical and sexual abuse, and substance abuse, are magnified for aboriginal women in prison (CSC 1997a: 11). The analysis in this paper examines the general plans and narratives informing the development and operation of the new regional prisons for women. While these plans are generally applicable to the aboriginal healing lodge (designed to meet the needs of aboriginal women prisoners), this prison has some separate policy guidelines that are not discussed in this paper.

10 The phrase 'will to empower' is taken from B. Cruikshank (1994).

11 The growing mass of policy and academic literature in education, health, legal, and labour reform and indeed penal reform confirms the widespread acceptance of empowerment strategies. Scholars who have documented these shifts in policy include Cruikshank (1993), Kendall (1993b), Shaw (1996a, 1996b), and Townsend (1998), who analyse changes in

therapeutic regimes. Snider (1994) examines these shifts in terms of punishment. Kinsman (1995) examines AIDS activism, and Young (1994) analyses drug and alcohol programs for pregnant women.

12 To support these claims, the task force and related policy documents cite several studies and statistics that illustrate the high incidences of racism, and sexism, and violent victimization, and educational and employment barriers, facing women in society – and more acutely women in prison.

13 For a more detailed description and analysis of the 'prudent subject,' see P. O'Malley (1996).

14 For further elaboration on the idea of relegitimating prisons, see J. Pratt (1997), and Sparks (1994).

15 For a more detailed analysis of how prisoners are increasingly governed through risk-based actuarial technologies, see Hannah-Moffat (1999) and Feeley and Simon (1992, 1994).

16 For a detailed discussion of the incidents that took place at P4W in 1994, see Arbour (1996), Frigon (1999), and Pate (1999).

17 A fuller description of events can be found in Arbour (1996).

18 One of the most significant outcomes of the inquiry was the development of the senior position of Deputy Commissioner for Women. Nancy Stableforth was appointed to this position in June of 1996. While this appointment has resulted in some positive changes, recommendations of the Arbour Report that outline the position and its authority have not been fully implemented (see Arbour 1996: 251–2). Consequently, the wardens of each women's unit report to their respective regional deputy commissioners. There is no uniformity in institutional decision making about women's corrections across the country; each facility is marginalized by virtue of being a small, expensive women's unit administered in a large men's penitentiary.

19 A more detailed discussion of these incidents is available in the following Board of Investigation Reports (CSC 1995a, 1996b, 1996c, 1996d, 1997b, 1997c).

20 Correctional Service of Canada, 'backgrounder,' September 1999.

21 The Intensive Healing Program for Women in Ontario was originally to be implemented at the Regional Treatment Centre inside Kingston Penitentiary. The court challenge resulted in the program to being moved to P4W.

22 Correctional Service of Canada, 'backgrounder,' September 1999. Presentation at National Stakeholder's Meeting by Deputy Warden Lori Macdonald, 19 January 2000, Toronto, Ontario. For more detail on the history of these developments, see Whitehall (1995), Laishes and Lyth (1996), Rivera (1996), Laises (1997), and Warner (1998).

23 Correctional Service of Canada, 'backgrounder,' September 1999, Presentation at National Stakeholder's Meeting by Deputy Warden Lori Macdonald, 19 January 2000, Toronto, Ontario.
24 News Release, 3 September 1999, National Strategy for High Need Women in Federal Correctional Institutions.
25 For additional details about the maximum population, see McDonagh (1999) and Morin (1999).

Conclusion: Stumbling Blocks, Growing Pains, or More of the Same?

1 Howe (1994) discusses some of the possibilities for addressing the discredited category of 'woman' on a political level. For example, she cites the efforts of political prisoners and others who have sought to develop 'new bases for affiliation' with fellow inmates and other political detainees (Harlow 1986: 508–20; cited in Howe 1994: 169).
2 See, for example, McDonagh (1999).
3 The reference to a white, middle-class sensibility is not meant to suggest that the category 'white, middle-class individual' is homogeneous.
4 The experiences of aboriginal women prisoners are clearly different from those of nonaboriginal women prisoners. However, this discussion does not articulate the breadth and content of these differences and experiences. For further information on aboriginal women prisoners, see Sugar and Fox (1989, 1990), and Adelberg and the Native Women's Association of Canada (1993).
5 More recently, the Commission on Systemic Racism in the Ontario Criminal Justice System (1994) has begun to consider the experiences of racism in a wide variety of communities. However, the recent report of the commission, *Racism Behind Bars: The Treatment of Black and Other Racial Minority Prisoners in Ontario Prisons*, does not provide a detailed or systemic account of the experiences and problems of minority women prisoners.
6 For a detailed account of the recommendations of the 1996 Arbour report, consult the report itself.
7 See Lajeunesse and Jefferson (1998a, 1999b).

References

Adams, S.G. 1977. 'Female Offender – Selected Statistics.' Appendix to the Report of the National Advisory Committee on the Female Offender. Ottawa: Solicitor General Canada.

Additon, H. 1949. 'The Woman Offender.' *Proceedings of the Fifth Canadian Penal Congress*. Kingston: Canadian Penal Congress.

Adelberg, E., and C. Currie. 1987. *Too Few to Count*. Vancouver: Press Gang.

– 1993. *In Conflict with the Law: Women and the Canadian Justice System*. Vancouver: Press Gang.

Adelberg, E., and the Native Women's Association of Canada. 1993. 'Aboriginal Women and Prison Reform.' In E. Adelberg and C. Currie, eds., *In Conflict with the Law*. Vancouver: Press Gang, pp. 76–94.

Alderson, J., and K. Hogan Wingate. 1997. *Administrative Investigation – Minor Disturbance – Use of Force – NOVA Institution*. Ottawa: Correctional Service of Canada.

Allen, H. 1987a. *Justice Unbalanced: Gender Psychiatry and Judicial Decisions*. Milton Keynes: Open University Press.

– 1987b. 'Rendering Them Harmless: The Professional Portrayal of Women Charged with Serious Violent Crimes.' In P. Carlen and A. Worrall, eds., *Gender, Crime and Justice*. Milton Keynes: Open University Press.

Arbour Commission – Public Hearings. 1996. *Transcript of Proceedings – Commission of Inquiry into Certain Events at the Prison for Women in Kingston*. (Phase II – P.C. 1995–608; vol. 4). Toronto: Farr Associates Reporting Inc.

Arnup, K. 1994. *Education for Motherhood: Advice for Mothers in Twentieth Century Canada*. Toronto: University of Toronto Press.

Axon, L. 1989. *Model and Exemplary Programs for Female Inmates: An International Survey*. Ottawa: Solicitor General of Canada.

– 1989. *Model and Exemplary Programs Available to Federally Sentenced Women*. Ottawa: Correctional Service of Canada.

Bacchi, C.L. 1990. *Same Difference: Feminism and Sexual Difference.* Boston: Allen and Unwin.

Backhouse, C. 1991. *Petticoats and Prejudice: Women and the Law in Nineteenth Century Canada.* Toronto: The Osgoode Society.

Backhouse, C., and D.H. Flaherty. 1992. *Challenging Times: The Women's Movement in Canada and the United States.* Kingston: McGill-Queen's University Press.

Baehre, R. 1977. 'Origins of the Penitentiary System in Upper Canada.' *Ontario History* LXIX(3): 186–207.

Baines, B. 1981. 'Women, Human Rights and the Constitution.' In A. Doerr and M. Carrier, eds., *Constitution in Canada.* Ottawa: Ministry of Supply and Service, pp. 31–63.

– 1988. 'Women and the Law.' In S. Burt, L. Code, and L. Dorney, eds., *Changing Patterns: Women in Canada.* Toronto: McClelland & Stewart, pp. 157–83.

Bannerji, H. 1995. 'In the Matter of "X": Building Race into Sexual Harassment.' *Thinking Through Essays on Feminism, Marxism, and Anti-Racism.* Toronto: Women's Press.

Barne, K. 1962. *Elizabeth Fry.* London: Methuen and Company.

Barry, A., T. Osborne, and N. Rose, eds. 1996. *Foucault and Political Reason: Liberalism, Neoliberalism and Rationalities of Government.* Chicago: University of Chicago Press.

Beattie, J. 1977. *Attitudes Towards Crime and Punishment in Upper Canada, 1830–1850: A Documentary Study.* Toronto: University of Toronto, Centre of Criminology.

Bell, V. 1993. *Interrogating Incest: Feminism, Foucault and the Law.* London: Routledge.

Benson, M. 1973. 'Adult Female Offenders: An Examination of the Nature of Their Offences, the Criminal Process and Service Patterns.' Toronto: Toronto Elizabeth Fry Society.

– 1995. 'Maternal Influence: Inmate Culture in the Andrew Mercer Reformatory for Women, 1880–1915.' Unpublished discussion paper, Department of History, University of Toronto, Toronto, Ontario.

Bertrand, M.-A., 1998. *Prisons pour femmes.* Montréal: Éditions du Méridien.

– 1999. 'Incarceration as a gendering strategy.' *Canadian Journal of Law & Society,* 14(1): 45–60.

Berzins, L., and R. Collette-Carrière. 1979. 'La femme en prison: un inconvénient social!' *Santé mentale au Québec* 4(2): 87–103.

Berzins, L., and S. Cooper. 1982. 'The Political Economy of Correctional Planning for Women: The Case of the Bankrupt Bureaucracy.' *Canadian Journal of Criminology,* October: 399–416.

Berzins, L., and B. Hayes. 1987. 'The Diaries of Two Agents of Change.' In E. Adelberg and C. Currie, eds., *Two Few to Count: Canadian Women in Conflict with the Law*. Vancouver: Press Gang.

Biron, L. 1992. 'Les femmes et l'incarceration. Le temps n'arrange rien.' *Criminologie* XXV(1): 119–34.

Bloch, R. 1993. 'American Feminine Ideals in Transition: The Rise of the Moral Mother, 1785–1815.' *Feminist Studies* 19: 101–26.

Blomberg, T. 1995. 'Beyond Metaphors: Penal Reform as Net Widening,' in T. Blomberg and S. Cohen, *Punishment and Social Control*. New York: Aldine de Gruyer.

Blomberg, T., and S. Cohen. 1995. *Punishment and Social Control*. New York: Aldine de Gruyter.

Boritch, H. 1997. *Fallen Women: Female Crime and Criminal Justice in Canada*. Toronto: ITP Nelson.

Boyd, S., and Elizabeth Sheehy. 1989. 'Feminism and Law in Canada – Overview.' In T. Caputo, M. Kennedy, C. Reasons, and A. Brannigan, eds., *Law and Society: A Critical Perspective*. Toronto: Harcourt Brace Jovanovich.

Braun, C. 1998. Colonization, Deconstruction and Renewal: Stories from Aboriginal Men at the Pe'Sakastew Centre. Masters thesis, Saskatoon, University of Saskatchewan.

Brodsky, G., and S. Day. 1989. *One Step Forward or Two Steps Back? Canadian Charter Equality Rights for Women*. Ottawa: Canadian Advisory Council on the Status of Women.

Brown, D., H. Kramer, and M. Quinn. 1988. 'Women in Prison Task Force Reform.' *European Group for the Study of Deviance and Social Control*, Norway conference papers, 1988. Reprinted in M. Findlay and R. Hogg, eds., *Understanding Crime and Criminal Justice*. Sydney: The Law Book Company.

Brown, W. 1996. *Doing Justice, Doing Gender: Women in Law and Criminal Justice Occupations*. London: Sage Publications.

Canada. 1849. Report of the Royal Commission to Inquire and then Report upon the Conduct, Economy, Discipline, and Management of the Provincial Penitentiary (Brown Commission).

– 1868. Annual Report of the Directors of Penitentiaries. Ottawa: King's Printer.

– 1894. Annual Report of the Inspector of Penitentiaries (1893–1894). Ottawa King's Printer.

– 1914. Report of the Royal Commission on Penitentiaries (MacDonnell Report). Ottawa: King's Printer.

– 1921a. Report on the State and Management of the Female Prison at Kingston Penitentiary (Nickle Commission). Ottawa: King's Printer.

– 1921b. Report of the Committee Appointed by the Right Honourable J.C.

Doherty, Minister of Justice to Advise Upon the Revision of the Penitentiary Regulations and the Penitentiary Act (Biggar, Nickle and Draper Report). Ottawa: Department of Justice.

– 1938. Report of the Royal Commission to Investigate the Penal System in Canada (Archambault Report). Ottawa: King's Printer.

– 1947. Report of General R.B. Gibson Regarding the Penitentiary System in Canada (Gibson Report). Ottawa: King's Printer.

– 1956. Committee Appointed to Inquire into the Principles and Procedures Followed in the Remission Service of the Department of Justice (Fauteux Report). Ottawa: Queen's Printer.

– 1977a. Report of the National Advisory Committee on the Female Offender (Clark Report). Ottawa: Ministry of the Solicitor General of Canada.

– 1977b. *Report of the Subcommittee on the Penitentiary System in Canada* (MacGuigan Report). Ottawa: Supply and Services Canada.

– 1978a. Report of the Joint Committee to Study the Alternatives for the Housing of the Federal Female Offender (Chinnery Report). Ottawa: Ministry of the Solicitor General of Canada.

– 1978b. Report of the National Planning Committee on the Female Offender (Needham Report). Ottawa: Ministry of the Solicitor General of Canada

– 1988. *Task Force on Aboriginal Peoples in Federal Corrections.* Ottawa: Ministry of the Solicitor General.

– 1990. *The History of Federal/Provincial Exchange of Service (Federal/Provincial Policy Review) Agreements.* Ottawa: Correctional Service of Canada.

– 1996. *Commission of Inquiry into Certain Events at the Prison for Women in Kingston.* (Arbour Report). Ottawa: Public Works and Government Services of Canada.

Canadian Association of Elizabeth Fry Societies (CAEFS). 1978. *Report of the Study Group on Clarke Report.* Ottawa: Canadian Association of Elizabeth Fry Societies.

– 1994. *Annual Report.* Ottawa: Canadian Association of Elizabeth Fry Societies.

– 1995. *Annual Report.* Ottawa: Canadian Association of Elizabeth Fry Societies.

– 1996. Annual Report. Ottawa: Canadian Association of Elizabeth Fry Societies.

– 1997. Annual Report. Ottawa: Canadian Association of Elizabeth Fry Societies.

– 1998. Annual Report. Ottawa: Canadian Association of Elizabeth Fry Societies.

– 1999a. Annual Report. Ottawa: Canadian Association of Elizabeth Fry Societies.

- 1999b. *Brief on Five-Year Review of the Corrections and Conditional Release Act*. Ottawa: Canadian Association of Elizabeth Fry Societies.
Canadian Centre for Justice Statistics. 1999. *The Juristat Reader*. Toronto: Thompson Educational Publishing.
Canadian Committee on Corrections. 1969. Report of the Canadian Committee on Corrections (Ouimet Report). Ottawa: Queen's Printer.
Canadian Penal Congress. 1949. *Proceedings of the Fifth Canadian Penal Congress Held at Kingston, Ontario*. Toronto: Canadian Penal Congress.
Carlen, P. 1983. *Women's Imprisonment*. London: Routledge and Kegan Paul.
- 1988. *Women, Crime and Poverty*. Milton Keynes: Open University Press.
- 1990. *Alternatives to Women's Imprisonment*. Milton Keynes: Open University Press.
- 1994. 'Why Study Women's Imprisonment? An Indefinite Article.' *British Journal of Criminology* (special issue – 'Prisons in Context'), 34: 131–40.
Carlen, P., and A. Worrall. 1987. *Gender, Crime and Justice*. Milton Keynes: Open University Press.
Carpenter, M. 1872; 1967. *Reformatory Prison Discipline, As Developed by the Rt Honourable Sir Walter Crofton in the Irish Convict Prison*. New Jersey: Patterson Smith.
Castel, R. 1991. 'From Dangerousness to Risk.' In G. Burchell, C. Gordon, and P. Miller, eds., *The Foucault Effect: Studies in Governmentality*. Chicago: University of Chicago Press.
Chandler, E. 1973. *Women in Prison*. New York: Bobbs-Merrill.
Cheriton, L. 1957. *Let's Face Our Responsibility to the Woman Offender*. Montreal: Canadian Congress of Correctional Proceedings.
Chunn, D. 1992. *From Punishment to Doing Good: Family Courts and Socialized Justice in Ontario, 1880–1940*. Toronto: University of Toronto Press.
Chunn, D., and R. Menzies. 1990. 'Gender, Madness and Crime: The Reproduction of Patriarchal and Class Relations in a Psychiatric Court Clinic.' *Journal of Human Justice* 1(2): 33–54.
Cohen, S. 1985. *Visions of Social Control*. Cambridge: Polity Press.
Comack, E. 1996. *Women in Trouble*. Halifax: Fernwood Publishing.
Commission on Systemic Racism in the Ontario Criminal Justice System. 1994. *Racism Behind Bars: The Treatment of Black and Other Racial Minority Prisoners in Ontario Prisons* (interim report). Toronto: Queen's Printer for Ontario.
Connor, D., and D. Fischer. 1994. *Evaluation of the Public Consultation for the Federal Women's Facility, Edmonton*. (Prepared for Correctional Service of Canada.) Victoria: Connor Development Services Ltd.
Cooper, S. 1987, 1993. 'The Evolution of the Federal Women's Prison.' In E. Adelberg and C. Currie, eds., *In Conflict with the Law*. Vancouver: Press Gang.

Correctional Service of Canada. 1991. *Symposium on the Future of Federal Corrections*. Ottawa: Correctional Service of Canada.
- 1992. 'Operational Plan' (draft). Ottawa: Correctional Service of Canada.
- 1993. *The Healing Lodge – Final Operating Plan*. Ottawa: Correctional Service of Canada, Federally Sentenced Women's Program.
- 1994a. 'Draft Correctional Program Strategy for Federally Sentenced Women' (abridged version). Ottawa: Correctional Service of Canada.
- 1994c. 'Implementing the FSW Task Force Report: Theory Into Practice.' *Let's Talk*. Ottawa: Correctional Service of Canada.
- 1995a. *Board of Investigation – Major Disturbances and Other Related Incidents – Prison for Women from Friday, April 22 to Tuesday, April 26, 1994*. Ottawa: Correctional Service of Canada.
- 1995b. *Substance Abuse Program for Women*. Ottawa: Correctional Service of Canada.
- 1995c. *Briefing Notes – Strategy to Manage Federally Sentenced Women Who Behave Violently*. Ottawa: The Federally Sentenced Women Program Committee.
- 1996a. *The Correctional Strategy*. Ottawa: Correctional Service of Canada, Federally Sentenced Women Program.
- 1996b. *Board of Investigation Report into a Suicide in February 1996, and Other Major Incidents at Edmonton Institution for Women*. Ottawa: Correctional Service of Canada. #1410-2-318.
- 1996c. *Board of Investigation Report into the Suicide of an Inmate at Prison for Women in February 1996*. Ottawa: Correctional Service of Canada. #1410-2-314.
- 1996d. *Major Inmate Disturbance: NOVA Institution, September 5, 1996; Board of Investigation into the Disturbance on the Federally Sentenced Women Unit, Saskatchewan Penitentiary*. Ottawa: Correctional Service of Canada.
- 1997a. 'Okimaw Ohci Healing Lodge.' *Let's Talk* 22(4): 11–12. Ottawa: Correctional Service of Canada.
- 1997b. *Board of Investigation into Alleged Inappropriate Application of Use of Force by the Cell Extraction Team on a Female Inmate at Springhill Institution from March 1, 1997 – March 9, 1997*. Ottawa: Correctional Service of Canada.
- 1997c. *Board of Investigation into the Disturbance on the Federally Sentenced Women's Unit Saskatchewan Penitentiary July 12, 1997*. Ottawa: Correctional Service of Canada.
- 1998a. *Board of Investigation into Allegations of Mistreatment by a Former Inmate at the Prison for Women between March 22, 1960 – August 1, 1963*. Ottawa: Correctional Service of Canada.
- 1998b. *Community Strategy for Women on Conditional Release – Discussion Paper*. Ottawa: Correctional Service of Canada.

– 2000. *Enhancing the Role of Aboriginal Communities in Federal Corrections.* Ottawa: Correctional Service of Canada.

Cott, N. 1989. 'What's in a Name: The Limits of Social Feminism.' *Journal of American History* 76: 809–29.

Coulson, G. 1993. 'Using the Level of Supervision Inventory in Placing Female Offenders in Rehabilitation Programs.' *IARCA Journal* 5: 12–13.

Cousineau, M.-M., D. Laberge, and B. Théorêt. 1986. *Prisons et prisonniers: une analyse de la détention provinciale québécoise durant la dernière décennie.* Montréal: Université du Québec à Montréal, Département de sociologie.

Cowley, B. 1978. 'The Political Effectiveness of Phyllis Haslam' (unpublished paper). Toronto: Toronto Elizabeth Fry Society Library.

Crawford, V., N. Joyce, and K. Becker. 1990. *Five Year Plan for Female Inmates.* Illinois: Illinois Department of Corrections, Bureau of Administration and Planning.

Crenshaw, K. 1992. 'Whose Story Is It, Anyway? Feminist and Antiracist Appropriations of Anita Hill.' In T. Morrison, ed., *Race-in Justice, Engendering Power*, pp. 402–36. New York: Pantheon.

Cruikshank, B. 1993. 'Revolutions Within Self Government and Self Esteem.' *Economy and Society* 22: 327–43.

– 1994. 'The Will to Empower: Technologies of Citizenship and the War on Poverty.' *Socialist Review* 93(4): 29–55.

Culhane, C. 1979. *Barred from Prison: A Personal Account.* Vancouver: Pulp Press.

– 1985. *Still Barred from Prison.* Montreal: Black Rose.

– 1986. 'Civil Disobedience at the Prison Gate: The Movement for Abolition of the Prison System in Canada.' In Brian Maclean, ed., *The Political Economy of Crime.* Scarborough: Prentice Hall.

– 1991. *No Longer Barred from Prison.* Montreal: Black Rose.

Cullen, F., and K. Gillbert. 1982. *Reaffirming Rehabilitation.* Cincinnati: Anderson Publishing.

Daly, K. 1989. 'Criminal Justice Ideologies and Practices in Different Voices: Some Feminist Questions About Justice.' *International Journal of the Sociology of Law* 17: 1–18.

Daubney, D. 1988. *Taking Responsibility: Report of the Standing Committee on Justice and the Solicitor General on Its Review of Sentencing, Conditional Release and Other Related Aspects of Corrections.* Ottawa: Solicitor General of Canada.

Dean, M. 1999. *Governmentality: Power and Rule in Modern Society.* Thousand Oaks: Sage Publications.

Dobash, R.E., R.P. Dobash, and S. Gutteridge. 1986. *The Imprisonment of Women.* New York: Routledge.

Drouin, M.-A. 1997. 'Rethinking Women Imprisonment: A Canadian Perspective.' In S. Hayman, *Imprisoning Women: Recognising Differences*. Proceedings
of a Conference. U.K.: Institute for the Study and Treatment of Delinquency.

Druar, L., P. Carrington, and J. Goyder. 1998. 'Community Reactions to the
New Prison for Women in Kitchener.' *Forum on Corrections Research*, 1998,
Vol. 10, No. 2, pp. 48–51.

Duff, R.A., and D. Garland, eds. 1994. *A Reader on Punishment*. Oxford: Oxford
University Press.

Edwards, S. 1981. *Female Sexuality and the Law*. Oxford: Martin Robertson.

– 1984. *Women on Trial*. Manchester: Manchester University Press.

Ekstedt, J., and C. Griffiths. 1988. *Corrections in Canada: Policy and Practice*.
Toronto: Butterworths.

Eveson, M. 1964. 'Research with Female Drug Addicts at the Prison for
Women.' *Canadian Journal of Corrections* 6: 21–7.

Faguy, P. 1973. 'Role of the Behavioural Scientist in the Canadian Federal
Penitentiary System.' Unpublished paper. Address given to the American
Psychological Association. NCJRS: 014-884.

Faith, K. 1993. *Unruly Women: The Politics of Confinement and Resistance*. Vancouver: Press Gang.

Faith K., and K. Pate. 2000.' Personal & Political Musing on Activism' In K.
Hannah-Moffat and M. Shaw, eds., *The Ideal Prison: Critical Essays on
Women's Imprisonment in Canada*. Halifax: Fernwood Publishing.

Federally Sentenced Women Program (FSWP). 1994a. *Literature Review*. Ottawa:
Correctional Service of Canada, Federally Sentenced Women's Program.

Feeley, M., and J. Simon. 1992. 'The New Penology: Notes on the Emerging
Strategy for Corrections and Its Implications.' *Criminology* 30: 49–74.

– 1994. 'Actuarial Justice: The Emerging New Criminal Law.' In David
Nelken, ed., *The Futures of Criminology*. New Delhi: Sage Publications.

Feinman, C. 1986. *Women in the Criminal Justice System*. 2nd ed. New York:
Praeger.

Female Offender Study Committee. 1985. 'Providing Institutional Services for
the Female Inmate.' A Report to the Minister of Department of Health and
Social-Corrections Division. Ottawa: Consultation Centre, Ministry of the
Solicitor General of Canada.

Finateri, L. 1999. 'The Paradox of Pregnancy in Prison: Resistance, Control
and the Body.' *Canadian Woman Studies* 19(1&2): 136–44.

Foucault, M. 1977. *Discipline and Punish: The Birth of the Prison*. New York:
Vintage.

– 1980. *Power/Knowledge: Selected Interviews and Other Writings*. Edited by
Colin Gordon. New York: Pantheon Books.

– 1981. 'Omnes et Sinulation: Towards a Critique of Political Reason.' In S.M.

McMurrin, ed., *Tanner Lectures on Human Values*. Cambridge: University of Cambridge Press.

- 1983. 'The Subject and Power.' In H. Dreyfus and P. Rainbow, eds., *Michel Foucault: Beyond Structuralism and Hermeneutics*. 2nd ed. Chicago: University of Chicago Press.
- 1990. *History of Sexuality*. New York: Vintage Books.
- 1991. 'Governmentality.' In G. Burchell, C. Gordon, and P. Miller, eds., *The Foucault Effect – Studies in Governmentality*. Chicago: University of Chicago Press.

Freedman, E. 1979. 'Separation as a Strategy: Female Institution Building and American Feminism, 1870–1930.' *Feminist Studies* 5(3): 512–29.

- 1981. *Their Sisters Keepers: Women's Prison Reform in America, 1830–1930*. Ann Arbor: University of Michigan Press.
- 1990. 'Theoretical Perspectives on Sexual Difference: An Overview.' In D. Rhode, ed., *Theoretical Perspectives on Sexual Difference*. New Haven: Yale University Press, pp. 257–61.
- 1996. 'The Prison Lesbian: Race, Class, and the Construction of the Aggressive Female Homosexual, 1915–1965.' *Feminist Studies* 22(2): 397–423.

Friedland, M. 1988. *Sentencing Structure in Canada: Historical Perspective*. Research Reports of the Canadian Sentencing Commission, Ottawa: Department of Justice.

Frigon, S. 1997. 'Sexe, mensonge et vidéo.' *Journal of Prisoners on Prisons* 8(1&2): pp. 105–12.

- 1999. 'Une radioscopie des événements survenus à la Prison des femmes de Kingston en Ontario en avril 1994: la construction d'un corps dangereux et d'un corps en danger.' *Canadian Women Studies/Les cahiers de la femme* 19(1&2). Toronto: York University Publications.

Fry, K., and R.E. Cresswell. 1848. *Memoir of the Life of Elizabeth Fry: Extracts from Her Journals and Letters*. London: John Hatchard and Son.

Garland, D. 1985. *Punishment and Welfare: A History of Penal Strategies*. Brookfield: Gower Publishing.

- 1990. *Punishment and Modern Society*. Oxford: Oxford University Press.
- 1996a. 'The Limits of the Sovereign State: Strategies of Crime Control in Contemporary Society.' *British Journal of Criminology* 36(4): 445–71.
- 1996b. '"Governmentality" and the Problem of Crime?' Unpublished paper, University of Toronto, Centre of Criminology.
- 1997. 'Governmentality and the Problem of Crime: Foucault, Criminology and Sociology.' *Theoretical Criminology* 1(2): 173–214.

Gilligan, C. 1982. *In a Different Voice: Psychological Theory and Women's Development*. Cambridge: Harvard University Press.

Gosselin, L. 1982. *Prisons in Canada*. Montreal: Black Rose Books.

Griffiths, N.E.S. 1993. *The Splendid Vision: Centennial History of the National Council of Women, 1893–1993*. Ottawa: Carlton University Press.

Hamelin, M. 1985. 'Les Québécois et Québécoise pénalisés.' *Cahier de l'École de criminologie* 18. Montréal: Université de Montréal, École de criminologie.

– 1987. Les fouilles à nu et les fouilles vaginales-rectales, le cas de la prison Tanguay ou un exemple de pouvoir discrétionnaire en milieu carcéral. Toronto: Yull Publications.

– 1989. *Femmes et prison*. Montréal: Éditions du Méridien.

Hann, R., and W. Harman. 1989. *Release Risk Prediction: Testing the Nuffield Scoring System For Native and Female Inmates* Ottawa: Correctional Service of Canada.

Hannah-Moffat, K. 1995. 'Feminine Fortresses: Woman-Centred Prisons?' *The Prison Journal* 75(2): 135–64.

– 1997. 'From Christian Maternalism to Risk Technologies: Penal Powers and Women's Knowledges in the Governance of Female Prisons.' PhD thesis, University of Toronto, Centre of Criminology.

– 1999. 'Moral Agent or Actuarial Subject: Risk and Women's Imprisonment.' *Theoretical Criminology* 3(1): 71–94.

– 2000. 'Reforming the Prison: Rethinking Our Ideals.' In K. Hannah-Moffat and M. Shaw, eds., *The Ideal Prison: Critical Essays on Women's Imprisonment in Canada*. Halifax: Fernwood Publishing.

Hannah-Moffat, K., and M. Shaw, eds. 2000a. *The Ideal Prison: Critical Essays on Canadian Women's Imprisonment*. Halifax: Fernwood Publishing.

– 2000b. *Gender, Diversity and Risk Issues Relating to Classification of Federally Sentenced Women*. Final Report. Ottawa: Status of Women Canada.

Hannah-Moffat, K., and M. Valverde. 1996. 'Saving the Prison or Saving the Prisoner? Penality and the Salvation Army in Turn-of-the-Century Ontario.' Unpublished manuscript.

Haq, R. 1999. 'Ontario's Regressive Approach to Prisons: The Negative Impact of Super Jails on Women and Their Children.' *Canadian Woman Studies* 19(1&2): 133–5.

Harris, K. 1987. 'Moving into the New Millennium: Towards a Feminist Theory of Justice.' *Prison Journal* 67: 27–38.

Hart, D. 1959. 'Elizabeth Fry Yesterday and Today.' *Telescope* 9: 23–5.

Haslam, P. 1969. 'The Damaged Girl in a Distorted Society.' Toronto: Toronto Elizabeth Fry Society Library.

– 1970. 'The Woman Offender.' Toronto: Toronto Elizabeth Fry Society Library.

Hattem, T. 1986. *Le recours à l'isolement cellulaire dans quatre établissements de détention du Québec*. Université de Montréal: Centre International de Criminologie Comparé.

– 1991. 'Vivre avec ses peines.' *Déviance et Société* 15 (1): 137–56.

Hawkes, M.Q. 1994. *Excellent Effect: The Edna Mahan Story.* Arlington: American Correctional Association.

Hawthorn, H. 1955. *The Doukhobors of British Columbia.* Vancouver: J.M. Dent and Sons.

Hayes, B. 1983. 'Presentation to the Saskatchewan Association of Criminology and Corrections.' Unpublished paper. Ottawa: Women for Justice.

Hayman, S. 2000. 'Prison Reform and Incorporation: Lessons from Britain and Canada.' In K. Hannah-Moffat and M. Shaw, eds., *The Ideal Prison: Critical Essays on Women's Imprisonment in Canada.* Halifax: Fernwood Publishing.

Heidensohn, F. 1981. 'Women and the Penal System.' In A. Morris and L. Gelsthorpe, eds., *Women in Crime.* Cambridge: Cambridge Institute of Criminology.

– 1986. 'Models of Justice: Portia or Persephone? Some Thoughts on Equality Fairness and Gender in the Field of Criminal Justice.' *International Journal of the Sociology of Law* 14: 287–98.

Hernandez, N.H. 1970. *La femme incarcérée à Montréal: typologie psycho-sociale.* Mémoire de maîtrise et sciences (criminologie). Montréal: Université de Montréal, École de criminologie.

Hindus, B. 1996. *Discourses of Power: From Hobbes to Foucault.* London: Blackwell.

Horii, G. 1994. 'Disarm the Infamous Thing.' *Journal of Prisoners on Prisons* 5(2): 10–23.

– 2000. 'Processing Humans.' In K. Hannah-Moffat and M. Shaw, eds., *The Ideal Prison: Critical Essays on Women's Imprisonment in Canada.* Halifax: Fernwood Publishing.

Hornblum, A.M. 1998. *Acres of Skin: Human Experiments at Holmesburg Prison.* London: Routledge.

Howe, A. 1987. 'Social Injury Revisited: Towards a Feminist Theory of Social Justice.' *International Journal of the Sociology of Law* 15: 423–38.

– 1994. *Punish and Critique: Towards a Feminist Analysis of Penality.* London: Routledge.

Hudson, B. 1998. 'Punishment and Governance.' *Social and Legal Studies* 7(4): 581–7.

Ignatieff, M. 1978. *A Just Measure of Pain.* London: Penguin Books.

Jaccoud, M. 1992. 'Le Droit, l'exclusion et les Autochtones.' *Revue canadienne droit et société* 11(1): 217–34.

Jackson, M. 1988. *Justice Behind Walls: A Report to the Canadian Bar Association Committee on Imprisonment and Release.* British Columbia: University of British Columbia Law School.

Jackson, M., and C. Griffiths. 1991. *Canadian Criminology: Perspectives on Crime and Criminology*. Toronto: Harcourt, Brace and Company.

Jagger, A. 1990. 'Sexual Difference and Sexual Equality.' In D. Rhode, ed., *Theoretical Perspectives on Sexual Difference*. New Haven: Yale University Press, pp. 239–54.

James, J.L.T. 1990. *A Living Tradition: Penitentiary Chaplaincy*. Ottawa: Correctional Service of Canada.

Johnson, H. 1963. 'The Doukhobors of British Columbia.' *Queens Quarterly* 70: 528–41.

Joliffe, K. 1984. 'Penitentiary Medical Services, 1835–1983.' (Report No. 1984–19.) Ottawa: Solicitor General Canada.

Karrys, E. 1952. 'The Work of the Psychologist in the Training School for Girls, Galt, Ontario.' *Ontario Psychological Association Newsletter* 4(4): 4–7.

Kealey, L. 1979. *A Not Unreasonable Claim: Women and Reform in Canada, 1880–1920*. Toronto: Women's Press.

Keip, E. 1994. *Staff Training in Issues for Federally Sentenced Women* (workshop outline). Ottawa: Correctional Service of Canada.

Kendall, K. 1993a. *Program Evaluation of Therapeutic Services at the Prison for Women*. Ottawa: Correctional Service of Canada.

– 1993b. *Literature Review of Therapeutic Services for Women in the Prison for Women*, volumes 1–3. Ottawa: Correctional Service of Canada.

– 1994. 'Creating Real Choices: A Program Evaluation of Therapeutic Services at the Prison for Women.' *Forum on Corrections Research*. Ottawa: Correctional Services of Canada.

– 2000. 'Psy-ence Fiction: The Moral Regulation of Female Prisoners through Psychological Sciences.' In K. Hannah-Moffat and M. Shaw, eds., *The Ideal Prison: Critical Essays on Women's Imprisonment in Canada*. Halifax: Fernwood Publishing.

Kent, J. 1962. *Elizabeth Fry*. New York: Arco Publishing.

Kershaw, A., and M. Lasovich. 1991. *Rock-a-Bye Baby: A Death Behind Bars*. Toronto: McClelland & Stewart.

Kinsman, G. 1995. 'Responsibility as a Strategy of Governance: Regulating People Living with AIDS and Lesbians and Gay Men in Ontario.' Unpublished paper. Laurentian University, Department of Sociology and Anthropology.

Koven, S. 1993. 'Borderlands: Women, Voluntary Action, and Child Welfare in Britain, 1840 to 1914.' In S. Koven and S. Michel, eds., *Mothers of a New World: Maternalist Politics and the Origins of the Welfare State*. London: Routledge and Kegan Paul.

Koven, S., and S. Michel. 1993. *Mothers of a New World: Maternalist Politics and the Origins of the Welfare State.* London: Routledge and Kegan Paul.

Kunzel, R. 1993. *Fallen Women and Problem Girls: Unmarried Mothers and the Professionalization of Social Work, 1890–1945.* New Haven: Yale University Press.

Labrecque, R. 1995. *Study of the Mother–Child Program.* Ottawa: Correctional Service of Canada.

Lacombe, D. 1991. 'Power, Knowledge and the Law: The Politics of Pornography Law Reform in Canada.' PhD thesis, University of Toronto, Department of Sociology.

Laishes, J. 1997. *Mental Health Strategy for Women Offenders.* Ottawa: Federally Sentenced Women's Program, Correctional Service of Canada.

Laishes, J., and S. Lyth. 1996. *Intensive Healing (Mental Health) Program.* Ottawa: Correctional Service of Canada, Federally Sentenced Women Program.

Lajeunesse, T., and C. Jefferson. 1998. 'The Cross Gender Monitoring Project.' First Annual Report – Federally Sentenced Women's Facilities. Ottawa: Federally Sentenced Women Program – Correctional Service of Canada.

– 1999. 'The Cross Gender Monitoring Project.' Second Annual Report – Federally Sentenced Women's Facilities. Ottawa: Federally Sentenced Women Program – Correctional Service of Canada.

LaPrairie, C. 1996. *Examining Aboriginal Correctional in Canada.* Ottawa: Aboriginal Corrections, Ministry of the Solicitor General.

LeClair, D. 1998. 'Correctional Service of Canada – Developing Aboriginal Community Partnerships.' In *Restore*, Ottawa: CSC and Aboriginal Multi-Media Society.

Legal Education and Action Fund. 1991. *LEAF Lines.* March, p. 5.

– 1993. *LEAF Lines.* Summer, 5(3): 16–17.

Lemonde, L. 1995. 'L'évolution des normes dans l'institution carcérale.' *Revue canadienne de droit et société* 10: 125–70.

Lewis, G.K. 1909. *Elizabeth Fry.* London: Headley Brothers.

Lowe, M. 1992. *One Woman Army: The Life of Claire Culhane.* Toronto: Macmillan.

MacKinnon, C. 1982. 'Feminism, Marxism, Method and the State: An Agenda for Theory.' *Signs* 7(3): 515–44.

– 1983. 'Feminism, Marxism, Method and the State: Towards Feminist Jurisprudence.' *Signs* 8(4): 635–58.

– 1986. 'Making Sex Equality Real.' In Lynn Smith et al., eds., *Righting the Balance.* Toronto: Carswell.

– 1987. *Feminism Unmodified: Discourses on Life and Law*. Cambridge: Harvard University Press.

– 1990. 'Legal Perspectives on Sexual Difference.' In D. Rhode, ed., *Theoretical Perspectives on Sexual Difference*. New Haven: Yale University Press, pp. 213–25.

Maloff, P. 1957. *In Quest of a Solution (Three Reports on the Doukhobor Problem)*. Vancouver: Hall Printing.

Marie-de-Saint-Benoît, Sœur. 1953. La prison des femmes catholiques à Montréal 1876–1952. Dissertation inédite. Montréal: Université de Montreal, École de service social.

Martel, J. 2000. 'Women in the Hole: The Unquestioned Practice of Segregation.' In K. Hannah-Moffat and M. Shaw, eds., *The Ideal Prison: Critical Essays on Women's Imprisonment in Canada*. Halifax: Fernwood Publishing.

Martin, D.L. 1993. 'Casualties of the Criminal Justice System: Women and Justice Under the War on Drugs.' *CJWL/RFD* 6: 305–27.

Maurutto, P. 1998. 'Philanthropic Governance: Church and State in Toronto's Catholic Archdiocese 1850–1950.' PhD thesis, York University, Department of Sociology.

McCormick, K., and L. Visano, eds. 1992. *Canadian Penology: Advanced Perspectives and Research*. Toronto: Scholars Press.

McDonagh, D. 1999. *Not Letting the Time Do You*. Federally Sentenced Women Maximum Security Interview Project. Ottawa: Correctional Service of Canada.

McGowen, R. 1986. 'A Powerful Sympathy: Terror, the Prison, and Humanitarian Reform in Early Nineteenth Century Britain.' *Journal of British Studies* 25: 312–34.

– 1987. 'The Body and Punishment in Eighteenth Century England.' *Journal of Modern History* 59: 651–79.

– 1988. 'The Changing Face of God's Justice: The Debates Over Divine and Human Punishment in Eighteenth Century England.' *Criminal Justice History* 9: 63–99.

McGrath, W.T. (Ed.). 1976. *Crime and Its Treatment in Canada*. Toronto: MacMillan Canada.

McMahon, M. 1999. *Women on Guard: Discrimination and Harassment in Corrections*. Toronto: University of Toronto Press.

McNeil, G., and S. Vance. 1978. *Cruel and Unusual: The Shocking Reality of Life Behind Bars in Canada*. Ottawa: Deneau and Greenberg.

Mitford, J. 1973. *Kind and Unusual Punishment*. New York: Alfred A. Knopf.

Moffat (Hannah), K. 1991. 'Creating Choices or Repeating History: Canadian Female Offenders and Correctional Reform.' *Social Justice* 18(3): 184–203.

Monture-Angus, P. 1995. *Thunder in My Soul: A Mohawk Woman Speaks*. Halifax: Fernwood Publishing.

– 2000. 'Aboriginal Women and Correctional Practice: Reflections on the Task Force on Federally Sentenced Women. In K. Hannah-Moffat and M. Shaw, eds., *The Ideal Prison: Critical Essays on Women's Imprisonment in Canada*. Halifax: Fernwood Publishing.

Morin, B. 1993. *Aboriginal Women's Healing Lodge*. Ottawa: Native Women's Association of Canada.

Morin, Sky Blue. 1999. *Federally Sentenced Aboriginal Women in Maximum Security: What Happened to the Promises of Creating Choices?* Ottawa: Correctional Service of Canada.

Moulds, E.F. 1980. 'Chivalry and Paternalism: Disparities of Treatment in the Criminal Justice System.' In S. Datesman and F. Scarpitti, eds., *Women, Crime and Justice*. New York: Oxford University Press, pp. 277–99.

Myrda, A., and V. Klien. 1993. 'Women's Two Roles.' In H. Exley, ed., *The Best of Women's Quotations*. New York: Exley Publications.

Nahanee, T. 1995. 'Gorilla in our Midst: Aboriginal Women and the Inhumanity of the Canadian Criminal Justice System.' MA thesis, Queen's University, Faculty of Law.

Needham, H.G. 1980. 'Historical Perspectives on the Federal Provincial Split in Jurisdiction in Corrections.' *Canadian Journal of Corrections* 22: 298–306.

Newburn, T., and E.A. Stanko. 1994. 'When Men are Victims.' In T. Newburn and E.A. Stanko, eds., *Just Boys Doing Business? Men, Masculinities and Crime*. Routledge.

Oliver, P. 1994. 'To Govern by Kindness: The First Two Decades of the Mercer Reformatory for Women.' In J. Phillips, T. Loo, and S. Lewthwaite, eds., *Essays in the History of Canadian Law: Crime and Criminal Justice* (vol. v). Toronto: The Osgoode Society for Canadian Legal History.

– 1998. *Terror to Evildoers*. Toronto: University of Toronto Press.

O'Malley, P. 1992. 'Risk, Power and Crime Prevention.' *Economy and Society* 21(3): 252–75.

– 1994. 'Penalising Crime in Advanced Liberalism.' Melbourne: Department of Legal Studies, La Trobe University. Unpublished paper.

– 1996. 'Risk and Responsibility.' In A. Barry, T. Osbourne, and N. Rose, eds., *Foucault and Political Reason: Liberalism, Neo-liberalism and Rationalities of Government*. Chicago: University of Chicago Press, pp. 189–208.

– 1998. *Crime and the Risk Society – The International Library of Criminology, Criminal Justice and Penology*. Australia: Ashgate Dartmouth.

Ontario. 1995. *Women's Voices, Women's Choices* (Report of the Women's Issues Task Force – Ministry of the Solicitor General). Ontario: Queen's Printer.

Ontario Court – General Division, Statement of Claim. 1998. *Dorothy Mills Proctor and Her Majesty The Queen In Right of Canada, The Attorney General of Canada, George Scott, Institute of Psychotherapy Limited, Mark Eveson and Gerald Wilson.* Court File Number: 98: cv-6618.

Palumbo, D., and J. Palumbo. 1992. *What Is Their Truth?: Listening to the Voices of Aboriginal Federally Sentenced Women.* Unpublished paper. Saskatchewan: University of Saskatchewan.

Parr, J. 1995. *A Diversity of Women: Ontario, 1945–1980.* Toronto: University of Toronto Press.

Pate, K. 1999. 'CSC and the 2 percent solution: The P4W Inquiry.' *Canadian Woman Studies* 19(1&2): 145–53.

Pate, K., and K. Faith. 2000. 'Personal and Political Musing on Activism – a Two-Way Interview.' In K. Hannah-Moffat and M. Shaw, eds., *The Ideal Prison: Critical Essays on Women's Imprisonment in Canada.* Halifax: Fernwood Publishing.

Pennington, D. 1986. *Agnes Macphail Reformer: Canada's First Female MP.* Toronto: Simon and Pierre.

Phillips, J. 1994. 'Women, Crime and Criminal Justice in Early Halifax, 1750–1800.' In J. Phillips, T. Loo and S. Lewthwaite, eds., *Essays in the History of Canadian Law: Crime and Criminal Justice* (Volume V). Toronto: The Osgoode Society for Canadian Legal History.

Pitch, T. 1992. 'A Sexual Difference Approach to the Criminal Question.' *Social and Legal Studies* 1: 357–69.

Pitman, E.R. 1969. *Elizabeth Fry.* New York: Greenwood Press.

Pollack, S. 1999. 'Moving "Inside": The Role of Law-breaking in Black Women's Attempts to Gain Economic Independence.' Paper presented at American Society of Criminology Meeting, November 1999. Toronto.

– 2000. 'Dependency Discourses as Social Control.' In K. Hannah-Moffat and M. Shaw, eds., *The Ideal Prison: Critical Essays on Women's Imprisonment in Canada.* Halifax: Fernwood Publishing.

Pollock-Byrne, J. 1990. *Women, Prison and Crime.* California: Brooks/Cole Publishing.

Pratt, J. 1997. *Governing the Dangerous.* Sydney: The Federation Press.

Prentice, Alison, et al. 1988. *Canadian Women: A History.* Toronto: Harcourt Brace Jovanovich.

Prison Association of New York (PANY). 1867. *Report on the Prisons and Reformatories of the United States and Canada.* Albany: Van Benthuysen and Sons' Steam Printing House.

Pringle, R., and S. Watson. 1992. '"Women's Interests" and the Post-Structuralist State.' In J. Butler and J. Scott, eds., *Feminists Theorize the Political.* London: Routledge.

Proudfoot, P. Report of the British Columbia Royal Commission on the Incarceration of Female Offenders. Vancouver: Royal Commission on Incarcerating of Female Offenders.

Rafter, N.H. 1982. 'Hard Times: Custodial Prisons for Women and the Example of New York State Prison for Women at Auburn, 1893–1933.' In N.H. Rafter and E. Stanko, eds., *Judge, Lawyer, Victim, Thief: Women, Gender Roles and Criminal Justice*. Boston: Northeastern University Press.

– 1983. 'Chastising the Unchaste: Social Control Functions of a Women's Reformatory, 1894–1931.' In S. Cohen and A. Scull, eds., *Social Control and the State: Historical and Comparative Essays*. Oxford: Martin Robertson.

– 1992. *Partial Justice: Women, Prison, and Social Control*, 2nd ed. New Brunswick: Transaction Publishers.

Ransom, J. 1997. *Foucault's Discipline: The Politics of Subjectivity*. London: Duke University Press.

Razack, S. 1991. *Canadian Feminism and the Law: The Women's Legal Education and Action Fund and the Pursuit of Equality*. Toronto: Second Story Press.

– 1993. 'Exploring the Omissions and Silence in Law around Race.' In J. Brockman and I.D. Chunn, eds., *Investigating Gender Bias: Law Courts and the Legal Profession*, pp. 37–47. Toronto: Thompson Educational Publishing.

– 1994. 'What Is to Be Gained by Looking White People in the Eye? Culture, Race, and Gender in Cases of Sexual Violence.' *Signs: Journal of Women in Culture and Society* 19(4): 894–923.

Reynolds, B. 1996. *Federally Sentenced Women in Canada*. Ottawa: Correctional Service of Canada. Unpublished paper presented to Commonwealth Corrections Administrators, 25–8 November, Australia.

Rhode, D. 1990. *Theoretical Perspectives on Sexual Difference*. New Haven: Yale University Press.

Rice, M. 1992. 'Challenging Orthodoxies in Feminist Theory: A Black Feminist Critique.' In L. Gelsthorpe and A. Morris, eds., *Feminist Perspectives in Criminology*. Milton Keynes: Open University Press.

Richie, B. 1996. *Compelled to Crime: The Gender Entrapment of Battered Black Women*. New York: Routledge.

Richmond, G. 1975. *Prison Doctor*. Surrey, B.C.: Nanaga Publishing.

Riley, D., and P. Mayhew. 1980. *Crime Prevention Publicity: An Assessment*. Home Office Research Study No. 63. London: Home Office.

Rivera, M. 1996. *Giving Us a Chance: Needs Assessment Mental Health Reserves for Federally Sentenced Women in the Regional Facilities*. Ottawa: Correctional Service of Canada, Federally Sentenced Women Program.

Rock, P. 1996. *Reconstructing a Women's Prison: The Holloway Redevelopment Project, 1968–1988*. Oxford: Clarendon Press.

Rose, N. 1989. *Governing the Soul: The Shaping of the Private Self*. London: Routledge.
– 1993. 'Government, Authority and Expertise in Advanced Liberalism.' *Economy and Society* 22(3): 283–300.
– 1996a. 'Governing "Advanced" Liberal Democracies.' In A. Barry, T. Osbourne, and N. Rose, eds., *Foucault and Political Reason: Liberalism, Neoliberalism and Rationalities of Government*. Chicago: Chicago University Press, pp. 37–64.
– 1996b. 'The Death of the Social? Re-figuring the Territory of Government.' *Economy and Society* 25(3): 327–56.
Rose, N., and P. Miller. 1992. 'Political Power Beyond the State: Problematic of Government.' *British Journal of Sociology* 43: 173–205.
Rose, N., and M. Valverde. 1998. 'Governed by Law?' *Social and Legal Studies* 7(4): 569–79.
Rosen, E. 1977. *An Evaluation of the Report of the National Advisory Committee on the Female Offender*. Ottawa: Advisory Council on the Status of Women.
Rothman, D. 1980. *Conscience and Convenience: The Asylum and Its Alternatives in Progressive America*. London: Scott Foresman and Company.
– 1990. *The Discovery of the Asylum: Social Order and Disorder in the New Republic*, rev. ed. Boston: Little Brown and Co.
Royal Commission on the Status of Women. 1970. Report of the Royal Commission on the Status of Women. Ottawa: Queen's Printer.
Ruemper, W. 1994. 'Locking Them Up: Incarcerating Women in Ontario 1857–1931.' In L. Knafla and S. Binnie, eds., *Law, Society, and the State: Essays in Modern Legal History*. Toronto: University of Toronto Press.
Sangster, J. 1999. 'Criminalizing the Colonized: Ontario Native Women Contract the Criminal Justice System, 1920–1960.' *The Canadian Historical Review*. 80(1): 32–60.
Sauvé, J. 1977. Task Force on the Role of the Private Sector in Criminal Justice. Ottawa: Solicitor General of Canada.
Sawicki, J. 1991. *Disciplining Foucault: Feminism, Power and the Body*. New York: Routledge, Chapman, and Hall.
Shaw, M. 1991a. *The Female Offender: Report on a Preliminary Study*. Ottawa: Ministry of the Solicitor General.
– with K. Rodgers, J. Blanchette, T. Hattem, L.S. Thomas, and L. Tamarack. 1991b. *Survey of Federally Sentenced Women: Report to the Task Force on Federally Sentenced Women on the Prison Survey*. Ottawa: Ministry of the Solicitor General.
– with K. Rodgers and T. Hattem. 1991c. *The Release Study: Survey of Federally Sentenced Women in the Community*. Ottawa: Ministry of the Solicitor General.

– 1992a. 'Issues of Power and Control: Women in Prison and Their Defenders.' *British Journal of Criminology* 32(4): 438–52.
– with K. Rodgers, J. Blanchette, T. Hattem, L.S. Thomas, and L. Tamarack. 1992b. *Paying the Price: Federally Sentenced Women in Context*. Ottawa: Ministry of the Solicitor General.
– 1993. 'Reforming Federal Women's Imprisonment.' In E. Adelberg and C. Currie, eds., *In Conflict with the Law: Women and the Canadian Justice System*. Vancouver: Press Gang.
– 1994. *Ontario Women in Conflict with the Law: A Survey of Women in Institutions and Under Community Supervision in Ontario*. Ontario: Ministry of Correctional Services.
– 1996a. 'Conflicting Agendas: Evaluating Feminist Programs for Women Offenders.' Unpublished paper.
– 1996b. 'Is There a Feminist Future for Women's Prisons?' In R. Mathews and P. Francis, eds., *Prisons 2000: An International Perspective on the Current State and Future of Imprisonment*. Hampshire: Macmillan Press.
– 2000. 'Women, Violence and Disorder in Prisons.' In K. Hannah-Moffat and M. Shaw, eds., *The Ideal Prison: Critical Essays on Women's Imprisonment in Canada*. Halifax: Fernwood Publishing.
Shaw, M., and S. Dubois. 1995. *Understanding Violence by Women: A Review of the Literature*. Ottawa: Correctional Service of Canada.
Shaw, R. 1957. *Proud Heritage: A History of the National Council of Women of Canada*. Toronto: Ryerson Press.
Sim, J. 1990. *Medical Power in Prisons: The Prison Medical Service in England, 1774–1989*. Milton Keynes: Open University Press.
Simmons, A., M. Cohen, J. Cohen, and C. Beitz, eds. 1995. *Punishment*. Princeton: Princeton University Press.
Simon, J. 1993. *Poor Discipline: Parole and the Social Control of the Underclass, 1890–1990*. Chicago: University of Chicago Press.
– 1994. 'In the Place of the Parent: Risk Management and the Government of Campus Life.' *Social and Legal Studies* 3: 15–45.
Smart, C. 1979. 'The New Female Criminal: Reality or Myth?' *British Journal of Criminology* 19(1): 50.
– 1990. *Feminism and the Power of the Law*. New York: Routledge.
– 1995. *Law, Crime and Sexuality: Essays in Feminism*. London: Sage Publications.
Smillie, E.M. 1980. *Elizabeth Fry*. Ontario: Belstan Publishing.
Smith, A. 1962. *Women in Prison*. London: Stevens and Sons.
Smith, B. 1990. 'The Female Prisoner in Ireland, 1855–1878.' *Federal Probation* 54: 69–81.
Smith, D. 1987. *The Everyday World as Problematic*. Boston: Northeastern.

Snider, L. 1990. 'The Potential of the Criminal Justice System to Promote Feminist Concerns.' *Studies in Law, Politics and Society* 10: 143–72.
– 1994. 'Feminism, Punishment and the Potential of Empowerment.' *Canadian Journal of Law and Society* 9: 75–104.
Solicitor General of Canada. 1998. *CCRA 5 Year Review – Women Offenders*. Ottawa: Solicitor General of Canada.
Solicitor General's Special Committee on Provincially Incarcerated Women. 1992. *Blueprint for Change*. Halifax: Nova Scotia Correctional Services.
Sommers, E. 1995. *Voices from Within: Women Who Have Broken the Law*. Toronto: University of Toronto Press.
Sparks, R. 1994. 'Can Prisons Be Legitimate?' In R. King and M. Maguire, eds., *Prisons in Context*. Oxford: Oxford University Press.
Sparling, L. 1999. 'A Suitable Place: Positive Change for Federally Sentenced Aboriginal Women in Canada.' *Canadian Woman Studies* 19(1&2). 116–21.
Spierenberg, P. 1984. *The Spectacle of Suffering: Executions and the Evolution of Repression*. Cambridge: Cambridge University Press.
Splane, R.B. 1965. *Social Welfare in Ontario, 1791–1893: A Study of Public Welfare Administration*. Toronto: University of Toronto Press.
Stableforth, N. 1997. 'Women Offenders.' *Let's Talk*. Ottawa: Correctional Service of Canada.
Stewart, L. 1993. *Women Who Volunteer to Go to Prison: A History of the Elizabeth Fry Society of British Columbia, 1939–1989*. Victoria: Orca Books.
Strange, C. 1983. 'The Velvet Glove: Maternalists Reform at the Andrew Mercer Reformatory, 1872–1927.' Unpublished master's thesis, University of Ottawa.
– 1985. 'The Criminal and the Fallen of Their Sex: The Establishment of Canada's First Women's Prison, 1874–1901.' *Canadian Journal of Women and the Law* 1: 79–92.
– 1990. 'Mothers on the March: Maternalism in Women's Protest for Peace in North America and Western Europe, 1980–1985.' In G. West and R.L. Blumberg, eds., *Women in Social Protest*. New York: Oxford University Press.
Strong-Boag, V. 1976. *Parliament of Women: The National Council of Women of Canada 1893–1929*. Ottawa: Carlton University Press.
Sugar, F., and L. Fox. 1989. 'Nistum Peyako Séht'wawin Iskwewak: Breaking Chains.' *Canadian Journal of Women and Law* 3: 465–82.
– 1990. *Survey of Federally Sentenced Aboriginal Women in the Community*. Ottawa: Native Women's Association of Canada.
Sumner, C. 1990. 'Foucault, Gender and the Censure of Deviance.' In L. Gelsthorpe and A. Morris, eds., *Feminist Perspectives in Criminology*. Milton Keynes: Open University Press.

Task Force on Federally Sentenced Women. 1990. Report of the Task Force on Federally Sentenced Women – Creating Choices. Ottawa: Ministry of the Solicitor General.

Thompson, G. 1972. 'Report of the Correctional Consultation Committee Appointed to Study Correctional Services for Women in the Maritime Provinces, 1972' (Coverdale Report). Ottawa: Department of the Solicitor General Canada.

Tietolman, R. 1972. *A Study of the Female Offender in Quebec and Ontario Prison Community*. Ministry of Solicitor General Canada – Library HV 6046–55 1972. Ottawa: Department of the Solicitor General – Consultation Centre.

Toronto Elizabeth Fry Society. 1978. 'Newsletter in Honour of Miss Phyllis Haslam, Executive Director of Elizabeth Fry Society of Toronto, 1953–1978.' Toronto: Toronto Elizabeth Fry Society Library.

Townsend, E. 1998. *Good Intentions Overruled: A Critique of Empowerment in the Routine Organization of Mental Health Services*. Toronto: University of Toronto Press.

Vallières, D., and H. Simon. 1988. Quand la prison devient abri: une analyse des femmes admises à l'infirmerie de la prison Tanguay en 1987. Montréal: Société Fry de Montréal.

Valverde, M. 1995. 'Building Anti-delinquent Communities: Morality, Gender, and Generation in the City.' In J. Parr, ed., *A Diversity of Women: Ontario, 1945–1980*. Toronto: University of Toronto Press.

– 1996. *Governing Out of Habit*. Unpublished paper, University of Toronto, Centre of Criminology.

– 1998. *Diseases of the Will: Alcohol and the Dilemmas of Freedom*. Cambridge: Cambridge University Press.

Valverde, M., R. Levi, C. Shearing, M. Condon, and P. O'Malley. 1999. *Democracy in Governance – A Socio-legal Framework*. Toronto: A Report for the Law Commission of Canada on Law and Governance Relationships.

Van Nijnatten, D., and S. Wray Gregoire. 1993. 'Report on Community Consultation Exercises.' Kingston: School of Policy Studies, Queen's University. Contract No. 93-93-ONT-333.

Vickers, J.M. 1986. 'Equality Seeking in a Cold Climate.' In L. Smith et al., eds., *Righting the Balance: Canada's New Equality Right*. Saskatoon: Canadian Human Rights Reporter.

Waldram, J. 1997. *The Way of the People: Aboriginal Spirituality and Symbolic Healing in Canadian Prisons*. Toronto: Broadview.

Walford, B. 1987. *Lifers: The Stories of Eleven Women Serving Life Sentences for Murder*. Montreal: Eden Press.

Warner, A. 1998. *Implementing Choices at Regional Facilities: Program Proposals for Women Offenders with Special Needs*. Ottawa: Correctional Service of Canada.

Watkins, R.E. 1992. 'A Historical Review of the Role and Practice of Psychology in the Field of Corrections.' Ottawa: Correctional Service of Canada – Research Statistics Branch.

Watson, C.M. 1980. 'Women Prisoners and Modern Methods of Prison Control: A Comparative Study of Two Canadian Prisons.' PhD thesis, McGill University.

Watson, S. 1990. *Playing the State: Australian Feminist Interventions*. Sydney: Allen and Unwin.

Webb, J. 1965. 'Not by Salads Alone.' *Federal Corrections*. Kingston: Regional Headquarters, Correctional Service of Canada.

Weedon, C. 1987. *Feminist Practice and Poststructuralist Theory*. Oxford: Basil Blackwell.

Weibe, R., and Y. Johnson. 1998. *Stolen Life Journey of a Cree Woman*. Toronto: Alfred A. Knopf Canada.

Wetherell, D.G. 1979. 'To Discipline and Train: Adult Rehabilitation Programmes in Ontario Prisons, 1874–1900.' *Histoire Sociale /Social History* 12(23): 145–65.

Whitehall, G.C. 1995. *Mental Health Profile and Intervention Strategy for Atlantic Region Federally Sentenced Women*. Correctional Service of Canada, Federally Sentenced Women Program.

Whittingham, M. 1984. *The Role of Reformers and Volunteers in the Advance of Correctional Reform in Canada Since Confederation*, no. 1984–70. Ottawa: Ministry of the Solicitor General Canada.

Woodcock, G., and I. Avakumovic. 1977. *The Doukhobors*. Toronto: McClelland & Stewart.

Woodrow, R. 1998. *Women on the Inside Need Friends on the Outside. A report on the needs of incarcerated females in Newfoundland and Labrador* for Emerging Elizabeth Fry Society of Newfoundland and Labrador, St John's, Newfoundland.

Yerbury, C. 1984. 'The "Sons of Freedom" Doukhobors and the Canadian State.' *Canadian Ethnic Studies*, pp. 41–70.

Yerbury, C., and C. Griffiths. 1991. 'Minorities, Crime and the Law.' In M. Jackson and G. Griffiths, *Canadian Criminology*. Toronto: Harbourt Brace Jovanovich.

Young, A.F., and E.T. Ashton. 1956. *British Social Work in the Nineteenth Century*. London: Routledge and Kegan Paul.

Young, I. 1994. 'Punishment, Treatment, Empowerment: Three Approaches to Policy for Pregnant Addicts.' *Feminist Studies* 20: 33–57.

Zedner, L. 1991a. 'Women, Crime and Penal Responses: A Historical Account.' In M. Tonry, ed., *Crime and Justice: A Review of Research*, Volume 14. Chicago: University of Chicago Press.

– 1991b. *Women, Crime and Custody in Victorian England*. Oxford: Claredon Press.

Zimmer, L. 1986. *Women Guarding Men*. Chicago: University of Chicago Press.

Zubrycki, R.M. 1980. *The Establishment of Canada's Penitentiary System: Federal Correctional Policy 1867–1900*. Toronto: Faculty of Social Work, University of Toronto.

Index